JFK
The Last Dissenting Witness

Portrait of Jean Hill, autumn 1962

JFK
The Last Dissenting Witness

By Bill Sloan with Jean Hill

Foreword by OLIVER STONE

PELICAN PUBLISHING COMPANY
Gretna 1992

The word "Pelican" and the depiction of a pelican are trademarks of
Pelican Publishing Company, Inc., and are registered in the U.S. Patent
and Trademark Office.

Library of Congress Cataloging-in-Publication Data

Sloan, Bill
    JFK : the last dissenting witness / by Bill Sloan with Jean Hill ;
with a foreword by Oliver Stone.
        p.   cm.
    ISBN 0-88289-922-8
    1. Kennedy, John F. (John Fitzgerald), 1917-1963—
Assassination.
    2. Hill, Jean. I. Hill, Jean. II. Title.
E842.9.S55   1992
973.922'092—dc20

                                                                91-42275
                                                                   CIP

Manufactured in the United States of America

Published by Pelican Publishing Company, Inc.
1101 Monroe Street, Gretna, Louisiana 70053

Contents

Foreword

Jean Hill is a pretty terrific lady with a unique perspective on the Kennedy assassination. When you talk to Jean, you get a feeling of rock-solidness. She communicates Texas down to her bones, and she also communicates the truth. She's a woman you believe, a woman you can trust. She has given me a bird's-eye view of the assassination. I believe her.

When we began working on our film about the assassination, Jean told us her story in her colorful colloquial dialect, which I tried to match in the film. She served as a technical adviser for the historic events in Dealey Plaza. She helped us set the mood and tone for those events. She also helped us catch details of the assassination that few other people know. She told us how her interrogators roughed her up, how angry they were, and that makes me wonder what they could be covering up.

Jean is one of the key witnesses to the assassination and an important character in our film. Former New Orleans district attorney Jim Garrison, portrayed by Kevin Costner, runs across her story and it sets up a flashback into the past. In the film as it was originally shot, Jean herself played a stenographer at her own inquisition. I had the scene framed with the actress playing Jean Hill and the real Jean Hill taking her testimony side by side. Jean and I both thought that was an interesting touch, and I was sorry that the scene had to be cut in the interest of time.

11

While we were filming in Dallas, I went to Jean's house for dinner and had an incredible meal. She does old-fashioned country cooking, and we all enjoyed it very much. We liked Jean from the beginning and grew to appreciate her even more as the filming progressed. She's fun. She has a good sense of humor, as well as a good sense of history, and she's as honest as the day is long.

OLIVER STONE

Preface

Millions of Americans have seen Jean Hill without ever realizing it. Anyone who views Abraham Zapruder's classic film of the Kennedy assassination is likely to notice her red-clad figure close beside the presidential limousine as the fatal shots strike JFK. Not knowing her name, many of those who have watched the Zapruder film refer to her simply as "the lady in red." She has appeared on TV any number of times, and countless readers have come across her photograph and/or references to her in authoritative books on the assassination.

And yet, even today, 28 years after the calamity in Dallas, virtually no one really knows who Jean Hill is. Few beyond a small "inner circle" of assassination investigators have any grasp of the long, bitter, traumatizing ordeal through which she has lived—much less of her potential importance to the modern history of the United States.

Now, thanks to the prominence she has been given in the widely acclaimed new Oliver Stone-directed motion picture, *JFK*, Jean Hill is becoming a familiar name to tens of millions more Americans. Through the film, they are learning of her role as an assassination eyewitness—the most important one still living—and as a stubborn dissenter to the findings of the Warren Commission.

The principal purpose of this book is to tell the rest of Jean Hill's story, the part to which the movie merely alludes. Here, for the first time anywhere, the last surviving assassination eyewitness openly to dispute the Warren Commission's verdict that Lee Harvey Oswald acted alone in murdering JFK reveals the long-kept secrets which federal authorities feared and tried desperately to suppress.

This book is a portrait of an ordinary citizen caught up in a monstrous web of intrigue and conspiracy, an innocent bystander thrust into the midst of the century's most shocking and horrifying event; but it is also much more. It is a story of romance and remorse, fear and bravery, sacrifice and deter- mination. It spans almost three decades, and with the excep- tion of one or two names that have been changed to protect innocent parties, it is the factual, unvarnished story exactly as Jean Hill lived it.

But the troublesome witness, whose courageous commit- ment to the truth puts her in constant fear of her life, repre- sents only one small aspect of Jean Hill's total character. Over the years, there have been many others: Jean Hill, a woman desperately in love with a policeman she could never marry; Jean Hill, a struggling single parent trying to raise two chil- dren; Jean Hill, a dedicated schoolteacher, determined to give her best to her profession in spite of her personal turmoil; Jean Hill, a human being entangled in a savage, inhuman dilemma.

Along with the mysterious "lady in red," they all come to life in the following pages.

JFK
The Last Dissenting Witness

CHAPTER ONE

The Shots and "The Shooter"

It is a bright, crystal-clear afternoon in April 1991, but to anyone standing in Dallas's historic Dealey Plaza, it could just as easily be November 1963. In reality, the Texas School Book Depository, from which Lee Harvey Oswald allegedly assassinated the president of the United States, has long since been converted into a county office building. But through the magic of Hollywood, the structure looming above the intersection of Elm and Houston Streets once more looks just as it did when Oswald supposedly fired his mail-order rifle from its notorious sixth-floor window.

Above the brown brick facade of the depository, the sky is pale blue and cloudless as director Oliver Stone and his camera crew pack dozens of actors, extras and vintage automobiles into one small sunlit corner of the plaza to film a climactic scene for the movie, *JFK*.

"Okay, we're rolling!" yells an assistant director. "Everybody quiet."

In the hush that follows, a bespectacled Dallas grandmother stares in silent awe from a short distance away and watches a simulated motorcade creep toward her. She is Jean Hill, a Dallas schoolteacher who is an integral part of this scene, both the original version and the one now being recreated by Oliver Stone.

Flanked by police motorcycles, a long blue Lincoln limousine—identical to the one in which John Fitzgerald Kennedy rode to his death more than 27 years ago—slowly ap-

17

proaches, and Jean Hill is filled with a rising sense of unease. She feels her insides coil into knots as the actor portraying Kennedy waves to the well-wisher extras lining the sidewalk. Despite the coolness of the day, she begins to sweat, and her whole body tenses as she awaits the shots she knows are coming.

"It's only a movie," she whispers to herself, vainly trying to control the shaking in her hands. "It's only a movie."

As a key consultant and technical advisor to Stone and his production company, Jean realizes full well that what she is witnessing is mere make-believe. But despite her attempts to stay calm and self-controlled, she is gripped by the same pervasive, paralyzing fear that has assailed her so many thousands of times before.

She closes her eyes, dreading the shots, even though she knows they are only blanks, and struggles against the stifling fear and the irrational desire to run away and hide.

"It's only a movie," she keeps reminding herself. "It's only a movie. It's only a movie . . ."

And as the phrase repeats itself monotonously inside her head, she finds herself being drawn irresistibly backward through time. Back across the years to this identical spot on a long-ago autumn noon. Back to a day that the world will never forget. Back to the very instant when the relentless, unending terror first began . . .

It was a bright, crystal-clear Indian-summer day in Dallas. The sky above the brown brick facade of the Texas School Book Depository was pale blue and virtually cloudless. On top of the building, the digital Hertz Rent-a-Car sign alternately flashed a temperature of 66 degrees and a time of 12:25 P.M.

It was Friday, November 22, 1963, a perfect day for a parade in a city that fancied itself as nearly perfect as any American city could be. Although it was less than a week before Thanksgiving, there was no hint in the air that winter's chill would soon descend—much less that it would be the most painful, soulwrenching winter that Dallas had ever experienced.

Below, in Dealey Plaza, a fan-shaped, park-like area where three major downtown thoroughfares converge before entering a railroad underpass at the western edge of the central business district, the crowds were smiling and eager. After all, it wasn't every day that you had a chance to see the president of the United States in person during your lunch hour, and downtown office workers had turned out by the thousands to take advantage of the opportunity.

Jean Hill and her companion, Mary Moorman, didn't work downtown, but they had come there anyway, attracted by the prospect of getting a close-up look at the president and taking his picture with Mary's new Polaroid camera. For Jean, an attractive, 32-year-old mother of two children who had recently separated from her husband, there was an extra added incentive: J. B. Marshall, the Dallas motorcycle patrolman whom she had been dating regularly for the past several weeks, was to be riding on the outside rear wheel of the presidential limousine. A romance had rapidly started to bloom between Jean and the handsome young officer, and her fondest hope at the moment was to be able to catch him in the same photograph with JFK.

She wanted J. B. to see her too. That was the reason she had worn the full-length red raincoat in spite of the sunny skies. There was to be nothing inconspicuous about Jean Hill on this fateful day.

To achieve her goals, she and Mary had charmed a young policeman into letting them into the open, triangle-shaped area bounded by Main, Elm and Houston Streets where they now stood. The triangle, which was directly across Elm Street from the spot where the main crowd had gathered in front of the school book depository, was normally off-limits to civilians, and Jean and Mary were virtually the only ones occupying it at the moment. It provided an unrestricted vantage point for snapping pictures of the motorcade, and the two women had established themselves in an ideal spot, squarely on the curb of Elm Street, where Jean calculated they would be no more than ten feet from the president's car and J. B.'s motorcycle when they passed.

She and Mary had taken turns running back and forth to the other side of the triangle to glance up Main Street toward the advancing motorcade as it drew nearer and nearer. And now the excitement and anticipation of the moment was building to such a fever pitch that Jean could hardly keep still.

For Jean Hill, like most of those gathered in the plaza at that precise moment, life seemed pleasant, satisfying and uncomplicated. In Dallas, a city largely unburdened by the problems besetting many other urban centers and a community that had long sensed itself favored by divine providence, life in general was good, and almost everybody expected it to keep right on getting better.

Although "Big D" was much larger and far more glamorous than Oklahoma City, where Jean had lived before moving to Dallas in August 1962, the lifestyle here seemed no less simple and easygoing—at least in the circles in which Jean moved. During her brief association with J. B., she had become acquainted with many of his fellow motorcycle officers. They were a laid-back lot, who were well known throughout the Dallas Police Department for their rakish escapades, and dropping a few of their names and badge numbers had been a key factor in persuading the young cop to let her and Mary go where they wanted to go today.

The digital sign atop the school book depository said 12:28.

As little as Jean realized it at that instant, the good, simple life in Dallas, Texas, was destined to last for approximately two more minutes. After that, it would never be the same again. Certainly not for any of those happy, excited Dallasites in Dealey Plaza—and least of all for Jean Hill.

"Look, Jean!" she heard Mary shout. "Here they come!"

Jean turned just as the lead motorcycle, ridden by Off. Len McGuire, another close acquaintance, came roaring around the corner of Main Street and turned onto Houston Street. It was closely followed by the first car in the Kennedy motorcade—the one bearing Dallas police chief Jesse Curry and county sheriff Bill Decker—which was now moving directly toward Jean and Mary and preparing to turn west again onto Elm Street.

Then the long, blue, open-topped limousine swung into view, flanked by four motorcycles, its flags fluttering in the slight breeze. Jean could see someone waving from inside the car, but as yet, the figures were blurred and indistinct. As the limo rounded the corner, Jean noticed dozens of excited people pouring out of Main Street, ignoring the police lines and spilling into the triangular area which she and Mary had had to themselves until now. She was acutely aware of their presence behind her as they charged toward the spot where she and Mary stood.

"Get started, Mary!" Jean yelled impatiently. "Let's get some pictures."

Mary raised the Polaroid and snapped a series of photos as the big Lincoln started down the slight incline into Dealey Plaza. As the fresh prints slid from the camera, Jean grabbed them quickly to peel away the paper coverings and brush them with fixative. As she completed this process, she shoved the pictures into the pocket of her long red coat, scarcely taking time even to glance at them.

She would have plenty of time to look at them later, she told herself. But she was wrong.

As nearly as Jean remembers today, Mary clicked off four or five photos as the limousine rolled toward them. Then, suddenly, the car was virtually on top of them, and Jean could see every occupant with amazing clarity. She saw tight-lipped Secret Servicemen, Texas governor John Connally with one hand raised, Mrs. Connally turning to say something to the president, Jackie Kennedy in a flash of pink, glancing down at something in her lap. None of them looked to be more than a dozen arm's lengths away. Just behind the limo and to her right, she could see J. B. in his white "ostrich egg" helmet, coaxing his rumbling cycle forward. In another second or two, it was going to be absolutely perfect.

But, as luck would have it, JFK himself was facing in the wrong direction, his attention totally occupied, it seemed, by the throngs in front of the school book depository. This would never do, Jean thought. She had to do something to make him turn around.

"Hey, Mr. President," Jean shouted impulsively when the car was almost abreast of her. "Look over here. We want to take your picture."

In her desperation and excitement, she stepped off the curb into the street as she spoke, almost touching the front fender of the limousine before she instinctively drew back.

An inner voice seemed to be admonishing her: No! Don't get too close. They won't like it if you get too close.

Whether Kennedy heard her or not is uncertain, but at that moment, he turned in Jean's direction. He seemed to smile directly at her, and he waved.

What a great picture this is going to be, Jean thought, as Mary raised her camera. She sighted through the viewfinder, and . . .

CRACK!

. . . almost simultaneously, Jean heard a shot.

Mary hesitated as an expression of pain and confusion crossed the president's face. His hands jerked convulsively toward his throat.

CRACK!

Jean saw the president driven backward and sideways as a second shot struck him with tremendous force. The whole back of his head appeared to explode and a cloud of blood-red mist filled the air and spattered down on the windshield of J. B.'s motorcycle.

Approximately an eighth of a second later (as investigators would later determine), as the president was falling toward his wife, Mary clicked the shutter of the Polaroid.

Then Jean heard Jackie Kennedy's anguished cry:

"My God, they've shot my husband!"

Within the space of a single split-second, Jean visually absorbed all this, and the stark, sudden horror of the scene etched itself into her memory for all time to come. But within that same split-second, her focus shifted to the area beyond the car, across Elm Street, and she saw something else—something even more unforgettably horrifying.

"Jean, get down!" Mary screamed, as she and the other panicked bystanders nearby threw themselves to the ground. But although she was every bit as convinced as Mary that they were directly in the line of fire, Jean stood there, immobilized by the shock of what she had seen, while her friend tugged desperately at her legs.

On the other side of the street, at the top of a little green mound universally known today as the "grassy knoll," Jean Hill had seen an incredible sight—one that no one else among the handful who shared her vantage point that day could see because all the others were sprawled face-down on the ground—and she was transfixed by it.

It was a sight that was destined to haunt her for the rest of her life: A muzzle flash, a puff of smoke, and the shadowy figure of a man holding a rifle, barely visible above the wooden fence at the top of the knoll, still in the very act of murdering the president of the United States.

For a stunned second or two after the sound of the shots faded, an eerie, motionless silence gripped the inhabitants of Dealey Plaza. During this fleeting, shell-shocked interval, Jean detected an abrupt flurry of movement to her right, and her eyes darted in that direction, fixing themselves on a point at ground level near the school book depository.

Somebody was running.

A lone man in a brown coat was running as hard as he could go, past the frozen, motionless figures of the stricken onlookers, straight toward the position of the shadowy gunman holding the rifle. Jean watched him run from a point near the west wall of the school book depository until he was almost to the near end of the wooden fence. Then he was lost in a sea of confusion as the crowd's momentary mass-paralysis dissolved and everyone suddenly started shouting, pointing, ducking and scrambling for cover.

As though in a dream, Jean watched her friend, J. B., turning his motorcycle around and around in tight circles, staring upward, his hand instinctively clutching at his service revolver.

She tried urgently to get his attention. "J. B.!" she cried. "It's me, Jean!"

There was no reaction from the officer. He gunned his roaring cycle, his eyes scanning the tops of nearby buildings, obviously searching for snipers and oblivious to her presence. Bobby Hargis, the motorcycle officer riding beside Marshall and nearest the limousine, wiped at the blood and brain tissue that covered his face and helmet, half-blinding him. He jumped off his cycle and stumbled up the hill at a crouch, drawing his pistol as he went.

Then, just as the limousine began speeding away with the mortally wounded president, something inside Jean Hill snapped, and she was suddenly running too. She raced directly across the street, narrowly avoiding being hit by J. B.'s still-circling motorcycle, and up the grassy knoll toward the fence where the shadow with the gun had been only an instant earlier.

She would later recall her own behavior with bewilderment and amazement, unable to offer any rational explanation for what made her decide to charge the position of an armed and ruthless killer.

"All I knew was that I had seen this man shoot the president right before my very eyes," she says, "and I had to stop him. That was the only thing I was thinking about right then."

But by now the entire area was one gigantic melee of confusion and hysteria, and Jean had to fight and claw her way through throngs of panicked, weeping, cursing, babbling people to get to the fence.

When she finally managed to reach the wooden barrier and ran behind it, she found herself in a parking area. She looked back at the point from which she thought the shots had come and saw a single uniformed policeman whom she did not recognize. The policeman seemed to be guarding something.

She noticed what looked like a rifle in the policeman's hand, and something far in the back of her mind told her to wonder why. None of the other officers she had seen was carrying a rifle. Why should this one be? And why should he be back here behind this fence?

She had no answers for her own questions, but as quickly as

Dealey Plaza in Dallas, Texas, with the former Texas School Book Depository in the background. Jean Hill stood in the grassy area to the extreme right when the fatal shot was fired. The "grassy knoll" is to the extreme left.

they formed in her brain, another part of her mind was telling her to disregard them. This was, after all, a policeman, an inner voice of reason said. His uniform and badge were symbols of law and order, and policemen were supposed to have guns, even rifles sometimes. Policemen were there to protect public figures and private citizens alike. And policemen didn't shoot at the president of the United States, not from behind wooden fences or anywhere else.

Did they?

Confused and breathless, Jean whirled away, her eyes frantically combing the plaza in search of either the man she now thought of as "the shooter" or the other man she had seen running toward him. Then, without warning, she heard a movement behind her and felt a hand clamp down on her shoulder in a numbing, vice-like grip.

"Secret Service," announced a low, authoritative male voice. "Where do you think you're going?"

She turned to see a burly man in plain clothes, who briefly flashed a badge of some kind at her, then stuck it back in his pocket, keeping a firm grip on her shoulder with the other hand.

"I've got to catch that man," Jean cried, struggling to free herself. "I saw him shoot the president."

"You're not going anywhere," the man snapped. "You're coming with me. We want to talk to you."

"Leave me alone," she howled, now on the verge of tears. "Don't you understand? I've got to go catch this man. They're getting away."

For one brief moment, she managed to break free. But before she could take more than two or three running steps, she was restrained by a second plainclothesman, whose grip on her other shoulder was even stronger than the first's.

"You'd better be still if you know what's good for you," he warned, as she slumped helplessly between them.

Unceremoniously, the second man jammed his hand into her coat pocket and deftly withdrew the handful of still-damp Polaroid prints she had deposited there a few minutes before.

"What are you doing?" Jean demanded. "Those are my pictures! Just who do you think you are?"

"We know who *we* are," the man said roughly, shoving the pictures into his own jacket pocket. "The question is, who are *you?* That's what we're going to find out, so just start walking and keep smiling—just like we were all real good friends. Otherwise, you're in big trouble."

Jean Hill never saw the pictures again. She never found the man with the gun either, but she can close her eyes today and see him with the same distressing clarity as she could see him then.

The sinister shadow . . .

The muzzle flash . . .

The sharp crack of the shots . . .

The president's head exploding . . .

Jackie screaming . . .

The running figure in the brown coat . . .

J. B.'s motorcycle turning and turning . . .

And although it is "only a movie" in 1991, the ongoing nightmare that began with those sounds and images is all too real for Jean Hill. It remains as real today as it was on that disastrous November noon in 1963.

As real as "the shooter" behind the fence.

The rest of that afternoon and evening seemed to stretch into an eternity for Jean. She was herded into a third-floor interview room in the Dallas County Criminal Courts Building, directly across Houston Street from Dealey Plaza, and by the time she found her way back into the outside world, she would feel as if she had been held captive there for days.

At first, she had no idea what had happened to Mary. The last time Jean had seen her, Mary was still hugging the ground in the grassy triangle. Jean had gone back to try to get Mary to come with her up the knoll, but Mary refused.

The two men representing themselves as Secret Service agents quickly turned Jean over to two other interrogators who sat staring out through some windows overlooking

Dealey Plaza. These men made no effort to identify themselves, but they neither looked nor acted like local officers, and Jean assumed that they were federal agents of some kind, although there was no way to know for sure.

At first, they were friendly and almost apologetic for detaining her, but they soon adopted a more menacing mood. They kept pecking away at her with the same probing, repetitive questions until she wanted to scream:

"Why did you come here today?"

"Why were you in the street just before the shots were fired?"

"How many shots did you hear?"

"Where did you think they came from?"

"Why did you run up the hill?"

"What did you think you saw?"

From the beginning, they seemed to want to hear answers that were impossible for her to give, and they made their displeasure evident when the "right" answers were not forthcoming. The more "wrong" answers she gave, the more hostile they became in their questioning, but there wasn't the slightest doubt in Jean's mind about what she had seen, and even in these increasingly unpleasant circumstances, she clung steadfastly to her story. The constant badgering made her angry and a little belligerent, but it in no way diminished the clarity or the terrible impact of what she had witnessed.

"I'm telling you, I saw somebody shooting at the president," she told them again and again. "He was standing behind the wooden fence at the top of the grassy knoll."

"The top of the what?"

"The grassy knoll." (Jean didn't realize it at the time, but she now believes she may have been the first person to use this term to describe the now-famous hillock in Dealey Plaza.)

"Well, you don't know what you're talking about," she was told sternly. "You couldn't have seen any such thing."

"How do *you* know?" she flared.

"Look, Mrs. Hill, you're only making trouble for yourself if you persist in this story."

"I know what I saw," Jean persisted.

"I don't think you do," the interrogator growled, "and if you know what's good for you, you'll keep quiet about it. It would be very foolish of you to ever repeat what you're saying outside this room."

Jean knew she could not possibly be the only eyewitness to be questioned by the authorities and wondered why she was the only person in the interview room. In point of fact, other witnesses who were also at the Criminal Courts Building that afternoon included Gail and Bill Newman, who had covered their two small children with their own bodies when the shots were fired, and Chalres Brehm, who had seen part of Kennedy's skull fly to the left rear of the limousine when the fatal bullet struck. Jean would become well acquainted with some of these witnesses later, but at the moment she had no idea who any of them were and they were not allowed to compare their accounts of the assassination during the course of the afternoon.

She wished desperately that she could somehow get in touch with J. B. Marshall, but she knew it was next to impossible. Adding to her uneasiness and frustration was the fact that J. B. was scheduled to leave on a 10-day deer hunting trip as soon as his shift ended that afternoon. Because of the assassination, he might not be able to go, since all police leaves might be canceled, but she was anxious to talk to him, and the thought of having to wait for 10 days was almost more than she could bear.

The questioners returned then, breaking into her thoughts and starting the interrogation all over again.

"Did you see a bullet hit the ground near you?" she was asked.

"Not that I remember. Why?"

"Then what made you jump back from the president's car so suddenly."

"I just realized that I shouldn't touch it, that's all."

"What were you doing out in the street in the first place?"

"I was trying to get him to turn toward me."

"Who?"

"President Kennedy."

"Why?"

"So Mary could take his picture. But just as he turned, the first bullet hit him."

"How many shots did you hear?"

"I'd say at least four to six. Maybe more."

The man stared coldly at her for a moment. "That's ridiculous," he said. "You had to be hearing echoes, not shots. We can account for only three bullets, and that means there were only three shots, maximum. The evidence shows they were all fired from a window in a building overlooking the site, not from this 'grassy knoll' of yours."

"All I know is I heard more than three shots and at least one of them came from behind the fence at the top of the knoll," Jean said. "Why are you treating me this way, like I'm a criminal or something? Why do you keep asking me these questions if you don't want to hear my answers?"

"Because your answers are wrong—and potentially dangerous," the interrogator said. "They'll only confuse matters, and they could cause you a lot of grief if you aren't careful." He shook his head in disgust and disbelief.

While Jean considered herself a virtual prisoner in the small interview room, all sorts of media people were apparently roaming at will among the law enforcement officers, federal agents and witnesses in the building. And when she was taken downstairs to the sheriff's office—and finally re-encountered Mary in the process—reporters and TV cameramen swarmed around the two women like flies. (It should be noted, and Jean readily admits, that Mary's recollections of the period immediately after the shooting do not necessarily coincide with Jean's own. Differences exist in their recollections of when and where they were reunited following Jean's run up the knoll.)

One of the reporters introduced himself as Jimmy Darnell, a newsman for WBAP-TV, Channel 5, the NBC affiliate for Dallas/Fort Worth.

"The network's pressing us to get some statements from eyewitnesses about the assassination," Darnell told Jean. "Do you mind if I ask you a few questions, ma'am?"

To Jean, the newsman's polite, soft-spoken approach was a pleasant contrast to the abrasive manner of the interrogators in the upstairs interview room. Brash, headstrong and feeling rebellious at the time (as well as being "a little wild" by her own admission), Jean conveniently forgot those interrogators' grim warnings not to repeat her story outside that room. And in doing so made what she now concedes was a terrible error in judgment.

"No, I don't mind," she said with a shrug, "as long as you promise not to call me a liar like everybody else I've talked to this afternoon."

Jean would not see or hear any of the television interviews she granted that afternoon for almost 25 years, but they would be broadcast to countless millions of other Americans within a few minutes. Jean's voice-only interview with Jimmy Darnell was the very first eyewitness account of the assassination to be carried by NBC News that afternoon, and an hour or so later the network followed up with on-camera interviews with both Jean and Mary. These were the only eyewitness interviews presented by the network during the first hours of its continuous coverage of the assassination.

The damage that would later cause Jean unlimited regret was done almost immediately at the beginning of the first interview.

"Could you give me your name and address, ma'am?" Darnell asked.

"I'm Jean Hill of 9402 Bluff Creek in Dallas."

"That's 9402 Bluff Creek?"

"That's right . . ."

It all seemed so inconsequential at the time. Only amid the agony that was to follow did Jean realize the import of what had happened. Her address had been broadcast—not once, but twice—on nationwide television. In essence, Jean Hill had suddenly become public domain, accessible to anyone who was curious enough, or hostile enough, to seek her out. And after the bizarre story of what she claimed to have seen that day was also aired, there would be plenty of the curious and the hostile alike. The doorway to trouble—in the form of threatening letters, crank telephone calls, midnight prowlers and all manner of unwelcome intrusions—had been left wide open.

That was only the start of it. In addition to the dozen or so newspeople whom Jean encountered that afternoon, she would soon be contacted by reporters from all three major U.S. networks and the British Broadcasting Corporation (none of whom had the slightest trouble locating her, for obvious reasons) and asked to elaborate on her story. Long before the storm of publicity died down, all hope of future privacy, security and peace of mind had died for Jean as well.

While Jean was in the sheriff's office, she was also asked to give a deposition detailing what she had witnessed, but Jean maintains that she was merely handed a blank form and told to put her signature on it. Later, she says, the same information that Mary had given was merely repeated on Jean's deposition form and she was never given an opportunity to read it at the time. This has led a number of people to question the authenticity of Jean's account of the afternoon, since no mention is made in the deposition of her being taken forcibly to the Criminal Courts Building and the impression is left that she, Mary, and reporter Jim Featherston of the *Dallas Times Herald* came to the building together.

In the bedlam following the shooting, Mary had already allowed Featherston to take possession of her only remaining Polaroid picture. It would be published in the *Times Herald* that weekend, along with an article based on Featherston's interviews with Jean and Mary. Later, the surviving photo would also be distributed to papers everywhere by United Press International and would become perhaps the single most widely published still photograph to capture the act of the assassination. It clearly told a graphic, gruesome story.

President Kennedy was still semi-upright and in the act of slumping toward Jackie, and a white-helmeted J. B. Marshall and part of his motorcycle were clearly visible in the foreground.

The photograph also showed the expanse of wooden fence at the crest of the grassy knoll, and at almost the same spot where Jean had seen the shadowy figure of "the shooter," a fuzzy, indistinct form of some kind was barely visible. It wasn't actually identifiable as a person, but merely as something that seemed not to belong at that particular spot.

Later, when Jean saw the photograph, she became more convinced that the strange shape behind the fence could actually be "the shooter" himself.

By shortly after 4:00 P.M., news vendors in downtown Dallas were getting up to $10 per copy for the edition of the *Dallas Times Herald* carrying details on the arrest of a suspect named Lee Harvey Oswald, an employee of the Texas School Book Depository, who was to be charged with both the murder of President Kennedy and the fatal shooting of Dallas policeman J. D. Tippit. Police had evidence that Oswald fired the fatal shots at the motorcade from a "sniper's nest" on the depository's sixth floor. On an inside page in the front section, the same edition also carried the reproduction of Mary's Polaroid picture and the story on Mary and Jean.

"Standing in the street at the triangle west of the Houston and Main Street intersection," the story read, "Jean Hill, of 9402 Bluff Creek, and her companion were eyewitnesses to the shooting of President Kennedy in Dallas Friday.

"Both heard a sequence of shots, saw the President slump over toward his wife, heard the piercing scream of Mrs. Kennedy.

"They glanced up to see a man run up the hill across the street from them . . ."

(Like many of the accounts published during those frantic hours following the assassination, the story was not totally accurate. Mary Moorman had never claimed to see either "the shooter" behind the fence or the running figure of the man in the brown coat. It was only Jean who had made this assertion.)

The report included this quote from Jean, who had been close enough to hear Jackie Kennedy's words distinctly at the moment the president was hit:

"Then the President looked up and just about that time he grabbed himself across the chest and looked like he was in pain. He fell toward Jackie across the seat.

"She (Mrs. Kennedy) said, 'My God, they've shot him,' and she fell across him. I would say about six shots rang out and everybody started screaming and falling down . . ."

Neither Jean nor Mary saw that edition of the *Times Herald* that evening, and apparently neither did any of the agents and officers who were questioning them—which was fortunate. Otherwise, the interrogation might have gone on all night.

Over the next few hours, circumstantial evidence steadily mounted against Oswald, who was being interrogated a few blocks to the east at the Dallas Police Department. In addition to the three spent cartridges found in the "sniper's nest," officers had also found a rifle with Oswald's palm print on it in the school book depository, and his prints were all over the boxes supposedly used to steady the weapon. The concept of a "lone assassin," which would subsequently blind the Warren Commission to masses of contradictory testimony and hundreds of unanswered questions, was already entrenching itself in the minds of law enforcement authorities.

But for some of them, Jean believes, the concept may have been there all the time.

As the emphasis shifted to Oswald, the officers at the Criminal Courts Building gradually seemed to lose interest in Jean and Mary. Finally, after they had been left alone for more than an hour and seemingly forgotten, the two women simply walked out of the Courts Building and kept going until they got to the car. Nobody actually gave them permission to leave, yet nobody tried to stop them either.

It was after 9:00 P.M. as they hurried the two blocks down

Houston Street to where they had parked Mary's 1961 Thunderbird that morning, crawled wearily into the car, and headed straight for home. Could it possibly have been only eight or nine hours since all this began? Jean asked herself disbelievingly.

At the moment, Jean was more concerned about her 12-year-old son, Billy, and her 10-year-old daughter, Jeanne, than anything else. Although she had a standing arrangement with a neighbor to care for the children after school if she wasn't home, she had never expected to be this late, and she had not even been able to get to a telephone to call and explain the situation. She also felt emptiness and disappointment at realizing that J. B. had probably left town without knowing of her problems and would not be back until a week from Sunday.

As the T-Bird glided east through a stricken and grieving Dallas, a sense of unreality seemed to hang in the very air. Jean was worried, exhausted and sick at heart, but she was also relieved that the most traumatic, unsettling incident she had ever experienced was finally over.

Mercifully, she could not know that the calamitous events of today were a mere prelude to what lay ahead. The greatest ordeal of Jean Hill's life had barely begun.

CHAPTER TWO

The Shock and
the After-Shock

When she first opened her eyes the next morning and looked out into the sunlit back yard, Jean felt calm and well rested, and her mind was briefly free of memories of the day before. The deep sleep into which she had finally fallen sometime after midnight had temporarily blotted out everything, but then the full comprehension of what she had witnessed in Dealey Plaza and experienced later in the upstairs interview room came back to her again, and she could almost feel the weight of it crushing her into the mattress. She lay there for a long time after that, mentally sorting through all the grim details, as she had already done a dozen times before. She fervently wished that she could pull the covers over her head and go back to sleep for the rest of the day—maybe even for the rest of the month—but that, of course, was out of the question.

Instead, she finally got up and dragged herself through some semblance of an ordinary weekend morning routine, throwing on her robe and making her way down the hall to the den, where she found Jeanne in front of the TV. Saturday morning fare normally consisted of reel after reel of animated cartoons, but today the nation was in mourning and nothing even remotely humorous was being shown on any of the channels. Billy was already off somewhere, doing what 12-year-old boys do on Saturdays, regardless of what might have happened the day before, but Jeanne was sitting and staring morosely at the small, flickering screen.

"I just can't understand why somebody would do something like that," Jeanne said, glancing up. "Why do you think they shot him, Mom? President Kennedy, I mean."

"I don't know, baby," Jean said woodenly. "I just don't know. Do you want some breakfast?"

"No, thanks, I already had some cereal," Jeanne said, "and I wasn't very hungry anyway. Hey, you know what? People have brought all kinds of flowers down there to Dealey Plaza where the assassination happened. They're piled up everywhere. They showed it on TV awhile ago. That's kind of nice, isn't it?"

"Yeah, it's real nice, baby," Jean said. In spite of herself, her eyes were drawn to the screen, which showed an endless line of mourners filing past Kennedy's coffin in the Capitol in Washington.

After a minute, feeling on the verge of tears, Jean forced herself to look away and went on into the kitchen to make coffee. She had voted for JFK in 1960, and although she had never been a strong supporter of many of his policies, she had always admired his personal charm and charisma. Now it was all gone forever and the thought filled her with a deep, aching sadness. She was sure she would have felt the same, even if she had not been standing a few feet away when Kennedy's head was blown apart.

While the coffee was brewing, she ventured outside more or less out of force of habit to pick up the newspaper—and realized immediately that she had made a mistake. On this day, November 23, 1963, looking at a newspaper was even worse than watching TV. It was like pouring salt into an open wound—especially if you lived in Dallas, Texas, and your name was Jean Hill.

There was a large, somber portrait of JFK in the center of the front page, and across the top were bold, blaring headlines which read:

KENNEDY SLAIN ON DALLAS STREET;
JOHNSON BECOMES PRESIDENT

Without really wanting to, Jean read for the first time about Lee Harvey Oswald, the prime suspect in the case, who was described as a 24-year-old ex-Marine, an avowed Marxist and a onetime defector to Russia. Oswald was accused of firing the fatal shots at the motorcade from a sixth-floor window in the Texas School Book Depository, and the authorities seemed to have little doubt that he was guilty as charged. Although, like Jean, several other eyewitnesses expressed the belief that some of the shots had come from the grassy knoll area, there was no official talk of other suspects. At the time the newspaper went to press, less than 12 hours had elapsed since Oswald's arrest, but it already was being made to sound like an open-and-shut case.

Almost before she realized what was happening—or even why—Jean's thoughts jumped back to an incident that had taken place several weeks earlier while she was in Oklahoma City. On that mid-October visit, she had had dinner with a close friend, who had recounted a very strange and unsettling story.

The friend had nervously told Jean of attending a speech by Herbert J. Philbrick, whose career as an FBI counterspy working within the Communist Party U.S.A. had been detailed in the best-selling book and TV series, "I Led Three Lives." The speech had been sponsored by the Oklahoma City Bar Association and after it was over, Jean's friend had been invited to stop by for a drink at the home of the lawyer with whom Philbrick was staying while in town. According to Jean's friend, Philbrick had gotten very drunk, begun cursing President Kennedy and his "New Frontier" programs, and accused JFK of "ruining" the country.

"But we're going to take care of all that," Jean's friend had quoted Philbrick as saying in the presence of the friend and Philbrick's lawyer host. "We're going to get rid of Kennedy for good when he goes to Dallas next month!"

Her friend had clearly been upset, but afterward, Jean had dismissed the threat as mere "drunk talk." The incident had slipped into the back of her mind and been forgotten—until now.

From there, Jean's mind skipped forward to yesterday, to "the shooter" behind the fence and the man she had seen running toward him. When she closed her eyes, she could almost recreate the exact scene in her mind. It made her shudder.

"Why are they concentrating so totally on Oswald?" she asked herself. "Why do they all seem so blind to any other possibilities?"

Did anybody else in Dallas besides Jean herself know anything about Philbrick's alleged threat? she wondered. Since Philbrick had worked for the FBI, was he referring to federal agents when he talked about what "we" were going to do? If Philbrick knew about the assassination plot weeks in advance, how many others knew about it too? And if others did know, how could Oswald be the only guilty party?

She pondered the same troubling questions over and over, but she couldn't come up with a single satisfying answer.

According to the newspaper, Oswald was being questioned by Capt. Will Fritz, head of the Homicide Bureau of the Dallas Police Department. Fritz, who looked more like somebody's granddaddy than a hardnosed investigator with a reputation for persuading even the most vicious criminals to confess, was a legend among Dallas cops. If Fritz was as good as everyone said he was, maybe he would get to the truth yet, Jean thought. She had heard J. B. Marshall mention Fritz's name more than once, and she knew that with J. B. and other young uniformed officers on the force, Fritz held almost god-like stature. Unlike many of the others, though, J. B. had actually worked for Fritz as an undercover officer when he first joined the force, and he considered "old Cap," as he called him, a good friend.

I ought to try to call J. B. right now, Jean thought abruptly. She was dying to tell him about all the things that had happened to her anyway, and maybe he could give her an idea of what was *really* going on at police headquarters . . .

Then the sudden, sickening realization hit her like a blow to the stomach: J. B. was gone—totally and irretrievably gone for the next eight and a half days. He was hundreds of miles away in the mountains of Colorado, where there were no telephones, no telegraph wires, and not even any mailboxes. Damn, she thought despairingly, he was utterly beyond her reach.

Thinking about J. B. had been another mistake, she told herself, as tears pushed against her eyelids. It was probably the biggest and worst mistake she could have made this morning.

All it did was add a load of aching loneliness to the burden of shock, grief and worry that was already weighing her down.

"I can't just sit here blubbering," she told herself sternly. "I've got to make myself do something."

She thought of calling Mary, but something told her that would be yet another mistake. Mary was a dear and trusted friend, but somehow the timing just wasn't right. They had already exchanged every scrap of information and every thought or semi-thought they had had about the assassination, but if Jean called, they would inevitably end up going back over everything again, bit by bit and piece by piece, and it could only make Jean feel worse under the circumstances. Naturally, she would call Mary later, but right now, if she couldn't be with J. B., she preferred total solitude.

So she finally wiped her eyes, pushed the newspaper away and stood up resolutely from the table. Then she walked across the kitchen and picked up an almost-new legal pad which she used for making shopping lists and writing notes to the kids. Since she couldn't talk to J. B. right now, she thought, she would write him a letter. Even though there was no way to mail it to him, she could at least put down all the puzzling, perplexing thoughts that were racing around in her head and let him read them when he came back.

Maybe putting it all down in black and white would help her make some sense out of what she had seen and heard. And in the bargain, she thought, it just might help keep her from going insane.

Outside of the sentences that flowed from her brain onto the pages of the legal pad in front of her, nothing that happened that day seemed to have any meaning. The sensation that she was actually communicating with J. B. grew and grew until it was almost as though he were right there in the same room with her. Jean wrote and wrote until her fingers ached and her hands cramped, and still she kept writing. Her words were spiced with references to the times they had spent together, especially the times when she and J. B. had gone target-shooting with .22 rifles along the Trinity River:

"It's one thing to pop away at a target, but since I saw JFK's head blown off, I've been wondering if I'll ever be able to fire a gun again . . ."

She also made a passing reference to the Philbrick story, which she had mentioned to J. B. previously:

"Do you suppose Philbrick could really be involved in this thing? His prediction about Kennedy certainly came true—in spades—and it just makes me wonder if he's not leading more lives than he ever admitted to . . ."

The hours crept by and Jean lost all track of time until the telephone rang at a little before four o'clock that afternoon.

The caller identified himself as a correspondent for CBS News.

"We're trying to interview as many assassination eyewitnesses as possible," he said. "If you wouldn't mind, we'd like to come to your home and shoot you sometime in the next day or so . . ."

"You'd like to *what*?"

"Shoot you. . . . I mean, film an interview with you at your home. That's 9402 Bluff Creek, right?"

"Yes, but . . . but how did you know where to find me?" Jean stammered.

"That was easy," he said. "When your name and address gets broadcast on network television, you can't be too hard to locate. Don't you remember being on NBC Friday afternoon?"

"Uh, not exactly," she said vaguely, hesitating at the idea of talking to any more media people, but intrigued by the prospect at the same time. "I know I talked to a bunch of reporters, but I didn't have a chance to watch much TV that day and I never got to see myself. I guess it'll be all right if you want to come out. Just tell me when . . ."

The CBS reporter wasn't the only caller that day, however, and the next one wasn't nearly as friendly.

"Are you Jean Hill?" he asked in a tone that was amiable enough at first.

"Yes, I am," she said, thinking it was probably another newsman. "What can I do for you?"

"For starters, you can learn how to see better and talk less," he snapped, his voice suddenly changing. "I saw all that bullshit about how you thought you saw a second assassin when Kennedy was shot—somebody besides Oswald, I mean."

"That's right, I did," she said firmly.

"In a pig's ass!" he snorted. "You saw a second assassin about like you saw a dog in Kennedy's car. You said that too, didn't you? You said you saw a *dog* in the president's limousine, for Chrissake! How crazy can you get?"

Jean suddenly felt a tingling wave of embarrassment, and she knew her face was flushing bright red. She had been afraid that her chance remark about the dog would come back to haunt her, and now it had. It was all so stupid, so totally insignificant—and yet so damning at the same time.

"I saw something . . . some kind of movement down in the seat of the car," she said lamely. "My attention was focused on something higher up, and I just caught a peripheral glimpse of it. Later, I asked somebody, 'Could it have been a little dog? Liz Taylor takes a little dog around with her, but I can't see Jackie Kennedy bringing one on a trip like this.' So in the confusion of the moment, with these reporters all yelling stuff at me at once, I said I saw a dog."

"There was no damned dog in the car, lady," the caller said coldly.

"Well, I guess I saw something else then. Maybe it was a bouquet of flowers or the paper they were wrapped in. All I know is I saw something moving."

(Jean had, in fact, seen a picture of what she now suspected was her notorious "dog" on an inside page of the *Dallas Morning News* that very morning. It was a large bouquet of yellow roses which had been given to Nellie Connally, the governor's wife. The photo showed the bouquet disheveled and abandoned in the floor of the presidential limousine as it stood outside Parkland Hospital.)

"I don't think you know shit, lady," the caller snarled. "And if you can't tell the difference between a dog and a bouquet of flowers, how the hell can you expect anybody to believe you saw somebody shooting at Kennedy?"

"Because that's where I was looking," Jean said helplessly. "I wasn't looking down at the seat of the car. I was looking up toward the grassy knoll."

"Well, I think you'd better just keep your mouth shut from now on," the caller yelled, "because you don't know what the hell you're talking about." He hung up with a crash that made Jean's ears ring.

She sat there for a long time afterward, shaking inside and cursing herself for saying something so thoughtless and inane. But Mary hadn't known what the flutter of movement in the car seat could have been either, and at the time, amid the constant storm of questions and the pressure-packed intensity of the interrogation, with the news people all rushing her, it hadn't seemed that important. "Just say what you saw," one of the reporters had urged. "If you think you saw a dog, say you saw a dog. What difference does it make?"

And so she had blurted it out, not once but several times.

Now it was clear that it *did* make a difference, she thought. It gave those who sought to promote Oswald as "the lone assassin" a convenient—if clumsy and inconclusive—tool to cast doubt on her reliability as an observer. In that sense, although Jean didn't fully realize it until much later, it would continue to make a difference for a very long time to come.

By Sunday morning, Jean was feeling somewhat better. Although a pall of gloom was draped like funeral crepe over the whole city and a cold knot of uneasiness still lurked beneath her ribs, the raw horror of Friday afternoon was now covered with a thin layer of scar tissue. The pain hadn't stopped, but it was slightly less excruciating. The shock was still there, but a kind of numbness was setting in. Even her chagrin over the "little dog that wasn't there" had diminished to manageable proportions.

To hell with them, she thought bitterly. She might not know what she hadn't seen, but she knew full well what she *had* seen. She would never forget it, not if she lived to be 100.

But even as the pain and shock eased, Jean sensed the beginnings of an entirely new emotion—fear. Never in her adult life had Jean Hill been accused of being shy, reticent or easily spooked. She had always been self-assured and never afraid to speak her own mind on any subject, but now she was beginning to regret her outspokenness about what she had seen in Dealey Plaza.

The man who had called about the dog had done more than chide or ridicule her; there had also been a strongly implied threat in his words. He was representative of countless people in Dallas who were reacting with heat and rancor, and possibly something worse, to what they perceived as attacks on their city. Newspaper editorial writers and TV commentators across the country were already referring to Dallas as a "city of hate," and that hate was starting to manifest itself in various ways. A number of Dallas clergymen had received anonymous telephone calls that weekend, warning them of dire consequences if they should say anything derogatory about Dallas or its leadership from their pulpits.

By the time the city's ministers had finished delivering their sermons that Sunday morning, however, the world would be handed the greatest evidence yet that Dallas was not only a "city of hate," but that it had not yet quenched its thirst for blood and vengeance.

As it did in most American homes, the TV in Jean's den

remained on constantly that morning of November 24, 1963. Even as Jean rushed around helping Jeanne get ready to attend a special children's matinee performance of the opera *Carmen* at Dallas's State Fair Music Hall, the TV continued a steady stream of coverage of the assassination's aftermath. The networks were alternating back and forth between memorial services in Washington for the slain president and the basement of the Dallas City Hall, where police were preparing to transfer Oswald to the county jail six or seven blocks to the west.

Jeanne was all dressed and they were about ready to leave when Jean called to her daughter: "Come on, baby. If we're going to get some lunch before the opera, we need to get started."

As she headed for the den to turn the TV off, Jean glanced up at the clock on the kitchen wall. It was precisely 11:20 A.M.

It was apparent as she approached the set that the long-awaited transfer was under way. She saw Oswald being led past throngs of newsmen and officers by a detective in a tall white hat, and she hesitated for a second as she reached out for the on-off knob. At that instant, the scene before her seemed to jump straight out of the screen and hit her squarely in the face.

She saw a stocky man in a hat and a dark suit dart from the right side of the televised picture with a pistol in his hand. She heard the pop of a gunshot. She saw Oswald cringe and grimace in pain as the bullet tore through him.

And in that phenomenal instant, she recognized the stocky man with the gun. She had never seen him but once before, but she recognized him as surely as she would have recognized her own face in a mirror.

Jean gasped wide-eyed as policemen converged on the gunman from all sides, struggling with him and wrestling for the pistol. She shrank back from the TV, feeling faint.

"Jeanne!" she cried. "For God's sake, Jeanne, come here quick!"

She sensed her daughter running toward her in alarm.

"What's the matter, Mom? What is it?"

"That man . . ." Jean choked, pointing at the screen. "He just shot Oswald. He shot the man they say killed Kennedy."

"Oh, no!" Jeanne said, crouching beside her mother. "What man?"

"I don't know his name," Jean whispered, "but I recognized him, Jeanne. I swear I did. He's the same man I saw running in Dealey Plaza right after Kennedy was shot."

Jean's 10-year-old daughter looked at her with an expression that she was destined to see innumerable times on other faces in the months and years to come.

"Are you sure, Mom?" Jeanne asked softly, the doubt obvious in her voice. "I mean, that seems awful weird, don't you think?"

"Yes," Jean admitted, shaking her head, "it does seem weird. It seems downright crazy and I don't know how it could be possible, but I swear to God it's true. I saw that man's face from almost the same identical angle Friday afternoon, and I know it's the same person—the same man I chased on the grassy knoll. I absolutely *know* it is!"

After she had somehow managed to get Jeanne to the music hall, Jean spent the rest of that afternoon wondering in all seriousness if she were losing her mind. Maybe the psychological stress and mental anguish of the last two days had simply driven her over the brink of insanity, she thought. She didn't *feel* crazy—disturbed and on edge, yes, but not crazy. On the other hand, though, what difference did that make? Most crazy people probably didn't *feel* crazy either, but that didn't make them any less so.

The earth seemed to be spinning wildly and out of control beneath her—so much so that it might fling her off into black, empty space at any moment.

How had she arrived at this haunting juncture in her life anyway? How could a simple "country girl," who had been born and spent all but the last few years of her life in rural or small-town Oklahoma, find herself squarely in the middle of one of the most earthshaking events of the century? How could naive, unsophisticated Jean Lollis Hill, who had never expected to catch so much as a single glimpse in her entire lifetime of anyone as important as the president of the United States, actually have been standing only a few feet away when John F. Kennedy was murdered? How had the fates conspired to make her perhaps the closest civilian eyewitness to one of the great crimes of all history?

Her mind whirled backward across the years in search of some sort of answer, but there was none. Up until she had moved to Dallas in the summer of 1962, nothing out of the ordinary had ever happened to Jean Lollis Hill. Up until then, her life had always seemed totally routine, utterly predictable, and without even the slightest clue as to what lay ahead.

The only child of Clarence and Irene Lollis, Jean had been born on February 11, 1931, at the tiny crossroads community of Ferguson, Oklahoma, some 75 miles southeast of Oklahoma City, and had remained there for the first dozen years of her life. Despite her parents' divorce while she was still a toddler and the ill feeling that had marked every contact between them after that, Jean remembered her childhood as being pleasant for the most part. Her mother had kept a comfortable home and taught young Jean the fundamentals of homemaking, and her father, a state game ranger, had taught her to fish, hunt and handle firearms as well as any boy, and to love the outdoors. But perhaps the major factor in her pleasant childhood memories revolved around her paternal grandfather, Jacob Lollis. She had spent much of her time with him during her transition from toddler to teenager, and still there had never seemed to be time enough when she was with him. Grandpa Jacob had been her hero of heroes, and it had been from him that she had learned the most about courage, strength, honesty and other basic values.

In 1943, she had moved with her father to the town of Wewoka, where Jean graduated from high school in 1948. That fall, Jean enrolled at Oklahoma Baptist University, some 40 miles down the road at Shawnee, to major in English, but dropped out of college two years later to marry Bill Hill, a young serviceman bound for the Korean War. It would be four years—and two babies—later before Jean returned to OBU to resume her education, finally earning a bachelor of arts degree and an elementary school teaching certificate in the spring of 1955. Soon after, the family moved to Oklahoma City, where Jean landed her first teaching position that fall.

For the next seven years, virtually all her time was occupied with being a mother, a wife and a teacher, more or less in that order. The time slipped past quietly and uneventfully for the most part, until mid-1962, when a job change for her husband, who by now was enjoying a lucrative career with Science Research Associates (SRA), had brought them to Dallas. They had built a ranch style house, which was virtually identical to the one they were vacating in Oklahoma City, on the far southeast side of the city, and had seemingly gotten off to a promising start in their new surroundings.

For the time being, Jean had given up her profession to devote full time to being a homemaker, but instead of making their life together better, this change only seemed to cause their relationship to deteriorate. Within a few months, severe marital difficulties had developed, and suddenly Jean was facing the greatest crisis of her life as she saw her marriage—and the limited-but-secure world she had always known—falling rapidly to pieces around her.

And now this, she thought. This insáne, unexplainable madness, engulfing her like a childhood nightmare, except that it was all too real. As bloody and bizarre as it was, it was actually happening, and there seemed no way to wake up from it. Especially now, after what she had seen today.

Time and again, she watched the TV replays of the first murder in history to be broadcast "live" on nationwide television. She watched the man who had now been identified as a Dallas nightclub operator named Jack Ruby as he materialized out of the crowd in the basement of the Dallas City Hall with a revolver in his hand and lunged toward Oswald. And each time the scene repeated itself, she felt the same burst of recognition as she saw Ruby's half-profile just as he pulled the trigger. To Jean, that was one of the oddest parts of all: She hadn't even gotten a full side view of the gunman, but in her mind there was no doubt whatsoever that he was the same man in Dealey Plaza.

"The feeling never faltered," Jean would recall many years later. "Every time I saw the scene replayed, the feeling was exactly the same. I knew this was the man in the brown coat, the one I had seen running toward 'the shooter' a split-second after the fatal shot hit JFK, the same man I had chased when I ran up the grassy knoll."

And yet, how could this be? Every practical fiber of her being shouted at her that it was utterly unbelievable, but the rest of her shouted defiantly back: Unbelievable, yes! Impossible, no!

Even today, Jean has no logical explanation for this remarkable case of déjà vu. But it is certainly worth noting that a number of other reliable witnesses also claimed to have seen Jack Ruby in Dealey Plaza at the time of the assassination. One of them was Victoria Adams, a school book depository employee, who told the Warren Commission that she and a woman co-worker, Avery Davis, saw a man in the plaza just minutes after JFK was shot who looked "very similar" to the photos of Jack Ruby that were published and televised after Oswald's death.

Cameraman Malcolm Couch of WFAA-TV, Channel 8, in Dallas, also testified that another newsman had seen Ruby near the depository right after the assassination. That other newsman was Wes Wise, who would later be elected mayor of Dallas, but who would never be called by the Warren Commission to confirm or deny Couch's testimony. Although Couch's hearsay account has been repeated in many assassination-related books, none of their authors apparently bothered to contact Wise for verification. (Wise told this author in June 1991 that his remarks had been misinterpreted and that he had actually seen Ruby in Dealey Plaza on November 23, 1963—the day *after* the assassination.)

In addition, there would be several other witnesses who produced testimony or evidence placing Ruby in Dealey Plaza at or around the time of the assassination. Among them were an off-duty Dallas policeman, a Dallas amateur photographer and a key witness discovered by New Orleans district attorney Jim Garrison during his investigation of an assassination conspiracy. But, unfortunately, many years would pass before any of these other witnesses became known to Jean.

At any rate, the sheer unbelievability of what she had seen, coupled with the indelible images burned into her consciousness, propelled Jean into another long, introspective letter-writing session with the legal pad that afternoon. If she could just get enough of her impressions down on paper while they were fresh, she thought, maybe she and J. B. could tie everything together in some logical way when they were able to sit down and discuss it later on.

"I had never seen this man in my life before last Friday, and then only at a distance," she wrote. "He was a total nonentity to me, so how could I remember his face so clearly when I saw him again on TV? And what caused me to be right there, no more than a couple of feet from the TV screen at the very second Ruby appeared? Was that just some kind of coincidence, or was it fate?"

As it had earlier, the subject of guns invariably cropped up from time to time in her writings:

"I'm getting leery of even having guns in my possession, and I'd certainly be afraid to leave the house with a gun, because someone would be bound to wonder who my target was. But I also wonder if anybody should go out in Dallas these days *without* a gun."

And later:

"With as many potshots as people are taking around this town, I only wonder if we'll ever get back to just shooting at turtles down on the riverbank. Oh, God, J. B., if only I could see you, even for a few minutes, it would make all the difference in the world . . ."

The week that followed was little more than one long blur for Jean, punctuated here and there by a few fleeting but sharply focused incidents.

She did three interviews at her home with representatives of major TV networks, carefully avoiding the subject of small dogs in all three. She prepared a Thanksgiving dinner for herself and the kids. She called Mary a time or two, but neither seemed to have much heart for long conversations. They talked listlessly about getting together, but the subject always seemed to die before any concrete plans were made. And Jean didn't even try to tell Mary about the similarity between Jack Ruby and the running man in Dealey Plaza.

She did make an attempt, however, to explain the similarity to a few close friends and members of her family in Oklahoma—with very unsatisfactory results.

"You need to relax and try to get yourself together," one friend advised. "Seeing something like the assassination can be an awful shock, and you sound like you're under a helluva strain."

She argued vehemently with her soon-to-be ex-husband when he came to pick up the children for an outing. He made his feelings crystal clear about her media interviews and her claims of multiple assassins.

"You're behaving like a total fool, Jean," he told her angrily. "I can't believe you'd say all these silly things to anybody, much less to all those reporters. If you don't have any respect for yourself, it looks like you'd care enough about the children not to embarrass them like this."

Early on the evening of Sunday, December 1, Billy and Jeanne were still staying with their father, and Jean was sitting alone in the den, nursing an aggravated case of the blahs, when the phone rang and she rose reluctantly to answer it.

"Hello," she sighed, half expecting it to be one of the kids calling with some problem.

A second later, her knees went weak as she heard J. B.'s low, rumbling drawl on the line. She hadn't allowed herself to expect him back before sometime early the next morning at the earliest. But here he was, calling her by the name no one else besides her mother ever used.

"Norma Jean, it's me," he said simply. "Are you okay?"

"I am now," she managed to say around the tight feeling in her chest and the lump in her throat. "God, you don't know how glad I am to hear your voice. It seems like you've been gone for a year."

"Yeah, I know," he said. "We're still out on the other side of Fort Worth, but we had to stop for gas and I couldn't wait any longer to call. We should be in Dallas in about an hour. Can you meet me someplace?"

"Sure, I think I can manage that," she said with a quaver in her voice. "Where?"

He mentioned the parking lot behind a service station near Forest Avenue and Central Expressway. They had met there several times before and she knew the place well. It was only about 15 minutes from her house.

"I can't wait to talk to you, J. B.," Jean said breathlessly. "Have you heard about everything that's happened? About Ruby and Oswald?"

"Yeah," he said grimly. "The first thing we did this morning when we got out of those mountains and back to civilization was buy a stack of newspapers. That was the first any of us had heard about it, but I read most of the way back when I wasn't driving. Damn, I can't believe something like that could happen right there in the city hall basement."

"I saw it on TV when it happened," Jean said, "and I still can't believe it either."

"It sure makes the Dallas police look like a bunch of damned morons," he said. (Like most other members of the force, he pronounced it "poh-leece"; it was a type of "inside humor" among Dallas officers.) "I bet there's going to be unmitigated hell to pay because of it."

"It'll blow over," Jean assured him. "At least you didn't have anything to do with it."

"Well, I'm sure not looking forward to going back to work," he said. "But I am glad to be home. I missed you, Norma Jean."

As he spoke, she could almost picture how he looked, leaning against the wall of a phone booth somewhere, most likely with a stubble of beard on his face, and a cigarette poking out from the corner of his crooked little grin.

"I missed you too," she said. "I've got so much to tell you I don't know where to start."

It was a classic understatement, she thought. She could never remember wanting to see anyone as badly as she had wanted to see J. B. Marshall for the past 10 days. Before that, it had been different. It had started as a mere flirtation, an exciting little game, but by the time of the assassination, she could already feel it ripening into something much more significant. During the interminable interval since, while J. B. had been so far away and seemed so totally lost to her, her feelings had grown steadily more intense.

And now, hearing him on the phone and knowing they would soon be together again, she felt herself totally consumed by them.

"Hey, I've got to go," he said, "but I'm heading that way. If we don't run into any problems, I should be there by 8:30 or so."

"I'll be waiting," she assured him above the thumping of her heart.

CHAPTER THREE

Living with the FBI

It was amazing, Jean thought, as she drove home in the early morning hours of Monday, December 2, 1963, how a little time could tarnish the brightest dreams and transform the most optimistic hopes into disappointment.

Only three or four hours ago, she had been convinced that she was falling in love—something she had vowed never to do again after her marriage had fallen apart—but now, if anything, she felt more lonely and demoralized than ever. She was assailed by doubt, confusion and perplexity, and she could only wonder if she should ever see J. B. Marshall again.

Her long-awaited reunion with J. B. could hardly have begun on a more romantic or exhilarating note. He had been as unshaven, disheveled and road-weary as she had expected, but he had seemed just as thrilled to see her as she was to see him. And for the first hour or so after they were alone together, there had been an abundance of physical and emotional communication between them, but very little of it had been of the verbal variety.

Eventually, though, she had gotten around to telling him what she had seen at the moment of the assassination, and they had taken time out from their lovemaking to relive those fateful moments and compare notes.

"I couldn't hear the shots over the noise of my cycle, but I could see what was happening," J. B. explained. "When that head shot hit Kennedy, I was sure it was coming from the right front because of the direction the blood flew. It looked to me like at least two people were firing from a forward position, and I thought there might be as many as six in all. The first thing I thought was, 'Oh, shit, they're going to pick all of us off like ducks in a gallery.' So I started circling, figuring a moving target would be harder to hit."

"That's what you were doing when I ran right past you," Jean said. "I saw a puff of smoke and a figure with a gun behind the wooden fence at the top of the grassy knoll, and I started running that way. You almost ran over me."

"Sorry," he said, "but I never knew you were there. I was too preoccupied with snipers. Are you saying you actually saw somebody fire at Kennedy from behind that fence?"

"That's what it looked like, and then I saw another man running toward him a second after the shots were fired." (She decided for the moment not to tell him that the running man had been an absolute double for Jack Ruby.)

"Could this other guy have been some kind of law officer? Maybe he was trying to grab the guy with the gun."

"No, I didn't get that feeling," Jean said. "I can't really explain why, but I had the distinct impression they were in it together and the second man was running up the hill to help the first one get away."

J. B. laughed and lit a cigarette. "I can just see you taking off after those two," he said. "I don't guess you caught either one of them, did you?"

"No," she admitted. "By the time I got there, there was total confusion, but . . ."

"Damned good thing, too," J. B. interrupted. "If you'd found them, you just might've got shot yourself, like poor old Tippit did."

"Well, I still might have found them," she said defensively, "except that two guys who said they were Secret Service collared me about that time and dragged me away."

"Oh, come on, Norma Jean, what're you talking about? There weren't any Secret Service on the ground in Dealey

Plaza—at least not as far as I know. I thought they were all in cars."

"Well, you'd better check again. These guys were either Secret Service or they were lying through their teeth."

She went on to recount in detail the tedious, exhausting, frustrating hours that had followed—the confiscated photos, the intimidating strong-arm tactics of the men who had detained her, the questioning in the Criminal Courts Building, the media interviews, and all the rest. When she finished, J. B. was no longer laughing; he wasn't even smiling.

"You need to keep quiet about this thing," he said gravely. "I don't think you ought to be talking to anybody about it anymore, okay? I'd just as soon nobody knew who Jean Hill is or what she saw."

"It's a little late for that, J. B.," she told him bluntly. "Good Lord, I've already been in the papers and on all the TV networks—at least I guess I have, because they all interviewed me and I told all of them what I saw. So everybody already knows about it, and people have been calling me from all over, wanting to talk . . ."

He looked at her and shook his head. "I wish you hadn't done that, Norma Jean," he said unhappily.

"But I was just trying to do my duty as a citizen," she protested. "What's so wrong about that?"

"Nothing, I guess," he said resignedly. "It's just that citizens who mind their own business have a habit of living longer than citizens who don't. That's all."

After that, some sort of invisible barrier seemed to have risen up between them to mar the intimate sense of closeness, almost of oneness, that they had experienced such a short time earlier. A little later, J. B. had said he was hungry and they had driven to an all-night coffee shop on Buckner Boulevard for post-midnight hamburgers and french fries.

The coffee shop was only about 10 minutes from where Jean lived, and as they sat there, she mentioned that the kids were gone and offered several none-too-subtle hints that J. B.

would be welcome to spend the rest of the night at her house.

"No, I guess I'd better go on to my place," he said. "I need to make sure everything's okay. Besides, I don't even have a fresh change of clothes with me and I've got to be at work early tomorrow." He glanced at his watch. "Today, I mean," he said. "God, it's after one o'clock, and it'll be close to two by the time I get home."

They didn't say much as they drove back to the parking lot where Jean had left her car. But when they got there, Jean asked J. B. to wait a minute and she ran over to her Volkswagen bug, unlocked the door on the driver's side and reached into the back seat, feeling around until she found the legal pad which she had spent much of the preceding week filling with her thoughts.

"Here," she said, thrusting the pad at J. B. through the open window of his GMC pickup. "It'll take you a while to read all this, but I wish you would anyway."

"What is it?" he asked, leafing through the tightly scribbled pages.

"It's some letters I wrote you while you were gone. Just ramblings about a bunch of different stuff, but I spent a lot of time writing it. I guess I did it for 'therapy' as much as anything—you know, something to keep me from going nuts until I could talk to you in person again. I think you might find some of it pretty interesting."

"Sure," he said, putting the pad in the seat beside him and slipping his arm around her. "I'll read every word. I promise."

"Am I going to see you tomorrow?" she asked.

He looked uncomfortable. "I don't know," he said. "I hope so. I'll give you a call."

"Is there some kind of problem?" she asked pointedly, frowning at him. "Is there something you're not telling me, J. B.?"

He made a wry face. "My, uh, wife's coming back from California tomorrow or the next day," he said. "I wish she wasn't, but she is."

"But I . . . I thought that was all over," Jean said, feeling queasy inside. "I thought you were permanently separated and getting a divorce."

"So did I," he said. "I've told her to go ahead with the divorce, and I thought she was going to, but. . . . Hell, Norma Jean, I don't know what she's trying to prove. Just wants to stir up some trouble, I guess."

Jean tried to smile, but it didn't work very well with the hot tears that were welling up in her eyes.

"Well, I guess she's sure doing that, all right," she said, turning quickly away and feeling utterly empty inside.

Toward the end of the first week in December, Jean received a telephone call from a polite, quiet-spoken man who identified himself as J. Gordon Shanklin, special agent in charge of the Dallas office of the Federal Bureau of Investigation.

"I understand you were an eyewitness to the assassination of President Kennedy," he said, then added unnecessarily: "Is that true, Mrs. Hill?"

Since it was clear that he already knew the answer to the question, there was no point in being evasive, Jean thought. "Yes," she said, "but I've already told the authorities everything I know about it."

"Well, I hate to bother you," he said ingratiatingly, "but it would be very helpful to us if we could just go over it with you again, just to make sure we have everything straight. We also have some photographs we'd like you to look at, if you don't mind."

Jean thought back to what J. B. had told her the previous Sunday night, and she hesitated. She hadn't seen J. B. since then, but she had talked with him twice by phone, and even though she had been decidedly cool toward him, he had repeated his urgings not to discuss anything she had seen in Dealey Plaza with anyone.

"I don't really have anything to add to what I've already said, Mr. Shanklin," she told the agent. "It was a very unnerving experience and I'd just as soon not talk about it anymore.

Couldn't you just leave me out of it?"

"I understand how you feel, Mrs. Hill," he assured her, "but I'm afraid that's impossible. I promise we won't take one more minute of your time than we have to, but we want to do everything in our power to determine exactly what happened that day, so I'm going to have to ask you to go back over the whole thing again."

"Well, all right," she said. "When do you want to talk to me?"

"I'd like to have you come down to our office tomorrow morning," he said. "I'll send a car for you, so you don't have to worry about finding your way."

"Isn't that an awful lot of trouble?" she asked. "I mean, can't you just talk to me here?"

"We have some very large photographic illustrations of the Dealey Plaza area that we'd like you to look at," he said, "and it will be much more convenient to do this at our office. By the way, we can explain the situation to your employer if you have to take time off from work."

"That's not necessary," she said. "I'm only working part-time as a substitute teacher right now, and I don't have an assignment for tomorrow."

Her voice was steady, but there was a discernible sinking feeling in the pit of her stomach. She had never dreamed they would make her go to FBI headquarters to be questioned; she had just assumed they would do it at her home. She felt like a third-grade pupil being summoned to the principal's office, and suddenly, without knowing why, she was scared.

"Very good," Shanklin said. "We'll pick you up at 10 A.M. sharp then—if that's agreeable with you."

It was odd, Jean thought, how people like Shanklin could make it sound as if you had a choice in something, when you actually had no choice at all.

"Okay," she said disconsolately and hung up.

The surroundings into which Jean was ushered the next morning bore little resemblance to the interview room in the Dallas County Criminal Courts Building where she had been questioned nearly two weeks earlier. The Dallas FBI headquarters was on an upper floor of the Federal Building on Commerce Street and several blocks removed from Dealey Plaza. But it was coldly impersonal, devoid of windows, and crowded with well-groomed men in stiff white shirts and conservative gray and dark-blue business suits, and in a way, its atmosphere was even more menacing than the other place.

The two men who had driven her there in a plain, unmarked Ford showed her into the office of Special Agent Shanklin, who turned out to be a kindly looking, middle-aged, slightly pear-shaped man in a rumpled, unstylish suit. To Jean, he looked more like a fatherly college professor than one of J. Edgar Hoover's top men, and she might have liked him if the circumstances had been different. As it was, his warm handshake and disarming smile were probably intended to set her at ease, she thought, but somehow they didn't quite get the job done.

"Thank you for coming, Mrs. Hill," he said, as though she had had some say-so in the matter. "We appreciate your cooperation."

It soon became apparent, however, that Shanklin would be only one of several agents participating in the questioning. She was led into a large room where two other men—neither of them showing the slightest trace of a smile—were seated at a long table beside a series of huge photographs that leaned against the wall. Each of the pictures looked to be half the size of the garage door on Jean's house, and each showed a portion of Dealey Plaza in such infinite detail that she could practically count the blades of grass.

Shanklin introduced the first man as a fellow FBI agent, but Jean was stunned to learn that the other man was with the Central Intelligence Agency. The thought of being interrogated by the FBI was scary enough, but the idea of the CIA was somehow even more awesome.

"We want you to look at these pictures very carefully," Shanklin said, "and show us as precisely as you can where you were in Dealey Plaza at the time the presidential motorcade arrived there on November 22."

She went to a photo taken from the north side of the plaza and pointed to the spot in the grassy triangle where she and Mary had stood. It was almost as if she could still see their footprints there, and she was certain that the spot she indicated was within a foot of their exact location. Could it have been only two weeks, she wondered, since the whole thing had happened? Sometimes it seemed more like two years.

"My friend and I were here," she said. "Right at the curb."

"I assume you're referring to Mary Moorman, Mrs. Hill," Shanklin said. "Is that correct?"

Jean nodded. "Yes, we were taking pictures."

"According to the Dallas police, that area was closed to civilians," the agent said, "so how did you happen to be there?"

"We, ah, persuaded one of the officers on duty that he should let us go in there to take our pictures."

"And how did you do that?"

"I guess you might say we flirted with him," Jean said, feeling her discomfort beginning to grow.

"I see," the agent said without changing expression. "And do you think the fact that you were well acquainted with other members of the Dallas Police Department had some bearing on his decision to let you in?"

The question caught Jean off-guard and she hesitated. "Well, I . . . I guess it might have," she finally managed to say.

"Did you mention J. B. Marshall's name to this officer," asked the other FBI man. "Is that one of the reasons he let you pass?"

"I might have," she said, growing steadily more unsettled. "Yes, I probably did."

"What exactly is your relationship with Officer Marshall, Mrs. Hill?"

Jean felt a light film of perspiration forming on her face. How did they know about J. B.? What else did they know? "He's a friend," she said.

"An *intimate* friend, Mrs. Hill?"

"You could say that."

"How long have you known him?"

"About a month, I guess. Maybe a little more."

"And would it be accurate to say that you are, uh, romantically involved with Officer Marshall?"

Jean felt something inside her snap and a wave of anger momentarily inundated her fear. "I don't think that's any of your business," she snapped. "What does all this have to do with the Kennedy assassination anyway?"

At that point, Shanklin interceded. "I apologize for my colleague," he said, smiling at Jean. "I think we should move on to another line of questioning for right now, Jim," he told the other agent. "We can come back to that later if necessary."

At this point, the man whom Shanklin had identified as a CIA agent assumed the lead role in the interrogation.

"You said you were 'right at the curb' on Elm Street as the presidential limousine approached," he began, "but weren't you actually in the street itself for several seconds?"

"Yes," she said, regaining some of her composure, "I jumped into the street and called out to the president to look in our direction. We wanted to take his picture."

"Is that the only reason you were in the street?"

She frowned. "Yes, of course," she said.

"And why did you suddenly jump back from the president's car at almost exactly the instant the shooting started?"

"I just realized I probably shouldn't be so close, and I decided I'd better get back."

"Did a bullet hit the ground near you? Was that one reason you jumped back?"

"No. I mean, if it did, I didn't see it or hear it."

"But you do claim to have seen someone fire at least one shot from almost directly across Elm Street from where you were standing, right?"

"Yes. From behind the wooden fence at the top of the grassy knoll."

The agent named Jim picked up an oversized photo of the knoll area and the fence and put it down beside her.

"Show us where you think this gunman was at the time," he said.

Jean pointed to a spot near the corner of the fence at its eastern end. "Right about there," she said, feeling a little of her confidence returning. If they wanted to talk about "the shooter," she had no doubts about what she had seen.

"And you believe this shot you say you saw was one of the shots that hit the president?"

"Well, I can't be sure," Jean said. "All I know is I saw the puff of smoke just as the president was hit in the head."

"I understand you also saw someone else acting suspiciously," Shanklin asked in his usual "let's-be-friends" tone. "Why don't you tell us about that?"

"I saw a man running from the direction of the school book depository toward the spot where I saw the shot fired."

"Did you get a good look at this person?" the CIA man asked. "Good enough to identify him if you saw him again?"

"Yes, I saw him very clearly."

"Had you ever seen him before?"

"Not that I remember." She tensed suddenly, anticipating the next question.

"Have you ever seen him since?"

Cold, sticky panic rose up inside her. Did she risk being called an idiot by telling them she believed the man to be Jack Ruby? Or did she deliberately lie to the FBI and run the risk of something far worse?

She looked desperately toward Shanklin, hoping to find some kind of reassurance in his face. He was smiling expectantly at her and clearly had no inkling of her dilemma.

"Yes," she said in a hoarse whisper. "I'm almost sure I have."

The CIA man raised his eyebrows in surprise. "You have? Where?"

"On TV," she said miserably. "I saw him shoot Lee Harvey Oswald on TV."

The CIA man's jaw dropped perceptibly. The FBI agent named Jim looked as if he had just swallowed something distasteful. Shanklin chuckled softly, stubbed out his cigarette and immediately lit another.

"I want to make sure I understand this," Shanklin said finally. "You're telling us that the man you saw running in Dealey Plaza was Jack Ruby, but you didn't realize who it was until you saw him shoot Oswald on TV. Am I getting it right?"

Jean nodded. "Look, I know how stupid it sounds, but I honestly believe it was him," she said. "When I saw him run up and shoot Oswald, I almost fainted. You can ask my daughter."

Shanklin smiled at her again. "I'm sure you do believe it, Jean, but . . ." He paused. "You don't mind if I call you Jean, do you?"

She shook her head. At this point, she didn't care what anybody called her.

"I don't doubt your sincerity for a minute, Jean," he said gently. "But the fact is, it couldn't have been Ruby. We've got several witnesses who can place Ruby somewhere else at the time of the assassination."

"I don't know anything about that," she said. "All I know is what I saw."

"I don't think you saw *anything*," the CIA man said bluntly. "I think you've got an overactive imagination—plus maybe you like all the attention you've been getting lately. Could that be it, ma'am?"

"I'm not making this up, damn it," Jean insisted. "Whether it was Ruby or not, I know what I saw when Kennedy was shot."

For what seemed to Jean to be an hour or more, the questioning revolved slowly and tediously around the identity of the running man and the jumble of interwoven Dealey Plaza images that were burned into her brain. And, inevitably, the questioners came back to the same point again.

"You can't really be sure that this running man had anything to do with the assassination, now can you?" the CIA man asked.

"I . . . I felt sure about it at the time," Jean said.

"Since you know now that Ruby was somewhere else, are you willing to say it definitely *wasn't* Ruby then?" the second FBI agent pressed.

Jean's head was spinning and she felt totally bewildered.

"No!" she cried. "I mean, I still think. . . . Oh, God, I don't know."

Shanklin glanced at his watch. "It's all right, Jean," he said. "It's almost noon and I think we've put you through enough of this for one morning. Why don't you think about it over the weekend and we'll talk again next week. I'll call you on Monday."

"You mean I'm going to have to come back down here and do this again?" she asked brokenly.

Shanklin's smile never wavered. "Oh, yes, Jean," he said cheerfully. "The only thing for us to do is keep right on going over the whole thing. We have to go over it and over it and over it until we're sure we've got every single detail straight—regardless of how long it takes."

"The bastards are obviously trying to make you change your story," J. B. growled. "They want to break you down a little at a time until they get you so damned tired and confused that you don't know what you saw anymore, and don't care."

"Well, they're doing a pretty good job of that," Jean said wearily, "but I can't see what difference it makes. If they don't like what I have to say, why don't they just ignore me?"

It was Saturday night and they were sitting in his truck in the same service station parking lot where they had met nearly a week ago. As put out with him as Jean had been, she had felt a surge of excitement when J. B. had called and told her he urgently needed to see her.

"That's not the way these people operate," J. B. told her. "It looks to me like they've already decided the case they want to make, and they'll do their damnedest to completely discredit any witness whose testimony might weaken that case."

"You mean they want everybody to buy the idea that Oswald was the only one involved?"

"That's the way it looks."

"But why?"

"Just think about it for a minute. What if somebody high up

in the government was mixed up in this thing? Hell, what if some dissident faction in the FBI or the CIA decided Kennedy was too liberal and had to be eliminated? What if J. Edgar Hoover himself wanted to get rid of Kennedy?"

Jean stared at him horror-stricken for a few seconds. "Oh, come on," she said. "You don't really believe that. I mean, how could you?"

"I'm not saying I do," he said. "I don't really know what I believe right now, but I know that if enough people say there was somebody shooting besides Oswald—and if they keep saying it long enough—it could lead to a lot wider, more thorough investigation. And if there *was* a plot of some kind inside the government, that'd be the last thing the plotters would want. That's why the things you're saying could be so dangerous to them."

Jean reached out and caught his arm. "I wish you'd quit saying these things, J. B." she said. "You're scaring the hell out of me. It's bad enough being questioned for hours by the FBI without thinking the FBI's part of some kind of plot."

"Look, Norma Jean," he said, "I don't know what these people are up to, but some things have been happening at work this week that I don't like at all. There've been FBI agents all over the police department for the past few days. They're questioning everybody who had anything to do with the Kennedy motorcade, which is okay up to a point, I guess. But what really burns my butt is they've been going through the personal stuff in our lockers at the station. That's why I had to talk to you and warn you."

"You think they went through your locker?"

"You're damned right they did," he said through clenched teeth, "and I might as well tell you, they took some things too."

"What kind of things?"

He looked into her eyes for a second, then glanced quickly away. "They took that note pad you'd written all those letters and stuff on while I was out of town," he said heavily. "I think they got a couple of pictures too, but the letters were the most important thing."

Jean felt a chill travel up her backbone. She had expressed thoughts and feelings in those letters that had never been intended for any eyes except J. B.'s. But it wasn't the emotional, deeply personal things she had written that worried her most right now; it was the references she had made to the assassination and a possible conspiracy.

"Maybe you just lost the pad somewhere," she suggested hopefully. "Maybe you put it somewhere else and forgot."

"No," he said, "it was definitely in my locker. I'd been reading at least three or four pages in it every day before I went on my shift. Then, when I opened the locker yesterday, it was gone. I know the bastards took it. They're the only ones who could have."

Jean laid her head against the back of the seat and closed her eyes, wondering how everything in her life could get so screwed up and twisted out of shape in such a short time. It made her cringe to think of the FBI reading what she had written on the legal pad.

"Okay, so what do we do now?" she asked after a long silence.

"We're just going to have to be damned careful," he said. "It would've been better if you'd just kept quiet in the first place about what you saw, but the best thing you can do now is make the FBI think they're shaking your story. Make them think you've changed your mind and had second thoughts."

"Hey, wait!" she protested. "The president of the United States got his brains blown out and I think I saw two of the people responsible. How can I lie now and say I didn't see anything? I just won't do it, J. B.—not for you or the FBI or anybody else."

"All right," he said resignedly, "I can't make you do it. But I don't think you understand what you're dealing with here, Norma Jean. These people have only just started with you, and they're liable to make a lot more trouble for you before they're through. They'll invade your whole life if they feel like it, and there's not a thing you can do to stop them."

"But there's no way I can be that important to them," she

said disbelievingly. "Why would they waste so much time and energy on me?"

"Don't kid yourself," he said. "They'll keep on for as long as it takes, until they've either discredited you—or destroyed you."

It took only a matter of a few minutes for J. B.'s grim predictions to start coming true.

When Jean returned home shortly after 9:00 P.M. that night, her headlights picked up the shape of an unfamiliar car parked a half-block down the street from the cul-de-sac in front of her house. For an instant, as she rapidly approached the car from the rear, then whipped past it, she was almost sure she could see two dark figures inside the car.

The next morning, as Jean backed out the driveway en route to a nearby supermarket to pick up a few things she needed for Sunday breakfast, she again noticed a strange car parked in almost the identical spot where she had spotted the car the night before. It was definitely not the same vehicle, because this one was light beige, whereas the other had been a dark color, probably either black or navy blue.

On an impulse, she turned in that direction, although the opposite way was the most direct route to the store. A second later, she passed the car head-on and got a clear view through the windshield of the two men sitting in the front seat. They were young, well groomed and dressed in white shirts, conservative ties and dark suits. The car was plain, unmarked and equipped with ordinary Texas license plates, but it might as well have had "Federal Bureau of Investigation" printed on its sides in six-inch letters.

On her return trip, the car was still there, and she noticed that, once she had pulled into the driveway, it was effectively screened from her view by the slight curve in the street and the cover of some shrubs and a telephone pole. Jean realized, however, that any vehicle entering or leaving her driveway would be readily apparent to the occupants of the parked car, and with binoculars, they would have no trouble at all reading license numbers from that distance, even at night. Each time she bothered to check for the rest of the day, the car was still there.

The two young, crew-cut FBI men who arrived on Monday morning to take Jean back downtown for her second round of questioning were in a dark blue Ford that bore a marked resemblance to the first car she had seen parked down the block Saturday night. But much as she felt like confronting them with shouted accusations, she bit her tongue and said nothing until she was seated in Special Agent Shanklin's office.

"Why are you spying on me?" she demanded then. "Why were your men constantly watching my house all weekend?"

She had half-expected Shanklin to feign innocence and deny the whole thing, so his bland straightforwardness took her by surprise.

"You have absolutely nothing to fear from FBI surveillance, Jean," he said, smiling. "We're there to protect you, that's all."

"Protect me from what?"

"From any threat that might come along," he said. "You're an important witness and we value your safety."

"Well," she responded petulantly, "I value my privacy, and I just wish you'd leave me alone."

"I'm afraid that's impossible under the circumstances," he said.

"But how long is this . . . this 'surveillance' going to last?"

"As long as necessary," Shanklin said, shrugging his rather stooped shoulders. "Now, if you don't mind, I think we should get on with our discussion of what you saw on the day of the assassination."

Shanklin led her into another room, where the same FBI agent who had participated in the first interrogation was waiting. She noted with some relief that at least there was no CIA representative present, but her relief was short-lived. As it turned out, this didn't mean that today's session would be any less wearing—or the questions any less loaded and insistent— than they had been the first time.

"How familiar are you with rifles and other types of firearms?" asked Shanklin's co-interrogator to begin.

"Fairly familiar," she said. "I've been around guns since I was a kid. My father was a game ranger."

"Do you own any weapons yourself?"

"Yes," she said, wondering where this line of questioning was leading, "I have a .22 rifle that I use for target-shooting. I also have a shotgun and a pistol that my father gave me."

"Can we assume then that you don't have the same fear of guns that some women do?"

"I guess so," Jean said, beginning to feel confused again.

"Does J. B. Marshall own a high-powered rifle? A larger caliber than a .22, I mean?"

"Yes, he has a deer rifle. I think it's a 30.06."

"Do you ever go target-shooting with J. B. Marshall?"

Jean hesitated momentarily. "Occasionally," she said, trying to keep her voice steady.

"Where do you go on these occasions, and what kind of targets do you ordinarily shoot at?"

"There's a place on the Trinity River below Seagoville where it's safe to shoot," she said. "I shoot at cans, floating logs, sometimes turtles." She was careful to say "I" and not "we."

"And how long has it been since you were down on the river taking potshots at the turtles?"

Jean felt a puzzled frown crease her forehead, not so much because of the question, which seemed to lead nowhere, but because of the particular phraseology used by the agent. For some reason, the term "potshots" sounded oddly familiar, but why?

Then she remembered. She recalled writing something about "potshots" in one of her unmailed letters to J. B. One of the letters on the legal pad that had disappeared from J. B.'s locker at the police station.

She glanced at Shanklin, who himself was glaring at the other agent.

"I don't see any point in all this," she flared, unable to contain her anger. "What difference does any of this make? What does shooting turtles have to do with shooting presidents, for God's sake?"

"I think we can move on to something else, Jean," Shanklin said brusquely. "Let's go back and review exactly what you saw and heard when the shots were fired in Dealey Plaza . . ."

As the days stretched into weeks and fall turned rapidly into winter, Jean had almost no contact with J. B. Marshall, except for a few brief telephone conversations. But the words of warning he had spoken to her that night in the parking lot often returned to torment her, as it became distressingly clear that he had been right.

The around-the-clock FBI surveillance of her home continued unabated. Now there were always at least one or two agents camped in a car a half-block or so down the street, waiting and watching. Sometimes, she felt like going down and sarcastically inviting them inside, but she didn't.

Meanwhile, Shanklin also continued to summon her periodically to his office for more questioning. And however far afield the questions might stray, they always eventually found their way back to what she had witnessed on November 22.

Not long before Christmas, Jean realized that the FBI's intrusion into her personal life had taken on yet another dimension. She now found herself being followed by agents in unmarked cars virtually every time she left the house.

She complained to Shanklin the next time she saw him, but he dismissed her complaints with a smile, a shrug and a single word:

"Protection, Jean," he said. "Protection."

Jean, however, had her own one-word definition for what was happening to her.

She called it "persecution."

CHAPTER FOUR

Eyewitness—
or Suspect

It was Saturday, December 21, 1963, exactly four days before Christmas. But when Jean thought of the date, she identified it less with the impending holiday and the spirit of peace and goodwill than with the rending, ongoing tragedy of the Kennedy assassination.

It was a month minus one day since the shots fired in Dealey Plaza—whether by a single solitary gunman or a team of a half-dozen—had irrevocably altered her life. She had scarcely found time even to think about the approaching Yuletide season, much less to carry out all the Christmas shopping and attendant chores that had always occupied her at this time of year. And, in fact, the only real reason she could find to anticipate the holiday was that it gave her an excuse to get away from Dallas for several days and escape the insane game she was being forced to play.

About the middle of that afternoon, several hours after Billy and Jeanne had left to spend the weekend with their father and while Jean was preparing for their upcoming trip to Oklahoma to spend the holidays with her family, she received an unexpected phone call from J. B.

And despite her hurt and disillusionment and the sense of doom she had felt hanging over their relationship, it was impossible to pretend that she didn't welcome his call.

"I figured you'd be going to Oklahoma pretty soon, and I was hoping we could get together for a while before you left," he said. "I miss you a lot, Norma Jean, and I'd sure like to see you."

Something about the sound of his voice made the coldness inside her melt like snow under a bright sun. "Well, I'd like to see you too," she admitted. "But I'll probably have an FBI escort if I come. They've been camping outside my house and following me everywhere."

"Knowing the way you drive, I'm sure you can shake 'em long enough to meet me someplace if you really want to," he said.

"I can try, I guess. Where?"

"Is your phone okay? Is it safe, I mean?"

"As far as I know. You don't think . . ."

"Who knows?" he said. "But just in case, I'll just say meet me at the first place at White Rock Lake where we ever went together. I know you remember where that is, don't you?"

She flushed slightly at the memory. "Yes, I remember. What time?"

"As soon as you can make it," he said eagerly. "I'll be halfway there by the time you hang up the phone."

As soon as they had been together for five minutes, Jean knew it was starting all over again. Only this time, it was deeper and wider and more turbulent than before. And she was drawn into it more irresistibly than ever.

"I told myself I was going to say no if you ever asked me out again," she said. "I told myself I wasn't knowingly going to stay mixed up with a married man. I must've told myself that a hundred times, for all the good it did."

"Don't worry," he assured her. "Things're going to work out. My wife's going to file for a divorce right after the holidays. I can practically guarantee it."

"Don't string me along, J. B.," she said. "I've got enough worry and heartache with the FBI without you dealing me any more misery."

"I mean what I say," he assured her, "but we *are* going to have to be careful about the Feds. I'd just as soon they didn't know any more about us than they already do."

"From what I can tell, they know way too much already."

"Yeah, they probably know a lot more than we want them to," J. B. admitted. "There's no question they took that notebook out of my locker—I know that as well as I know my own name—and God knows what else they've been able to find out."

"They've been asking me things about you," she told him, "and I know they can tell it upsets me. Every time they take me down there for questioning, your name comes up. Why is that, J. B.?"

"There's more than one way to skin a cat, Norma Jean—or nullify a witness," he said bitterly. "If they can't discredit you one way, they'll try some other way. They'll try ripping your character and making you look immoral or flighty or undependable. Linking you and me together can only help them do that, at least until I can get free. And even then, it might cause you trouble."

"I can't see why," she said.

His explanation was characteristically blunt. "From everything that's been going on in the department, I get the distinct feeling the Feds think somebody in the Dallas police had something to do with the hit on Kennedy," he said. "I can't see any other reason why they'd be spending so much time grilling so many of our people."

"What about?"

"Hell, about everything. The parade route, the way the cars were arranged, the way our escort formation was set up, the fact that so many Dallas cops knew Jack Ruby, the fact that somebody let Ruby into the basement right before he shot Oswald, the fact that some of the cops were heard cussing Kennedy for being a flaky liberal. It just goes on and on."

"Did *you* know Ruby?" Jean asked in spite of herself. "You never mentioned it if you did."

"No, I didn't actually *know* him. I'd been in his place two or three times, and once he even bought a round of beers for the table where I was sitting. But I can't hardly think of a cop on the force that didn't wander into the Carousel once in a while, mostly because Ruby was always good for a free drink. I never remember saying anything to the guy outside of 'Hi.'"

"I can't believe the FBI suspects Dallas police of killing JFK," Jean said. "From everything you've said, I would've thought it was the other way around."

"Well, it could be," J. B. said. "It's crazy, but the Feds seem to think we had something to do with it, and a lot of us think the same thing about them. It's like nobody trusts anybody anymore, and there's no way you can conduct a legitimate investigation under those conditions. That's why this damned case isn't ever going to be solved—and it's why hanging around with a Dallas cop, married or otherwise, isn't the smartest thing to do these days."

"I'd be glad to take my chances with a cop if he was single, but maybe we really shouldn't see each other any more until both our divorces are final," she said. The words were as unpalatable as a mouthful of chalkdust on her tongue, but she felt that she had to say them anyway.

"Maybe not," he said, staring into her eyes, "but I don't think I can stand not seeing you at all, Norma Jean."

"Well, to hell with the FBI then," she said, kissing him. "I can't stand it either, so we'll just have to get by the best way we can."

They spent the better part of five hours together, and before Jean left to return to her empty house and the empty prospects before her, J. B. took a small, brightly wrapped package out of the glove compartment of the pickup and handed it clumsily to her.

"Here's a little something from Santa Claus," he said. "But don't wait for Christmas morning. Open it now."

She pulled the bow off and peeled the paper away to reveal a small velvet-covered box from a jewelry shop. She opened it and caught her breath at the sight of a tiny carved silver turtle on a silver chain.

"In memory of all those turtles we shot on the river," he said simply.

"It's beautiful," she said, putting it around her neck and fumbling with the catch until she got it fastened. "I'll wear it every day from now on."

She leaned toward him, pressing the little turtle between them as she held J. B. tightly against her. The lights along the lakeshore became a blur then, as tears filled Jean's eyes, but she didn't mind. As long as she couldn't see clearly, she could pretend for a few minutes that they were alone on the riverbank again, far from the mystery and disaster now swirling around them and threatening to engulf them.

But she could only wonder if they would ever find their way back to that kind of calm, uncomplicated time and place again.

In one sense, the five-day interlude in Oklahoma was a welcome respite from the unyielding pressures with which Jean had been living. It gave her an opportunity to hold the situation at arm's length and examine it in a more rational, less emotional way. But in another sense, the holiday sojourn became a mere void in which she drifted and marked time, especially after the festivities of Christmas Day itself were past, until she could go home again. She enjoyed seeing her parents and other members of her family, and Billy and Jeanne always had a good time in Oklahoma, but thoughts of J. B. were never far from Jean's mind, and by the morning of the fourth day, she was agonizingly lonely. Even the prospect of the omnipresent FBI car parked down the street and renewed summonses to FBI headquarters for questioning seemed a small price to pay for the chance to be with J. B. again.

She passed some of the time by writing a long letter to J. B., in which she told him in all candor and frankness how much she cared about him, and generally poured out her feelings as she had never done before. The act of writing it all down and reading back over it was gratifying and comforting in itself, but even when Jean started homeward on the early afternoon of December 27, she was still not certain that she would actually give the letter to J. B. Maybe it was something she had needed to express, just to clarify her feelings in her own mind.

But she wasn't sure she was ready to reveal those feelings to him—at least not yet.

The kids had elected to stay behind to enjoy the attention of grandparents and the company of friends and cousins whom they didn't get to see very often nowadays, and for the sake of expediency and economy, Jean found herself making the 200-mile, four-hour trip back to Dallas alone in the same car with her estranged husband. It was a far-from-pleasant experience, and they argued most of the way, mainly about Jean's involvement in the Kennedy investigation and the effect it was having (at least as far as their father was concerned) on the children.

"You're subjecting those kids to all kinds of problems and embarrassment," he accused. "And it's all because of your big mouth and that cop you're sneaking around with."

"You know what you can do with your holier-than-thou attitude," Jean retaliated at one point. "I'll see who I want to see and do what I want to do. If you'd done a little less 'sneaking around' yourself over the past 15 years, we might still be happily married. But as it is, what I do is no concern of yours anymore."

Despite the gloomy chill of the overcast day, she had been steaming with anger for hours by the time she got home, and she was so grateful and relieved when her ex's car screeched out of the driveway and left her standing there that she could have danced a jig. (That should really have gotten the attention of the pair of federal "watchbirds" down the street, she thought.)

She unlocked the front door, hauled her suitcase into the house, and flopped down on the couch in the living room. She was finally home again—home without the children for once, for five whole days—but apart from J. B., there seemed to be no purpose in her being there. Without J. B., floating in limbo at home would be no different from floating in limbo in Oklahoma.

She looked at the clock. It was a few minutes past six on a Friday afternoon, which meant he would be getting off in less than an hour. She wondered where he was working today. Probably manning a speed trap in one of three or four regular locations, but there was no way to tell which one.

"Oh, God," she whispered aloud, "I've got to see him. I've just got to. I think I'll crack up if I don't."

At that moment, as if by answer, the telephone rang.

Jean's heart was pounding furiously as she lifted the receiver, but her heart sank momentarily when she heard Mary Moorman's voice at the other end of the line, rather than J. B.'s. Then, when she realized what Mary was saying, her heart leaped all over again.

"J. B.'s been trying to get you all afternoon," Mary said.

"I just got in from Oklahoma," Jean gasped.

"Well, he wants you to meet him if you can. He's working a stakeout at the east end of the Corinth Street viaduct. He'll be there till seven o'clock."

"I'm on my way," Jean yelled.

She grabbed her purse and was about to run straight out to the driveway, where her Volkswagen was parked, when she caught herself. She strode briskly into the master bathroom, flipped on the light and looked at herself in the mirror.

"Umm, not too good," she told her reflection. "Better do a few quick repairs before I head out."

As usual, the repair work with the makeup, mascara and lipstick took longer than she anticipated. When she realized it was after 6:30, she called an abrupt halt, shoved the makeup kit into her purse and ran for the door, irritated at herself for wasting so much time.

She was further agitated when she reached the front porch to find that it had started raining. It was a cold, driving rain that pelted down in fat drops and was already making puddles in the street, but if it had been a few degrees colder, the rain would have been sleet, and that would have been even worse.

She had mentally plotted a route that would take her north on St. Augustine Road to Military Parkway, then west to Haskell Avenue, around the corner of Fair Park, then down through the near south side to pick up Corinth Street. It wasn't that far, as the crow flies, but with the rain and the Friday night traffic, it was going to take close to 25 minutes at best. She had to hurry.

The engine of the VW sprang to life and accelerated with a steady purring hum as she splashed out of the driveway into the street. If nothing else, the rain would make it easier to shake the FBI tail, she thought, and she was right. Within ten blocks, the pursuing headlights had vanished behind her and she was alone. Got to hurry, she told herself. Don't want him to leave before I get there. Got to hurry.

It was raining harder than ever as she turned left on Military, so hard that the windshield wipers had trouble keeping pace with the downpour, even on high speed. But the parkway was four lanes wide, with a broad median down the center, and there weren't many cars around, so now was her chance to make up some lost time. It was now or never, she knew, because once she passed Fair Park, she would be lucky to get above 30 miles per hour again. She gave the VW the gas and watched the speedometer needle climb past 50, then past 55.

Now she was almost to Forrester Field, a high school football stadium just north of the parkway. It seemed especially dark along this stretch of road, but she could dimly make out the lights along Buckner Boulevard a quarter-mile ahead through the pouring rain.

Suddenly, she thought she detected something in the roadway 20 or 30 yards in front of the speeding VW. She leaned forward, straining to see through the water cascading across the windshield.

At that instant, Jean's headlights illuminated the shape of a car. It was crossways in the road, squarely blocking her path, and—Oh, no! she thought—there were four or five teenagers behind it, trying to push it onto the median.

Jean hit the brakes desperately, but it was too late. The VW fishtailed on the slippery pavement with a sickening lurch, and then it was skidding straight toward the group of teenagers, now scrambling wildly to get out of the way.

She saw their white, terror-filled faces. She heard herself

scream. Then she jerked the steering wheel as hard as she could to the right, away from the teenagers, but toward the looming outline of the car.

Jean felt the grinding impact of the crash. She felt herself being hurled forward like a projectile. She was aware of the windshield shattering around her as she crashed through it head first.

"So this is what it feels like to die," she thought with curious detachment.

Then everything went black.

The sights, sounds and sensations of the living world came back to her slowly and from a great distance. She heard vague, mumbling voices coming from somewhere, but she couldn't decipher what they were saying. She forced her eyes open a narrow slit and saw a blur of light. She seemed to be lying on a bed of some kind, surrounded by a cloud of pale-beige fog. She wondered for a moment if this were the hereafter, but somehow it seemed too forbidding to be heaven and too bland to be hell. Then she realized that her head was filled with dull, throbbing pain and there was a swath of bandages running across her forehead and down one cheek.

Not heaven or hell, she thought. More like a hospital.

A white-clad figure materialized out of the fog and a face peered down at her.

"She's coming out of it now. She's coming around."

"Thank God," said somebody else.

The voices still had a mumbly, monotonous sound to them, but they were becoming clearer. With maximum effort, she managed to bring into focus the face of the nurse hovering above her.

"What's going on?" Jean heard her voice asking.

"You're in the Baylor Medical Center emergency room," the nurse said. "You went through the windshield of your car, but you were lucky. You've got yourself a pretty good concussion and your face is sprayed with glass, but it looked a lot worse when they first brought you in."

"What time is it?" Jean asked.

The nurse glanced at her watch. "It's 8:35 on Friday night," she said, looking slightly bemused. "Why?"

A hundred different concerns could have crowded Jean's mind at that moment: Was anyone else hurt in the accident? How long was she going to have to stay in the hospital? Would her face be permanently scarred? Was her car demolished beyond repair? Would her insurance cover the damage? But as it was, none of these questions even occurred to her.

There was only one thing on her mind right now—one overriding concern that obliterated all else.

"Good Lord," Jean moaned despairingly, "I've totally missed J. B."

For some reason, the nurse grinned.

"I don't think so," she said. "Not if you mean that big motor-cycle jockey who's been hanging around here for the past hour or so, looking like he'd lost his last friend. He's right here if you feel like seeing him."

"I do," Jean said. "Oh, yes, I really do."

Slowly, a tall, dark-blue uniform came into focus beside the bed, and then, as incredible as it seemed, she was looking up into J. B.'s face. She couldn't believe he was actually there. In spite of the nurse's assurances, she still wondered if she were having a dream or some kind of hallucination.

"Hello, Norma Jean," he said softly, leaning down over her. "You sure know how to scare the hell out of a guy, don't you?"

"How did you get here?" she whispered as the nurse moved discreetly away. "God, I hardly know where I am, myself, so how did you know?"

"I heard the accident report on my radio," he said. "It sounded like your car and it was in a location where I thought you might have been. Then, when I heard them call for an ambulance and say 'possible fatality,' I damned near burned the tires off my Harley getting over here."

"I'm so glad to see you," she said. "I didn't kill anybody, did I?"

"No, I talked to the ambulance driver and the investigating

officer. You tore hell out of a couple of cars, but nobody else was hurt."

"Get me out of here, J. B.," she said, trying to sit up. "I want to get out of here."

"But, honey, you're pretty banged up. Besides your face and head, you've got a bad sprain in one ankle. I think they want to keep you overnight."

"No," she said firmly. "I need the kind of treatment I can't get in this hospital—not in any hospital." She paused and looked deeply into his eyes. "Unless you've got to go home tonight, I mean."

He shook his head. "I'm not going anywhere," he said solemnly. "I'm staying with you. Wherever you are. For as long as you want."

She laughed softly, even though the motion made her headache worse.

"Gee," she said, smiling at him, "if I'd known I'd get that kind of results, I might have thrown myself through a windshield a long time ago."

The period of almost four days, beginning at the moment Jean and J. B. arrived at her house shortly before 11:00 P.M. that Friday night until he reluctantly went back to work his shift on New Year's Eve afternoon, ranked as one of the most idyllic and unforgettable interludes of Jean's life. For the most part, the weather remained threatening and inclement, with overnight temperatures hovering just above freezing, and they rarely ventured outside the house.

Even before they had left the hospital, Jean had dug in her purse, found the letter she had written J. B. in Oklahoma—now crumpled and sprinkled with tiny fragments of glass from the windshield—and given it to him to read. He had reread it several times and seemed deeply touched by it. She was equally touched when he told her how he had felt as he rushed toward the hospital that evening.

"When I walked into that emergency room and saw you were still alive, I knew there was no backing out for me," he said. "No matter what happens, I love you, Norma Jean, and I want to be with you from now on."

When they weren't in each other's arms, they had time to talk about things that had almost been forgotten during the calamitous six weeks just past. Jean hobbled around the kitchen on her sore ankle, cooking elaborate meals for them, which they consumed with boundless appetites. They laughed, they sang, they toasted each other. And then they made love some more.

For up to a day at a stretch during this time, Jean was able to forget completely about the FBI surveillance, although it was apparently continuing without pause (as an occasional glance out one of the front windows attested). And although the double garage was totally empty, J. B. left his truck parked in plain sight in the driveway to illustrate his unconcern about what the agents might see or think. For the first time in weeks, they were able to rediscover that there were more important things in their lives than the assassination and its lingering aftermath.

Not that they didn't talk about the Kennedy case and the increasingly tangled web of conflicting, confounding evidence being woven around it. On the contrary, they discussed it at greater length, and in a more thoughtful, analytical way than they had been able to do at any time previously. And as they did, Jean became more convinced than ever that a coverup of massive proportions was taking shape.

Up to now, she had tried hard to believe that the seeming inability of federal authorities to develop any conclusion beyond that of "Lee Harvey Oswald, lone assassin" was the result of honest mistakes, investigative carelessness, jurisdictional conflicts, lack of concrete evidence and sheer hardheadedness. But as J. B. gradually revealed the details of what had been going on in the inner sanctums of the Dallas Police Department over the past few weeks, she began to see a disturbing pattern emerging. It was a pattern that suggested not just a conspiracy with more than one assassin, but a monstrous coverup by someone high and powerful.

Jean had never realized until then just how worried J. B. really was.

"The Feds are tearing our whole department to pieces," he said. "They're slipping around and talking to guys' partners behind their backs, telling them a lot of lies about incriminating stuff their partners supposedly said about them."

"What kind of stuff?" Jean asked.

"You know, stuff like 'He's told us all about you and that kickback you took or that woman you're sleeping with.' Or anything else that might be incriminating in any way. Then, when they get something on some guy who might be able to cast some doubt on that 'Oswald-acted-alone' bullshit, they start leaning on him. I know of cases where they've told cops to alter their locations at the time of the assassination or deny something they might've heard over the radio. And they tell 'em, 'If you don't cooperate, we'll take your badge.'

"It's a kind of divide-and-conquer situation, and they've been especially rough on all the guys who were on motorcade duty that day. To tell you the truth, McGuire and I both expect to be kicked off the force just about any time now. So do a lot of other people. It's got everybody so damned on edge, they can't stand it. I've seen a half-dozen fistfights break out between guys I thought were best friends just in the past couple of weeks. One guy even tried to shoot his partner right there in the basement where Ruby killed Oswald."

"That's hard to believe," she said. "I always thought the Dallas poh-leece were like one big family."

"We were—with a few exceptions, of course. Lots of guys didn't like J. D. Tippit, for example, and now that he's dead, a lot of 'em still don't. I get the feeling the Feds think Tippit was in this thing with Oswald up to his armpits. That may be what started all this crap in the first place. On the other hand, it might not be."

"Why should the Feds want to mess up the whole department? What good does that do them?"

"Hell, they want to intimidate us to the point that no Dallas cop will dare dispute anything the FBI says about this case.

That means the Feds'll have a totally free hand in the investigation. Then, if they can't intimidate us, they're going to do their best to make us look like the biggest bunch of bumblers and clowns since the Keystone Kops. That way, if we come up with something counter to what the FBI claims, nobody'll believe anything we say anyway."

According to J. B.'s inside information, FBI sabotage and interference had not only been aimed at rank-and-file Dallas officers, but at its highest levels of leadership. Even Capt. Will Fritz, chief of the Homicide Bureau and the principal questioner of Oswald after his capture, had been subjected to official intimidation from Washington, J. B. claimed.

"The word is, 'old Cap' got a phone call from Washington right after Oswald was killed," J. B. said, "and whoever it was told him, number one, that Oswald was definitely 'his man' and he should consider the case closed. And, number two, they told him not to talk about anything pertaining to the Kennedy investigation with any other member of the department. Since then, 'old Cap's' drawn himself into some kind of damned shell and won't say a word to anybody, not even his best friends. I even went by and tried to talk to him, but he just ducked back into his office. I've also heard lots of rumors that Chief Curry was under heavy pressure from the Feds to back off the Kennedy thing once and for all."

"That really stinks," Jean said. "It'd stink even if it was just petty politics, but it sounds to me like they're really trying to hide something."

"They're going to get away with it too," he said, in one of the few glum moments of those memorable four days. "God knows how much evidence these people have destroyed or distorted by now, and when they get through, nobody'll know what to believe anymore."

"Tell me the honest-to-God truth, J. B.," she said. "Do you think anybody on the Dallas police force could've helped assassinate the president?"

"I just don't know," he said. "If you'd asked me that two months ago, I would've said 'Hell, no,' but now I'm just not sure."

Of all the interrogators who had questioned and badgered her, Jean had never told anyone about the uniformed policeman she had encountered behind the wooden fence on assassination day, just seconds before the so-called Secret Service agents had grabbed her. In fact, she had never mentioned the incident to anyone, not even J. B. But now she could no longer resist the need to talk about it.

"As far as you know, was there any reason for a Dallas cop to be carrying a rifle in Dealey Plaza the day Kennedy was shot?" she asked.

He gave her a strange look. "Not that I can think of," he said. "What makes you ask?"

"When I ran behind the fence, right after the shots were fired, I came face to face with this cop," she recalled. "At least I thought he was a cop. He definitely had a Dallas policeman's uniform on. And he had what looked like a rifle in his hands."

"Are you sure it was a rifle? I mean, could it have been a shotgun? I know there were some officers with riot guns there that day, at least a little later on. I don't know about right at the moment of the assassination."

"I can't be positive," she said. "At the time I was thinking 'rifle' because I knew those were rifle shots I'd just heard, but I guess it could've been a shotgun too. All I really know was it had a long barrel and a wooden stock."

Instead of going away, the strange look seemed to intensify on J. B.'s face. "I sure hope you never mentioned this to the FBI or the Secret Service," he said.

"I've never mentioned it to a single soul," she said, "not until right now. I honestly didn't think anything about it at the time, because in my own mind, I thought it was a situation where there were 'good guys' shooting back at the assassins. When I found out that wasn't true, I just sort of shoved the whole thing to the back of my mind."

"Thank God," he said, looking relieved. "If those people ever got ahold of something like that, it'd make every cop in Dallas a suspect."

"I don't think it's just the cops they're after," she said.

"Sometimes I feel more like a suspect than an eyewitness, my-self. Especially last week, when they started asking me if I owned any weapons and if you had a rifle and if I liked to shoot guns and things like that."

"That's part of the plan," J. B. said evenly. "That's the way these people want us to react. The more they can make us re-act like suspects—like we were the ones who did something wrong—the less they'll have to worry about us as witnesses."

Yes, Jean thought grimly, it was a ploy as old as crime itself: To divert suspicion from yourself, obliterate as much evidence as possible and point the finger of guilt at somebody else.

In that sense, they were all suspects.

CHAPTER FIVE

Subpoenaed
and Scorned

Like most other Americans, Jean had been aware that, just a week after JFK's death, Pres. Lyndon Johnson had signed an executive order creating a "blue ribbon" seven-member presidential commission, headed by Chief Justice Earl Warren, to investigate the assassination. But also like most other Americans during this period of confusion and consternation, Jean couldn't know of all the political manipulations that lay behind the creation of the Warren Commission.

At the time, she had no idea, for example, that by forming the commission and giving it almost unlimited authority, Johnson had successfully squelched moves in both houses of Congress, as well as by Texas attorney general Waggoner Carr, to launch independent inquiries that would have been beyond presidential control. Nor did she realize until much later that the Warren Commission's principal concerns were quashing rumors of an assassination conspiracy and reassuring the public that the "one man-one gun" premise being set forth by federal authorities was correct beyond the slightest doubt. Testimony to support this conclusion would be magnified by the commission, while witnesses offering contradictory information pertaining to Kennedy's murder would be ignored or disregarded and their testimony altered, twisted or suppressed.

As has been amply illustrated in the years since the Warren Commission's "investigation," uncovering and revealing the full, unvarnished truth about that murder was never a priority. Even though some members of the commission urged a wider, more thorough investigation, the commission itself had no investigative apparatus beyond the questioning of witnesses by its attorneys and had to rely on information gathered by the FBI, the Secret Service and local police agencies.

At the time, however, Jean had no knowledge of any of this, and it had certainly never occurred to her that she would be among the witnesses called to testify before this powerful body. That thought didn't cross her mind, in fact, until the day in early February 1964—not long after the commission hearings had officially opened with the testimony of Marina Oswald, widow of the alleged assassin—when she received an official Warren Commission subpoena in the mail.

When she opened the heavy, engraved envelope, Jean discovered that she was being summoned to give a sworn statement to a counsel for the commission in Washington, D.C., early the following month. Her first reaction was fright and nervousness, but after the initial shock wore off and she had some time to think about it, she actually became rather excited about the idea. The federal government would undoubtedly pay for her transportation and it would give her an opportunity to see the nation's capital for the first time without the encumbrance of two small children. But most important of all, maybe she would finally be granted a responsive, sympathetic hearing by someone in authority. Someone who would accept her story for what it was worth, instead of trying to make her change it, condemning her as a liar, or dismissing her as a moron.

"At first, I really wanted to go," she recalls today. "I thought, This is my chance to get my story on the record once and for all, a chance to make it official. If the commission really wanted to find out the truth, I was more than willing to help. I felt that it was my patriotic duty."

J. B. didn't share her enthusiasm, however. On the contrary, he seemed extremely upset when she told him about the subpoena.

"I got one of the damned things too," he said, "and I'll have to honor mine if I want to keep my job in the department, but it's different where you're concerned. They can't force a private citizen to go up there and testify. You could probably get away with just telling them to take their subpoena and stick it, but you can at least make 'em come to you."

"Do you have to go to Washington too?" she asked hopefully. "Maybe we could go together."

"Forget that," he said. "There's no way even the federal government's going to pay to fly half the Dallas police force to Washington. They're going to interview all the cops right here in Dallas, and if I were you, I'd just throw that damned subpoena in the trash and forget it."

"I don't see why I should," she said innocently. "I mean, these are very important people, J. B. They might be a lot different from those Secret Service goons or the FBI. I think they might listen to me."

"Oh, hell, use your head, Norma Jean," he scolded. "This whole thing's nothing but a setup. Look who appointed the Warren Commission, for God's sake. It's like the fox guarding the henhouse or letting your prime suspect pick his own jury. They're going to be a damned sight more interested in covering up than they are in investigating."

She looked shocked. "Are you saying you think President Johnson had something to do with what happened to Kennedy? I mean, I know cops are supposed to be cynical, but how could you really . . . ?"

He looked away. "I'm not saying he necessarily had anything to do with it personally or directly, but . . ."

"But what?"

"I don't know," he said, in an uncertain tone that was unusual for him. "I probably ought to just shut up about it. It doesn't do any good to talk about it anyway."

"I don't have the slightest idea what you're driving at," she said.

"Just forget it, okay?"

"But I don't *want* to forget it," she persisted. "Tell me what you mean."

"It's hard to pin down," J. B. said, still seeming hesitant. "It's just some stuff I've been reading, plus a lot of stories I've been hearing around the department. The gist of it's that somebody high up in the government wanted Kennedy out of the way and Johnson in the White House. Maybe not Johnson himself, but somebody powerful enough to pull it off."

"Well, sure, I've heard things like that too. You and I have even talked about it ourselves, but I still don't believe it. It's too far-fetched to think . . ."

"That's exactly what the damned Warren Commission's all about," he said bitterly. "To make you—and everybody else— believe it's too far-fetched."

"Well, why don't you go ahead and tell me what you've heard?" Jean demanded. "Then I can make up my own mind what to believe."

"No," he said, suddenly his firm, unequivocal self again. "At least not yet. Not until I can check some of it out further and make sure it's more than just rumors or scuttlebutt. In the meantime, though, I think you should forget about the Warren Commission—and especially about going to Washington. If you don't say what those people want to hear, you just might never come back again."

For the next few days, Jean kept the envelope containing the subpoena tucked away at the back of a dresser drawer, hoping that having it out of sight would help keep her from thinking about it. For the most part, though, the ploy didn't work. Occasionally, she would manage to forget it for an hour or so, only to have the knowledge of it suddenly descend on her again like a lead weight crashing down out of the blue. Still, she didn't mention it to anyone else, not even the kids. There would be time enough to tell them if she decided to honor the subpoena and make the trip to Washington.

She had no idea what the penalty might be for refusing to go. Maybe it would be like being in contempt of court or something, and if so, the commission probably could fine her if they wanted to make an issue out of it. As she agonized over it, her feelings swung back and forth like a pendulum. Sometimes, she admitted to herself that J. B. was almost certainly right, that, at best, it would be a waste of time to go to Washington, and, at worst, it might be downright risky. At other times, however, she still felt a strong urge to go and tell her story one last time. She had already been subjected to months of grief over what she had seen, and the only way to make it all worthwhile was to make sure that her eyewitness account became part of the official record.

Meanwhile, in the midst of all this turmoil, Jean was making a dedicated effort to get her life together and deal with an increasingly perplexing set of personal problems. With her lawyer preparing divorce papers, she was urgently in need of a full-time job to support herself and the children. So when she had heard that there might soon be an opening for a fourth-grade teacher at an elementary school not far from where she lived, she had put in her application with the Dallas Independent School District. While she awaited developments, she continued to substitute as much as possible and to watch her finances. It had cost several hundred dollars over and above the insurance coverage to have the Volkswagen fixed after the post-Christmas wreck, and this expense, on top of all the routine holiday bills, had left her savings pretty well depleted. Unless something happened soon, money was going to become a real problem.

To complicate matters further, she was again going through a frustrating, perplexing period with J. B., whose visits to her house had become more and more infrequent over the past few weeks. J. B. blamed the FBI surveillance and said that it wasn't wise for them to be seen together very often, but sometimes Jean couldn't help but wonder if their long separations actually stemmed from guilt feelings and second thoughts about the woman who was still legally his wife.

There was no remaining question in Jean's mind that she loved J. B. Marshall—that question had been clearly answered weeks earlier—and she knew she would have married him instantly if both weren't still entangled in other commitments. But two factors about her relationship with J. B. were deeply troubling to Jean. One was that, like many other husbands caught in a hopeless, dead-end marital situation, he seemed unable to make a complete psychological or physical break. Jean was sure that he wanted to, but that he was held in check by a warped sense of responsibility, especially toward his own two children. And the second was that he never seemed willing to let Jean make her own decisions. His protectiveness and concern for her were welcome, even cherished. But his continuing attempts to restrict her every thought, word and action—his "edict" concerning the trip to Washington being a prime example—often made her feel as if she had no freedom of choice anymore.

In some ways, she thought, J. B. was as much her "jailer" these days as the FBI agents who perpetually sat in the parked car down the street, even when he stayed away for days at a time. The difference was, she didn't rely on the FBI for emotional support the way she relied on J. B. And when restrictions and sternly repeated orders were the price of that support, they merely aggravated Jean's natural tendency to kick over the traces and exert her independence. Was he really trying to spare her some grief, or was he merely trying to control her?

As the days went by, she knew she would have to make a decision soon on the Washington trip. But for once, she wanted to be sure that it was truly her decision and not J. B.'s, so she decided not to discuss it with anyone until after the decision was made. In the meantime, she called the airlines for ticket information and departure times, quietly arranged for someone to look after Jeanne and Billy for a couple of days in the event she did go, and mentally sorted through the clothes and personal items she would need for the trip. And in the process, almost before she realized it, she convinced herself that she was, indeed, going to go.

Even so, she almost lost her nerve again when Special Agent

Shanklin called one morning with a pointed question.

"I know you've received a Warren Commission subpoena, Jean," he said, in his disarming, "big-brotherly" way. "Are you prepared to go to Washington to give testimony?"

She could feel the butterflies fluttering around in her stomach as she answered: "I guess so, if that's what I'm supposed to do."

"Good," he said. "We'll make your travel arrangements."

Later, she felt relief that the agonizing decision was finally behind her, and she fought off her recurrent bouts of uneasiness by spelling out to herself exactly what she intended to do. She would go through her story one more time, and if anyone chose to listen and take her seriously, fine. If not, she would at least have the comfort of knowing that she had made the effort and could wash her hands of the whole affair with a clear conscience. If she was bullied, ridiculed or rejected by the Warren Commission as she had been by the FBI, the CIA, the Secret Service and God knows who else, then she would simply give up. She would give up and quit trying to tell the truth to anyone, ever again.

At least J. B. would like that, she thought.

Several days before her scheduled departure for Washington, Jean awoke with a start to the sound of the clock-radio beside her bed blaring out a 7 A.M. newscast. And even before she was completely awake, she was amazed to hear her own name coming at her out of the speaker.

"New York attorney Mark Lane, who was hired by the mother of accused assassin Lee Harvey Oswald to represent her son, and who plans to write a book on the JFK assassination, is in Dallas today, talking to various assassination witnesses," the announcer was saying. "Among those Lane plans to interview are Dallas schoolteacher Jean Hill . . ."

Jean sat up groggily in bed, rubbing her eyes and wishing for a replay of what she had just heard—or thought she heard. The prospect of being interviewed by a writer was almost worse than that of being interrogated by Warren Commission lawyers, because it would mean more publicity, Jean thought, and every time she was the subject of more publicity, bad things started to happen. She wondered if her ears were playing tricks on her or if she had still been dreaming. If she hadn't, who was Mark Lane, and why should he be interested in her? What the hell was going on now?

The answers to her questions came later that day when the telephone rang. To the best of Jean's recollection, the ensuing conversation went something like this:

"Mrs. Hill, this is Mark Lane," a male voice said. "I'm gathering information on the Kennedy assassination, and I'd like very much to talk with you."

"What about?"

"About what you saw in Dealey Plaza the day the president was killed."

"I gave a deposition at the sheriff's office that day and I've talked to the FBI several times since. I don't really have anything else to say."

"Mrs. Hill, you were one of the people closest to the president's car when he was hit, and you claim to have seen a man who could have been involved in the assassination running away that day. This could be very important information, and I'd like to do a personal interview with you about that."

"Look, I'm scheduled to talk to the Warren Commission soon, and I don't think I should talk to anyone else about it beforehand," Jean said. "I think I've talked to too many people already."

"Well, I'd just like to know what the man looked like. You could tell me that, couldn't you?"

Jean felt the now-familiar queasiness forming inside her. "He was a heavy-set man," she said softly, "wearing a hat and a brown overcoat."

"How old would you say he was? How tall?"

"In his forties, I guess, and about average height."

"Did you ever see him before or since?"

"I . . . I don't know. I told you, I don't want to talk about it."

"Do you *think* you might have seen him somewhere else?"

Jean hesitated for a full five seconds before she answered. "Yes, I think so," she said, then added quickly: "Listen, I don't want this in any books or anything, but, well, I . . . I thought he looked a lot like Jack Ruby."

She had the distinct and instant feeling that she had made a mistake, but at the time she had no idea of its implications.

She could not know, for example, that Lane himself, who wanted to serve as Lee Harvey Oswald's posthumous legal counsel before the Warren Commission, would testify before the commission a short time later, on March 7, 1964, and would allude to his conversation with Jean in these words:

"She said further that after the last shot was fired, she saw a man run from behind the general area of a concrete facade on that grassy knoll, and that he ran on to the triple overpass."

Other than a misinterpretation by Lane or an attempt to stretch her remarks out of context, Jean can offer no explanation today for the last portion of this statement, since she had never, in all the hours of questioning she had undergone to this point, mentioned anyone running "on to the triple overpass."

Moreover, she could not conceive of the hatred and venom that would be directed at Mark Lane—particularly in Dallas—when his book, *Rush to Judgment*, was published more than two years later. There would be five separate references in the book to Jean's story, including her claim to have seen Jack Ruby in Dealey Plaza, augmented by statements based on her Warren Commission testimony. These references would include Lane's admission that Jean had later refused to permit a filmed interview and had told Lane that she could not discuss the case anymore "because I don't want the FBI here (at her house) constantly and I want to continue to teach here (in Dallas)." Whether it was done intentionally or not, some of her statements would be taken out of context or subtly changed in Lane's version of them. And by then, of course, it would be much too late to do anything about it.

In the days immediately following the Lane interview, another firestorm blew up in Jean's face. The first indications of its ferocity came from Gordon Shanklin.

"Jean, Jean, what am I going to do with you?" Shanklin fumed after sending two FBI agents to bring her to his downtown office. "We've told you over and over that the man you saw running in Dealey Plaza could *not* have been Jack Ruby, because we've established that Ruby was somewhere else at the time. But you keep right on saying it. You seem to say it every time you get a chance. Why, Jean, why? Why do you want to make trouble for yourself?"

"Maybe because I happen to think it's true," she said obstinately. "Besides, what makes you think I've been talking to anybody about it?"

"Mark Lane doesn't keep secrets very well, Jean," Shanklin said, lighting a fresh cigarette from an inch-long butt, then crushing out the butt among dozens of others in the overflowing ashtray on his desk. "Of all the people in the world you could have picked to tell this Jack Ruby pipedream of yours to, Mark Lane is probably the very worst."

"How did you even know I talked to him?" she demanded. "You wouldn't have known if you weren't always sneaking around."

"It's our business to know things," Shanklin said enigmatically.

"It's your business to mind everybody else's business," she snapped.

He smiled. "You're a very stubborn woman, Jean, but I like you. I like you a lot and I think you realize that. I'd really like to be your friend, if you'd only be reasonable."

"I always thought I *was* reasonable until I happened to see the president of the United States get his head blown off," she said sarcastically. "Then, all of a sudden, I lost my sense of reason, Mr. Shanklin."

"Why don't you call me Gordon?" he said, still smiling. "After all this time, I think we know each other well enough to be on a first-name basis."

"I can't argue with that," she said. "I think you and your men probably know me better than anybody else in the world by now."

"All right, then," Shanklin said, "let me set you straight on something once and for all. We have an unimpeachable witness who can place Jack Ruby in the advertising department of the *Dallas Morning News* at the time of the assassination. It's that simple. Now will you just try to forget it?"

Jean forced herself to smile back at Shanklin. Behind her smile, however, her mind was racing a mile a minute. When they had told her earlier that Ruby was somewhere else, she had assumed he was probably miles away on the other side of town. But even as unfamiliar with downtown Dallas as she was, Jean knew that the Dallas News Building was right at the corner of Houston and Young Streets, just three short blocks from the south end of Dealey Plaza and not even a brisk five-minute walk from the school book depository.

"I'll try," she said, "but what makes you so sure this other witness is right and I'm wrong?"

The hottest part of the firestorm, however, came from J. B. Marshall.

"Damn it, you can't go," he told her sternly two days before she was to leave for Washington. "I won't let you."

"Listen, J. B., you don't own me," she retorted coldly. "You can't keep me from going if I want to."

"No, I guess I can't," he said with a sigh, "not any more than I can keep you from spilling your guts to every opportunist and busybody that comes along. But I want you to know I'm scared, Norma Jean. And I'm not just fooling around; I mean it. I'm scared if you go, you won't come back."

The angry look on her face softened slightly as she realized he was genuinely worried. "Hey," she said, "people fly to Washington every day. Hundreds of people. What's the big deal?"

"You're booked to go on the same plane with Marina Oswald," he said bluntly. "I know because I had somebody check the passenger lists. A helluva lot of people in this town think Marina's every bit as guilty as her husband and they hate her just as much. We've had at least a hundred bonafide threats against her life since the assassination. What if there's a bomb on the plane, Norma Jean? What if somebody decides to do some unscheduled 'repairs' on the engines? What if there's a couple of hit men with automatic rifles waiting at the airport? Marina's got Secret Service to protect her, but you've got nothing. Do you really think it's worth the risk?"

She stared speechlessly at him for a long, tension-filled moment. Then her shoulders sagged, her eyes burned with tears, and she shook her head.

"No," she said finally, wiping her eyes. "No, I guess not."

And that was how Jean Hill came to defy the Warren Commission subpoena, cancel her trip to Washington, arouse the further wrath of the FBI, and incur the utter disdain of Warren Commission counsel Arlen Specter, who eventually traveled to Dallas to interrogate her.

Along the way, she also managed to attract the personal attention of FBI director J. Edgar Hoover himself.

On Saturday, March 21, 1964, Jean received a curt letter from the Warren Commission informing her that, since she had refused to keep her Washington appointment, she would be interrogated instead at Parkland Memorial Hospital in Dallas at 2:30 P.M. on the following Tuesday, March 24. The letter left little doubt that her failure to appear would lead to dire consequences, even though she was being given only three days' notice. This was further emphasized by a call from Shanklin on Monday, the day before her hearing.

"I'm sending two agents to pick you up tomorrow afternoon and drive you to Parkland," Shanklin said in as harsh a tone as she had ever heard from him. "They'll be there about 1:30, and there'll be no kidding around this time. Be ready."

"I'll be ready," Jean said tartly, "but I'm driving my own car. I don't want to ride with those guys."

"All right," Shanklin said, "but they're going to escort you and make sure you get there."

Jean was ready, as instructed, when the agents arrived, but she was far from prepared for the treatment she was to receive that afternoon at the hands of Arlen Specter, an assistant counsel for the Warren Commission and now a U.S. senator from Pennsylvania.

Soon after she was ushered into an office on one of the upper floors of the medical center, it became obvious that Specter had been fully briefed by the FBI and Secret Service on Jean's background, her personal life, and her history as a dissenting witness. Jean contends today that Specter purposely set out to humiliate and intimidate her in every way possible. Besides Jean herself, Specter and a stenographer were the only persons present, and Jean firmly maintains that none of the actual conversation that took place at the beginning of the interview was ever recorded.

She clearly recalls Specter telling her frostily, however, that he knew "all about" her. She says that he accused her of engaging in a "shabby extramarital affair," thirsting for publicity and notoriety, refusing to cooperate with federal authorities, and proving herself "totally unreliable" as a witness. Unless the commission received her full cooperation from now on, she remembers him telling her, she would be "very, very sorry."

At one point during this diatribe, Jean says she glanced at the stenographer, who kept her eyes averted and had thus far written nothing at all on the notepad in front of her.

"Are we talking off the record here?" she demanded, a mixture of fear and fury constricting her chest.

Yes, she was told, but once the conversation became "official," she would be expected to give "proper answers" based on fact, not on her overactive imagination or "what some talkative cop told you while you were in bed together."

Jean felt her face flush. She had prayed that this time would different, but it was going to be like all the rest. No, not like all the rest either. It was going to be worse—much worse.

"You can go to hell," she recalls yelling at Specter. "I know what I saw and what I heard."

His response, she says, was to taunt her about "a little dog that didn't exist" and a man running away, who "most likely didn't exist either"; about shots that were never fired, coming from locations where there were no weapons; about going into a restricted area where she didn't belong, then "flaunting" herself in front of the media, and making "silly claims" of being manhandled by federal officers.

Jean says she was warned of dire consequences if she persisted in this kind of behavior, to which she responded furiously:

"Oh, yeah, I'm sure people who can kill a president and get away with it can handle some insignificant 'nobody' like me with no trouble at all."

Jean says that Specter accused her of talking "insanity" and warned that if she continued with what she was saying, she would end up looking as "crazy" as Marguerite Oswald, mother of the accused assassin.

None of this unseemly exchange appears, of course, among the 19 pages of testimony by Jean Hill in Volume Six (pages 205-223) of the official report of the President's Commission on the Assassination of President Kennedy. What does appear is a heavily edited, completely distorted and shamelessly fabricated version of Jean's testimony, which she describes today as a "total travesty."

There were long intervals, she says, when, at a hand signal from Specter, the stenographer stopped taking notes. In countless instances, she charges, the meaning of her remarks were altered and her actual words were changed.

The very first introductory sentence of the document graphically points up the fallacious nature of the entire transcript. It reads: "The testimony of Mrs. Jean Lollis Hill was taken at 2:30 p.m. on March 24, 1964, in the office of the U.S. Attorney, 301 Post Office Building, Bryan and Ervay Streets, Dallas, Tex."

In point of fact, of course, Jean's testimony was actually given some five miles away from Bryan and Ervay Streets, in the very same building where President Kennedy had been pronounced dead. The fact that those who prepared the published transcript could make such a careless mistake—or be so unconcerned with the truth—seems utterly incredible under the circumstances. But it is no more incredible than the rest of the document.

Early in the transcript, for example, Specter said: "May the record show that a court reporter is present and is taking verbatim transcript of the deposition of Mrs. Hill . . . and that all of the report is being transcribed and has been transcribed from the time Mrs. Hill arrived. Is that correct, Mrs. Hill?"

To which Jean is alleged to have replied: "That is correct."

"That is a barefaced lie and a total misrepresentation of what really happened," Jean charges today. "The whole transcript is a pack of lies."

After the heated exchange that had just occurred—not one word of which appears in the transcript—this represents a flagrant falsification. And as a secondary point, there was no "court reporter" present, only a public stenographer, whose identity, incidentally, cannot presently be established.

The transcript shows Specter directing question after question at Jean concerning the location in the presidential limousine of Governor Connally and Connally's movements at the time of the shooting. Most of these questions came after Jean had clearly stated that, having just recently moved to Texas from Oklahoma, she did not even know Connally or recognize him by sight.

Whoever concocted the final version of the transcript was careful to include a shaky reference by Jean to the idea that the running man she had seen in Dealey Plaza looked like Jack Ruby, and they also took pains to make it seem that she was, in effect, discrediting her own observations.

Specter: Was he more than five feet tall, or can you give me any meaningful description of him?

Hill: Well, yes, but I don't want to.

Specter: Why is that?

Hill: Well, because . . . it seems that I am merely using a figure and converting it to my story, but the person that I saw looked a lot like—I would say the general build as I would think Jack Ruby would from that position. But I have talked with the FBI about this and I told them I realized that his (Ruby's) whereabouts had been covered at all times and of course I didn't—at that time I didn't realize that the shots were coming from the building. I frankly thought they were coming from the knoll.

Ample mention is also made, of course, of the nonexistent dog in the presidential limousine, of Jean's media interviews and conversation with Mark Lane, of people "making fun" of her and "laughing" at her, and of her estranged husband ridiculing her and saying: "Of all the people in the United States, you would have to see a dog!" It is clear to Jean that Specter did his utmost to carry out the threat of making her appear "crazy."

The "editors" of the transcript subsequently made a point of having Jean repeat several times the erroneous statement that she had had "only one" personal contact with the FBI, when she actually had had no fewer than nine or ten such interviews by this time, and had, in fact, been personally escorted to this very hearing by FBI agents.

One particularly interesting aspect of the deposition comes very near the end of the transcript. While many other witnesses testifying before the commission were routinely given an opportunity either to review the completed transcript at a later time and sign it to indicate its accuracy, or to waive that right, Jean was offered neither such option. At the end of the interview, Specter merely told her: "This transcript will be reviewed by me in Washington and by my colleagues in Washington and it is possible that you may be contacted again."

She was not contacted, however, and, as far as the Warren Commission was concerned, the issue of Jean Hill's testimony was apparently closed when she walked out of the interview room at Parkland Hospital. But the same cannot be said for the FBI's continuing preoccupation with certain of Jean's allegations.

As revealed by documents whose existence was unknown to

Jean prior to early 1991—and totally contrary to what she was being told at the time by Shanklin and other federal agents—the FBI took a remarkably keen interest in her report of seeing a Ruby look-alike in Dealey Plaza when Kennedy was shot. The reasons for this interest are open to speculation today, but if federal authorities were as certain as they indicated that Ruby could not have been at the assassination scene when Jean claimed to have seen him, they showed it in a most peculiar manner.

On March 13, 1964, Jean was once more grilled by the FBI, this time by Special Agents E. J. Robertson and Thomas T. Trettis, Jr., to whom she repeated her description of the running figure in Dealey Plaza. Again, she recalled the figure as being a white man wearing a brown raincoat and a hat, whom she had seen running west, away from the school book depository, toward the wooden fence and the railroad tracks beyond. Subsequently, Agent Robertson was assigned to conduct an investigation aimed at establishing the identity of this person.

On March 30, Robertson was advised by Capt. P. W. Lawrence of the Dallas Police Department that a review of police files failed to disclose any information that would assist in identifying the running man in the brown raincoat and hat. The following day, March 31, Dallas police patrolman James W. Foster, who had been on the railroad bridge above the triple underpass at the time of the assassination, and Dallas County sheriff's deputy Roger Craig, who had been on Houston Street near Elm at the time, also were questioned at length by Robertson. According to Robertson's report, neither Foster nor Craig recalled seeing a man fitting this description.

Robertson also questioned Dallas patrolman W. E. Barker, the same officer who had allowed Jean and Mary Moorman to enter the grassy triangle between Main and Elm Streets. Minutes after the president had been shot, suspicious bystanders had called Barker's attention to a man standing near the intersection of Elm and Houston Streets. Robertson reported, however, that Barker said the man could not have been the same person Jean had seen because of elapsed time and the fact that he had no hat.

The investigation did not stop in Dallas, however. It stretched all the way to Washington and to the highest echelons of the FBI. It reached its climax on May 6, 1964, when a letter on the official stationery of the Office of the Director of the Federal Bureau of Investigation was dispatched by courier to J. Lee Rankin, general counsel of the Warren Commission. Here is the text of that letter:

> Dear Mr. Rankin:
>
> Reference is made to my letter dated April 2, 1964, which enclosed copies of a memorandum revealing the results of a reinterview with Mrs. Jean Lollis Hill. Mrs. Hill commented she observed a white man, wearing a brown raincoat and a hat, running west away from the Texas School Book Depository Building following the shooting. Mrs. Hill did not closely observe this individual; did not know who he was; and never saw him again. Mrs. Hill described this man as "average height and heavy build."
>
> Additional investigation has been conducted by this Bureau endeavoring to identify this individual. This investigation included a review of all available film taken near the Texas School Book Depository Building following the shooting; a re-examination of the results of all interviews with individuals who were in the vicinity of the shooting; a review of an additional film taken by Mr. Thomas P. Alyea, WFAA-TV newsman; and interviews with Dallas Police Department and Dallas County Sheriff's Office personnel, none of which revealed the identity of the man described by Mrs. Hill.
>
> Investigative results appear on pages 43 through 49 in the report of Special Agent Robert P. Gemberling dated April 15, 1964. This report was furnished to you by letter dated May 4, 1964, and no further action is being taken in this matter.
>
> Sincerely yours,
>
> J. Edgar Hoover

The existence of the Hoover letter was unknown to Jean herself until the spring of 1991, when, in the process of conducting research for this book, the author discovered it among microfilmed documents and exhibits pertaining to the Warren Commission hearings.

The letter clearly indicates that this was at least Hoover's second communication with the Warren Commission concerning Jean's statements. But since the commission was supposedly finished with Jean by this time, why was Hoover still so concerned about what she claimed to have seen? Why did Hoover make no mention of Jean's belief that the running man might have been Jack Ruby? Why were no witnesses other than law enforcement personnel apparently asked about the man in the brown raincoat and hat? And what of Ruby himself, by this time being held in isolation in the Dallas County jail, awaiting trial for murder? Was he ever confronted directly with the question of whether he had slipped away from the Dallas Morning News Building long enough to show up in Dealey Plaza at the instant of the assassination?

No definitive answers to these questions are possible today, but one point is worth noting: Within a few days after writing this letter, Hoover would make his own momentous appearance before the Warren Commission as the hearings wound to a close. His purpose would be to emphasize the thoroughness of the FBI investigation and to assure the commission in the strongest and most persuasive terms possible that Lee Harvey Oswald had acted independently and alone, and that the "one man-one gun" premise was now ironclad and irrefutable.

But before that could be accomplished, Hoover needed to dispose, once and for all, of such "messy details" as Jean Hill's running co-conspirator, her insistence that up to six shots had been fired, and her dogged belief that at least some of the shots had come from a "shooter" atop the grassy knoll.

And from all remaining indications, that was the primary purpose of Hoover's letter.

CHAPTER SIX

Voicing the "Unthinkable"

It was after 3:00 A.M. on a weekday night, and the house was as quiet as a tomb. Billy and Jeanne had been fast asleep for hours, but Jean still lay wide awake, staring into the darkness above her bed and lost in a swirling maze of thoughts, half-thoughts, suspicions, doubts, worries and fears.

It was the third or fourth night within the past week that she had had trouble sleeping. One of the reasons for her insomnia was the lingering psychological trauma and the helpless, left-over anger from her head-butting session with Arlen Specter. But there was something else too—a dark, shadowy something that had been growing in her mind for weeks. The more it grew, the more all-encompassing it became. It not only blotted out sleep at night, but rational thought and practical action during the daytime, as well. And there seemed to be nothing Jean could do to control it.

At the center of the dark mental shadow was an idea that, on one hand, was so monstrous as to be almost unthinkable, but, on the other hand, was so arresting, so intriguing—and even so logical—that it was impossible to resist. There was nothing original about the idea; it had undoubtedly occurred to thousands, perhaps even millions, of other Americans over the past few months. And yet, there was something so vile and alien about it, something so contrary to every deeply held belief about her country, her government and the American system that it made Jean almost physically ill to dwell on it.

109

At the moment, though, she had been dwelling on it constantly for more than three hours, ever since she had turned off the TV shortly before midnight and gone to bed, and by now her brain was filled with it to the point that she thought her skull might burst from the pressure and she felt psychologically dominated by it to the point that she wanted to scream.

She couldn't remember the first time she had pondered the question, but since then, she had repeated it over to herself 10,000 times at least:

What one person stood to gain the most from John F. Kennedy's death?

Inevitably, the same answer always jumped out at her like a bogeyman—LBJ, of course. Behind the dark shadow in her mind lurked the face of Lyndon B. Johnson, 36th president of the United States.

Not only had Kennedy's death propelled Johnson, a man with enormous political ambitions, directly into the White House, with a near certainty of winning re-election, it had also given him greater temporary power to chart the nation's course without serious challenge than any president since Franklin Roosevelt. During this period of national mourning, Johnson could obtain virtually whatever he wanted, either from Congress and the rest of the power structure in Washington or from the American public, simply by invoking the name and memory of his martyred predecessor. Whether his wish was for a wider war in Southeast Asia, or passage of the most revolutionary civil rights bill in history, or the lowering—by an executive order issued immediately after JFK's death—of a 75-year veil of secrecy over many of the facts concerning the Kennedy assassination, it would be granted with few, if any, questions asked.

The mere fact that JFK's death had fulfilled LBJ's life could not be construed to mean, of course, that Johnson had consciously played some sinister role in the assassination. Such a thought was contrary to everything America stood for and it flew in the face of a pervasive popular mythology—that men who achieved high office were invariably men of equally high character, principles and morals, selfless men who were above reproach. Jean had always accepted this high-minded mythology with the same blind faith as most Americans, but over the past few months, the dark shadow in her mind had slowly begun to erode that faith. And each time she was rebuffed as a witness, each time she saw her story discounted or held up to ridicule, her faith had been eaten away a little more.

"If the Kennedy assassination had happened after Watergate, I think we would have seen a far different reaction on the part of the media and the public," Jean says today, "and consequently, we would have had a much more meaningful and intensive investigation. But in 1963 and 1964, we were just too naive to believe that our top political leaders could commit calculated, cold-blooded criminal acts. That made it far too easy to hide the truth."

Having lived most of her life up to that time in Oklahoma, Jean had little background knowledge of Texas politics. But with LBJ in the White House, she had taken an interest in what newspaper writers and TV commentators had to say about the controversy that marked his rise to political prominence. She became aware of vote-stealing charges in the 1948 election that had put Johnson in the U.S. Senate; vague claims of conflicts of interest and abuse of privilege over the years; documented associations with such shady characters as Billie Sol Estes, whose fraudulent empire had collapsed after Johnson became vice president.

To Jean, however, these all seemed to fall into the category of "political things." Certainly, there were breaches of ethics involved, and technically, perhaps, some crimes had been committed, or at least some laws had been broken. But a vice president conspiring to murder a president? That was a whole different matter. The idea was still unthinkable.

It might have always remained so, except for certain bits and pieces of information, liberally mixed with innuendo, that circulated freely among the ranks of Dallas policemen and eventually reached her by way of J. B. Marshall. Once that began to happen, Jean couldn't seem to get the "unthinkable" idea off her mind.

It had been during their after-Christmas interlude, when they had been talking about the strangeness of the FBI investigation and the overwhelming federal mistrust of Dallas cops, when J. B. had suddenly hit her with the first and most thought-provoking revelations about LBJ. She could still remember how oddly uneasy they had made her feel.

"According to the guys who were escorting his car in the motorcade, our new president is either one jumpy sonofabitch or he knows something he's not telling about the Kennedy thing," J. B. had drawled.

"What're you talking about?" Jean asked innocently. "I don't understand."

He chuckled, but it was a sound devoid of humor or mirth. "They say he started ducking down in the car a good 30 or 40 seconds before the first shots were fired," he said. "I'd say that's just a little peculiar, wouldn't you?"

"Oh, come on, J. B.," she said, thinking he had to be joking. "They obviously weren't serious—were they?"

"As far as I know, they were dead serious," he said. "One of them told McGuire he saw Johnson duck down even before the car turned onto Houston Street, and he sure as hell wasn't laughing when he said it."

"Maybe Johnson just dropped something in the floor and bent over to pick it up. I mean, there could be a simple explanation."

"Maybe so," J. B. said. "I don't claim to know what his reasons were, but this guy said it sure looked like he was expecting bullets to be flying. When I heard it, it made me start wondering about a whole lot of other stuff too."

"Stuff about Johnson?"

"Yeah, like what they told us out at Love Field right after Kennedy's plane landed."

"And what was that?"

He hesitated for a long moment. "If I tell you about this,

Norma Jean, you've got to promise me you'll never breathe a word of it to anybody," he said softly. "Not even to Mary or your mother or your kids. Not to anybody, understand?"

"Okay, sure," she said, a little taken aback by the gravity of his tone. "I won't tell a soul, I promise."

"Well, while Kennedy was busy shaking hands with all the wellwishers at the airport, Johnson's Secret Service people came over to the motorcycle cops and gave us a bunch of instructions. The damnedest thing was, they told us the parade route through Dealey Plaza was being changed."

"Changed? How?"

"It was originally supposed to go straight down Main Street," J. B. said, "but they said for us to disregard that. Instead, we were told to make the little jog on Houston and cut over to Elm."

Jean felt her mouth drop open. "My God," she said in amazement, "if you'd stayed on Main, Kennedy might've been completely out of range of whoever was shooting at him. My 'shooter' behind the wooden fence definitely wouldn't have had much chance to hit him from there."

J. B. stared at her with a straight face. "Maybe that's why they changed the route," he said bluntly, "but that's not all. They also ordered us into the damnedest escort formation I've ever seen. Ordinarily, you bracket the car with four motorcycles, one on each fender. But this time, they told the four of us assigned to the president's car there'd be no forward escorts. We were to stay well to the back and not let ourselves get ahead of the car's rear wheels under any circumstances. I'd never heard of a formation like that, much less ridden in one, but they said they wanted to let the crowds have an unrestricted view of the president. Well, I guess somebody got an 'unrestricted view' of him, all right."

"Are you sure it was Johnson's Secret Service that told you all this?" Jean asked. Surely, there had to be some mistake here, she thought. It all sounded so . . . so *premeditated*.

"I guess they were Secret Service," he said. "They were sure as hell acting like they were in charge, and I know they were with Johnson, because when they got through telling us what to do, they went back to his car. Oh, and that's another thing. They changed up the order of the cars in the motorcade before we started out. Originally, the car carrying Johnson was supposed to be right behind Kennedy's car, but they decided to put a carload of Secret Service in between the two main VIP cars. That didn't make a helluva lot of sense to me either, but it might at least explain why Johnson was so ready to duck."

She frowned. "How do you mean?" she asked.

"Well, maybe he forgot about putting that Secret Service car between him and Kennedy," J. B. explained. "If he knew there was going to be shooting, maybe he was thinking he was a lot closer to the intended victim than he really was."

The more Jean thought about it, the more certain she became that JFK's murder involved much more than two or three fanatics firing from ambush. By the time the Warren Commission was done with her, she was convinced not only of a well-planned conspiracy involving parties within the federal government, but of a massive ongoing effort to conceal their hateful secret. Why else would all the representatives of federal authority with whom she had come in contact—from the alleged Secret Service agents who had grabbed her on the grassy knoll right up to Arlen Specter himself—do their best to discredit her, threaten her with embarrassment, warn her to forget what she had witnessed with her own eyes, or try to twist or alter her story?

Whether it had been Jack Ruby or someone else, was the man she had seen running in Dealey Plaza an employee of the federal government? Was the mysterious "shooter" behind the fence on the payroll of the Secret Service, the CIA, the FBI or, God forbid, the man who was now president of the United States?

Suddenly, the "unthinkable" had become thinkable, after all. And until Jean could find some satisfactory answers to the questions that kept exploding in her brain, she feared there would be many, many sleepless nights ahead.

If the thread of conspiracy did lead all the way to the Oval Office, she probably would never feel secure again, but her need for more information now outweighed everything else, including her fear.

A day or two later, she went to the public library and began to search through several years of microfilmed back copies of daily newspapers for any articles that might tell her more about Lyndon Baines Johnson, his background, his political rise and his associations. It was as good a place as any to start.

She ran across numerous references to "Landslide Lyndon's" 87-vote victory in the 1948 Senate race and his ties to South Texas political boss George Parr. She also read all the stories relating to long-time LBJ friend Billie Sol Estes, a wheeler-dealer who had used non-existent fertilizer tanks as collateral for millions of dollars worth of government-secured agricultural loans.

One of the most interesting, and unnerving, of these stories involved a U.S. Department of Agriculture official named Henry Marshall, who was found shot to death on his farm near Franklin, Texas. He had been struck in the abdomen by five bullets, apparently from a bolt-action .22-caliber rifle discovered near the body. No autopsy had been performed before a local justice of the peace, in what had to be the most unforgivable disregard of law and common sense that Jean had ever encountered, ruled Marshall's death a suicide. There was a clear implication that, had he lived to testify against Estes, Marshall might have caused Johnson considerable damage in the process.

Later, Jean expanded her reading list to include coverage by *Time* and *Newsweek* of the bitter fight for the 1960 Democratic presidential nomination, which JFK had wrested from Johnson on the first ballot. She read about the campaign that followed, in which LBJ swallowed his pride to accept second place on his party's ticket, then provided the crucial margin of victory in six key states to give Kennedy the White House after the closest presidential election in U.S. history.

But perhaps the most eye-opening story of all appeared in

the *Dallas Morning News* on November 22, 1963, the very day of the assassination, under a headline which read:

NIXON PREDICTS JFK MAY DROP JOHNSON

The article quoted former Vice Pres. Richard Nixon, who had lost the presidency to John Kennedy, concerning the friction between Johnson and Kennedy's key advisors, including JFK's brother, Attorney General Robert Kennedy. It mentioned the frequent snubs of Johnson by White House insiders, who laughed at him and called him "Colonel Cornpone" behind his back. And Nixon speculated that, by 1964, Kennedy would feel strong enough to dump Johnson from the ticket and replace him with a vice president who was more in tune with the philosophy of JFK's "New Frontier."

If this were true, Jean told herself, Johnson would have been left with only two alternatives: One, to become a pathetic, powerless castoff of his party who would have sacrificed his exalted role as Senate majority leader for nothing and have no guarantee of ever regaining public office. Or two, to stop it from happening at all costs and by any means possible.

Knowing LBJ as well as she felt she now did, Jean had little doubt which course he would have chosen.

By mid-April 1964, Jean was settled in at the first full-time teaching job she had held since leaving Oklahoma City, and she welcomed the renewed sense of purpose that she derived from going to work each day and having students that she could think of as "her own." It was a satisfying feeling, one that substitute teaching had never afforded her, and dealing with a classroom filled with 27 nine- and ten-year-old youngsters all day was more than enough to take her mind off her other problems.

Evenings and weekends were another story, however. At times, she almost wished for more papers to grade or more bulletin boards to make—anything to keep her from thinking about the lingering aftermath of the assassination—and she still suffered through periodic bouts of sleeplessness. While she had heard nothing directly from the FBI since her Warren Commission testimony, the now-familiar car with the two agents inside remained a fixture on the street in front of her home, and although she had long since gotten used to its being there, it still gave her a furtive, unsettled feeling each time she passed it.

The car's constant presence also continued to deter J. B. from visiting her at home very often, although since his wife was currently gone again and he was once more intimating that this was the final breakup, he usually did show up at least twice a week. As for Jean, she didn't care who knew that J. B. was a regular caller. The kids had both accepted him by now as "Mom's friend," and paid no particular attention to his presence in the den or at the dinner table. Jean's divorce was well in the works by this time, and there was reason to hope she would soon be legally unbound from a marriage that had, in reality, ceased to exist almost a year ago. And at least when J. B. was there in the house and they could talk face to face, she didn't have to worry about anyone spying on their conversation. She frequently heard strange noises on her telephone, and she couldn't help but wonder who was listening in—and what use they would try to make of what they heard.

Late on a sunny Saturday morning, Jean and J. B. were sitting in the dining area, drinking coffee and looking out across the back yard, where birds were chirping and the trees along the creek were blooming and leafing out. The kids were off doing kid things, and the atmosphere was lazy and spring feverish. Jean felt as relaxed as she had at any time recently, but there was still a ball of suppressed tension coiled inside her, and, as so often happened these days, random thoughts kept nagging her, tugging at the back of her mind and refusing to let her enjoy the moment as fully as she would have liked.

"I want to ask you one question about the assassination," she said warily, filling his coffee cup. "Then I promise I'll drop the subject, okay?"

He grinned at her and shook his head. "Hey, with you there's no such thing as one question," he teased. "Let's don't even start."

"All I want you to do is refresh my memory about something," she said. "Something you told me a while back."

"All right," he said, "but let's make this short and sweet. I don't want to spend the day talking about that junk."

"You said you escorted Johnson back to Love Field from the hospital that day, after Kennedy was pronounced dead," she said. "I was just wondering how he acted."

He took a long sip of his coffee and furrowed his eyebrows at her over the rim of the cup. "It's hard to describe," he said then. "What makes you ask?"

"I don't know. It's just something I've been thinking about, something that's been bugging me. Why is it hard to describe?"

"Well," J. B. said, seeming to search for the right words, "he acted scared, but that's just it—it was like he was *acting*, not like he was really in fear of his life. I remember hearing him yell to somebody as he was getting in the car. He said, 'We've all got to be very careful. This could be a worldwide conspiracy to kill off all our leaders.' The thing that struck me was he seemed to be in total charge already. Everybody else was kind of numb and reeling with shock, but Johnson was in full control, giving orders and telling people what to do."

"I think that's very, very odd," she said. "What he said about a 'worldwide conspiracy,' I mean."

"What's so odd about it?" J. B. demanded. "I'd say he was pretty well hitting the nail right on the head."

"I think so too, but don't you see? At about the same time LBJ was talking about a 'worldwide conspiracy,' those federal agents who were questioning me were giving me a hard time over even suggesting there was more than one person involved."

J. B. laughed sourly. "Maybe in the excitement of the moment, the truth just slipped out of his mouth," he said. His words made it plain that he believed Johnson had known it was a conspiracy all along.

"Did he seem sorry?"

"What do you mean?"

"Did he seem sorry about what happened to Kennedy? Really sympathetic, I mean? Were there tears in his eyes? Did he seem choked up or anything?"

"I don't know, but I sure as hell didn't see any tears of grief. Matter of fact, he was almost rude to those guys he was talking to. Somebody asked him did he want to go back to Air Force Two, which was the plane he came in, and he said, 'No, take me to Air Force One. That's where I belong now.'"

"When you were escorting him back from Parkland to Love Field, you didn't ride in any unusual formations, did you?" she asked pointedly.

"No, it was all very standard procedure on that trip," he replied. "I think Lyndon had had all the high visibility he wanted for one day."

She sat silently, looking into J. B.'s eyes for several seconds before she spoke again. Then, for the first time, she put a horrifying thought into words. It was something to which each of them had alluded on many occasions over the past five months, but which neither had ever quite managed to verbalize before.

"You think he was personally mixed up in it, don't you?" she said. "You think Johnson knew exactly what was going to happen."

"We shouldn't talk about it," he told her. "You've asked way more than your quota of questions. I think we ought to just drop it."

"I *can't* drop it," she said nervously. "I can't get it out of my mind. I haven't been able to think about anything else for weeks."

He set his coffee cup down very deliberately and reached out with both hands, taking her by the shoulders and pulling her toward him.

"Okay," he said in a low growl, "I'm going to say this once, and it's the last time I'm ever going to say it, so just don't bring it up again, you hear?"

She nodded jerkily, shaken at the emotion in his voice.

"Yes, damn it, I think our new president's up to his neck in this mess," he said. "I don't think he actually hired the shooters, but I think he either caused it to happen or knowingly allowed it to happen. And when it was done, I think he did everything possible to make the Dallas police back off the case and leave it to his hand-picked 'investigators.' But the way I feel doesn't really have anything to do with how he acted or what he said that day at Parkland."

"Then what *does* it have to do with?"

"The thing that convinced me was what happened to Will Fritz," he said, referring to the Dallas Police Department's chief homicide detective. "I told you how 'old Cap' went into a shell and refused to talk to anybody after Oswald was killed. Well, he's been like that with most of us ever since, but I hear there's a couple of people outside homicide that he finally opened up to, and the department's been full of rumors for the past month about what he told them."

"What do you mean? What's he supposed to have said?"

"According to what I heard, less than three hours after Ruby shot Oswald, Fritz was ordered to scrap the investigation as of that minute and not go another step further with it. The rumor is, he said the order came straight from the White House. His exact words were supposed to have been, 'You can't keep running a homicide investigation when the president of the United States calls you on the phone and tells you point-blank to stop.'"

As J. B. spoke, it was as if the last piece of an intricate jigsaw puzzle had abruptly fallen into place in Jean's mind. Suddenly, all the isolated fragments she had struggled to assemble over the past weeks and months now came together in a complete and finished portrait—a portrait of such vile deceit and treachery in high places that it was agonizing to contemplate. And instead of relief or satisfaction, she felt only churning, oppressive fear.

In that instant, she wanted to tell J. B. everything she knew or thought she knew, everything she had read and heard and surmised about Johnson. She wanted to pour it all out at once in one great frenzied flood, but somehow she managed to hold herself in check.

"But are you sure you can believe it if it's only a rumor?" she asked in a surprisingly calm voice. "I mean, there's no way to know Fritz really got a phone call like that—is there?"

"Hell, yes, there is," J. B. said simply. "I know he got it because that's the only way 'old Cap' would've ever quit before he finished a job. The worst part is, he's the only man alive who could've gotten to the bottom of this damned thing. Now nobody'll ever know the truth."

"You and I will!" Jean said emphatically, clutching his hands in her own. "The two of us will know the truth and nothing can change that."

"Don't talk like a damned fool," he said. "When we don't have a shred of proof, what possible difference does it make what we know? When it's our word against the president of the United States, who do you think anybody's going to believe?"

"But between us, we know things that nobody else in the world knows, J. B.," she protested. "Somewhere, somehow, somebody'll listen to us—they'll have to. We can't just sit on our hands and do nothing. That's just as bad as . . ."

"Now you listen to me, Norma Jean," he interrupted. "We're going to forget every damned bit of what we know or might know. We're going to forget it right here and now. We're never going to talk about it again, not even to each other, and for damned sure we're never going to mention it to anybody else. You hear me?"

"If we do that, we'll just be part of the same stinking cover-up," she argued. "Can't you see how wrong that is, J. B.?"

"I don't give a good goddamn!" he yelled, banging his fist against the table and sending the coffee cups clattering. "I'm telling you to forget it!"

The scowl on his livid face eased a little then, and his voice was slightly calmer as he added:

"Think about it, Norma Jean. If I were you, I'd a whole lot

rather be wrong and alive than right and dead!"

Late one afternoon a few days later, Jean arrived home from work to find an unexpected visitor waiting for her. Except for the agents in the parked car on the street, she had had no face-to-face contact with anyone from the FBI in several weeks and had been hoping, now that the Warren Commission unpleasantness was over and done with, that they were growing tired of her and would leave her alone. But the presence of a smiling, chain-smoking Gordon Shanklin on her front porch made it obvious that she had been overly optimistic.

"Good afternoon, Jean," he said amiably. "You're looking well—very well. Going to work every day must agree with you."

"What are you doing here?" she said frostily. "What do you want now?"

"Well, you could invite me in for a start," he said, still smiling at her.

She reluctantly opened the door and ushered him into the living room. "Okay," she said, "what is it? I wish you'd make it quick. I'm tired and I have papers to grade."

He sat down on the couch without waiting to be invited and studied her for a long moment through a haze of cigarette smoke.

"I'm here to ask you a favor, Jean," he said. "It's a very big favor, and it would be an even bigger favor to you than it would to me, if you'd agree to do it."

She eyed him suspiciously. Once or twice before, she had had the feeling that Shanklin had something more than a mere professional interest in her. It was nothing she could pin down, but it was almost like intuition, and the feeling came back to her now, even stronger than before.

"What kind of favor?" she asked.

"First of all," he said, "let me tell you that we've conducted a very, very thorough investigation of the suspicious Jack Ruby look-alike character you claim to have seen in Dealey Plaza on the day of the assassination. We've talked to a number of other witnesses and none of them recall seeing a man fitting that description. Consequently, our investigation has hit a stone wall."

"Well, I'm sorry," she said, "but I *did* see him."

"Don't you think there's a chance you were mistaken, Jean?" he asked in a low, intimate voice. "In the shock of the moment, couldn't your eyes have been playing tricks on you?"

"No," she said firmly. "I'm telling you, I saw him."

"All right," he said, "I'm willing to concede that point, just between the two of us. But I want you to understand that, as far as the record is concerned, it would be to your very great advantage if you had *not* seen him. If you were to change your mind on that point, and if you were willing to sign a statement to that effect, I could promise you . . ."

"Is that the favor you're asking?" she demanded.

He nodded. "Yes," he said flatly. "If you could bring yourself to repudiate your earlier story and just say you made a simple mistake, it would make your life much easier from here on. It would be the best thing you could possibly do for yourself and your children. The safest thing."

"You're asking me to tell a lie!" she stormed. "And I think you're threatening me if I don't."

"No, I'm not," he responded mildly. "Appearances can be deceiving, especially in a moment of shock and stress. And any threat to your safety or the safety of your children won't come from me, Jean. I only want to help you."

"Why is it so almighty important to you, Gordon?" she asked. "Why is it important enough for you to ask me to make a false statement?"

"I'm not asking for myself, Jean," Shanklin said solemnly. "I'm asking you to do it for your country. The American people need reassurance right now, not alarm and confusion. They need to be confident that our government is secure and in good hands, and stories like yours tend to shake their confidence . . ."

She stood up, feeling the blood rushing to her face, and before she could stop herself, she was screaming out the most brazen accusation she had ever uttered.

"You people don't give a damn about the truth," she howled. "The only thing you care about is covering up for Lyndon Johnson and his friends!"

Shanklin looked as if she had just kicked him in the groin. His smile crumbled and his face went as pale as his starched white shirt. He seemed to be having difficulty sucking air into his lungs.

"I didn't hear you say that," he told her when he finally found his voice. "I didn't hear it and I pray to God you never say it again. Don't ever even *think* it."

"I can't help thinking it," she said stubbornly, "and I'll bet lots of other people think it too. If a few more of them spoke up and said something, maybe things would be different."

"Don't be stupid," he said. "The public won't buy that kind of garbage—not ever. But I warn you, Jean: You repeat it once too often to the wrong person, and all the FBI surveillance in the world won't be enough to keep you safe!"

CHAPTER SEVEN

Threats and Warnings

The instant Jean walked into the house that afternoon in early May 1964, she was gripped by an ominous feeling that something was wrong. Outside, the air was warm and alive with the sounds and smells of spring, but no sooner had she closed the front door behind her than she was seized by a cold sense of foreboding. She shivered as a slight chill passed through her.

There was a presence of some kind in the house. An unwelcome presence that had no business there. She couldn't see it or hear it or smell it, but she was certain it was there, nevertheless.

The kids, she knew, were visiting down the street. She had seen them just a few moments before in somebody's front yard as she drove past, so the presence, whatever it was, had nothing to do with them—or anyone else she knew, for that matter. On a rational level, Jean would have bet her last nickel that there wasn't another living soul on the premises. And yet, the eerie sensation that she was not alone persisted so strongly that she had to fight the urge to call out, "Hello, is somebody there?"

It was a feeling she had experienced all too often over the past month or more, ever since she had accepted a full-time assignment to teach a fourth-grade class at Annie Webb Blanton Elementary School in Dallas. Before that, except for a few occasions when she was called to substitute for another teacher, she had been home during the day for most of the time since the assassination. The school was less than a mile from the house as the crow flies, but she was away from early morning until late afternoon every day from Monday through Friday, and she had first begun to notice the feeling within a week or two of taking the job. Altogether, it had happened at least a half-dozen times, and although she couldn't begin to explain it, it was almost as if some sixth sense were trying to warn her:

"Someone's been here while I was gone. Someone's been right here in my house, going through my personal belongings. Why are they doing this? What are they looking for?"

She walked slowly through the rambling ranch-style structure, glancing carefully around as she entered each room, letting her eyes roam over each familiar object to see that it was exactly as it should be.

Billy, who was the most neatness-conscious 12-year-old boy Jean had ever encountered, had left his room as tidy as usual, with nothing out of place. By contrast, Jeanne's room was decidedly on the cluttered side, but there was nothing unusual about that either. The kids had clearly been in the house before Jean arrived, but the evidence they had left behind—some thrown-down schoolbooks, a wadded pair of socks, a dirty glass on the kitchen counter—were of no concern to her. The feeling had to do with something else. Something stealthy and sinister and impossible to define.

After one complete walk-through, however, she hadn't found a single thing out of the ordinary; every detail of the house seemed to be perfectly normal (if not exactly orderly), but still the feeling nagged at her. It nagged so demandingly that she retraced her steps through the house a second time, and it made her so intense that she caught herself holding her breath as she painstakingly repeated her visual examination.

She was beginning to feel foolish and was about ready to shout "Boo!" at herself in the mirror on her dresser, when, on an impulse, she opened the door of her bedroom closet, turned on the light and peered inside. Her clothes hung in perfect order on their hangers and her shoes were neatly stored in stacked boxes on the floor and the pockets of a plastic shoe bag on the door. Then she looked up at the wooden shelf which ran the width of the closet, just above the clothes rod, and she froze in her tracks.

Her cameras were gone.

She always kept the three cameras lined up side by side on the shelf—a Polaroid that was almost identical to the one Mary Moorman had used to photograph the motorcade, an aging movie camera that she had had since the kids were preschoolers, and a Kodak Instamatic that she had hardly touched since buying the Polaroid. For as long as she had lived in the house, the cameras had been there on the shelf, but now they were gone.

Her first reaction was perfectly predictable.

"I've been burglarized," she said aloud.

Even with two FBI agents perpetually sitting in a parked car and watching from a short distance down the street (they were in a nondescript gray Ford sedan today; she had spotted them easily as she drove by), it would have been entirely possible for someone to enter the house from the rear and not be noticed. She was well aware that the dry creek bed behind her property would provide a burglar with plenty of cover.

But before the echo of her own words had faded away, something told Jean she was mistaken. It just wasn't that simple. For one thing, there were no indications of forced entry— no shattered glass, jimmied windows, mangled locks or anything of the sort. Whoever had taken the cameras hadn't *broken* in; they had simply walked in.

There was something else too. As she looked back at the closet shelf, Jean noticed an expensive pair of binoculars and a box filled with rare currency and coins that she had collected over the years, both still sitting adjacent to where the cameras had been. Why would any burglar have taken the cameras, especially the old, next-to-worthless Kodak, and left these other valuables behind? It didn't make sense, but her rationalizations didn't make her feel any better either.

If anything, they only made her more skittish and jumpy than ever. An ordinary burglary would have been bad enough, but this was somehow worse. It was worse because it was abnormal—as abnormal as everything else in her life had become over the past six months.

After dinner that evening, when the kids were through with their homework and settled in front of the TV, Jean told them she was going out to run some errands. She promised to be back in an hour or less, warned them to keep the doors locked, and left to meet J. B. at one of the regular rendezvous points they used when they needed to talk.

As usual, she had to drive around for a while to shake the two agents in the gray Ford, who inevitably tried to follow her, but who seldom managed to stay in sight of her for more than a few minutes if she really set her mind to losing them. There was no way she could outrun them in her Volkswagen bug, but she could usually outmaneuver or outsmart them.

She smiled in spite of herself as she streaked through a changing signal light at Bruton and Prairie Creek Roads. In the rear view mirror, she saw the driver of the Ford slam on his brakes and stop for the light, then watched the Ford's head-lights fade rapidly into the distance behind her. She took a quick left, then another right and angled back to the south-east. It still amazed her how timid these FBI guys were when they were behind the wheel of a car. There was no way any of them was going to keep pace with Jean Hill, she vowed with a trace of satisfaction.

Five minutes later, she eased her car into the edge of a corn-field off Cheyenne Road, a narrow rural thoroughfare which marked the boundary between Dallas and the sparsely popu-lated suburb of Balch Springs. Her headlights picked up the shape of J. B.'s white GMC pickup just before she switched them off and pulled alongside it.

Amid a flurry of hugs and kisses, she gasped out the story of the three cameras and asked him what he thought she should do.

"Were there undeveloped pictures in any of the cameras?" he asked.

"I don't know," she said, shaking her head. "I can't remember. What difference does it make?"

"Maybe none," he said, "but I don't think I'd report this as a burglary if I were you. Why don't you just sit tight for a while and see what happens? In the meantime, though, you might check around to be sure nothing else is missing."

"I've already checked everything I could think of," Jean said. "Did you have anything special in mind?"

He shrugged. "Well," he mused, "if whoever took your cameras wanted to know what kind of pictures you'd been taking, they might have borrowed some of your photo albums too. They might even have been interested in any scrapbooks or diaries or old letters you had laying around."

Jean frowned at him, puzzled. "Why would anybody care about things like that?" she asked.

"To find out whatever they could about you," J. B. said. "About your personal life, your background, your family, your friends." He paused and she saw him wink at her in the red glow from his lighted cigarette. "Your deepest, darkest secrets," he added pointedly.

She stared at him, shaking her head again, this time in disbelief.

"You think it's the FBI," she said. "You think they're the ones who took the cameras, don't you?"

He gazed off through the cornstalks for a moment, then looked straight into her eyes. "Could be," he said. "They *did* take stuff out of my locker."

"But they don't have any right to prowl through my home," Jean flared. "They have to have a warrant to do things like that."

"These people don't give a damn about rights or warrants," he said. "They do whatever they feel like doing. You ought to know that by now."

"Well," she fumed, "I can't imagine what they could expect to find."

He grinned without looking at all amused.

"Who the hell knows?" he said bitterly. "Maybe pictures of you and me playing four-handed stud with Jack Ruby and Lee Harvey Oswald."

Two days later, Jean opened her closet door to find the three cameras safely back in their familiar spot on the shelf. If any of them had contained raw film at the time they vanished, whoever had taken them had kept it. All three were empty.

After J. B.'s warning, Jean had checked carefully through all her personal papers and photographs. As nearly as she could tell, nothing had been missing, but there was something peculiar about the way her photo albums had been stacked in the bookcase where she kept them. Ordinarily, they were placed in chronological order, with the latest ones on top, but now one of them was out of sequence.

Later, she made a point of asking Billy and Jeanne if either of them had been looking through the albums. Both children assured her that they had not.

The business with the albums could easily be her imagination, Jean readily admitted to herself, but the disappearance and reappearance of her cameras was definitely real. The problem was, now that the cameras had been returned, she had no proof they had ever been missing in the first place. Maybe she shouldn't have listened to J. B. after all, she thought. Maybe she should have gone ahead and reported a burglary. At least there would have been some record of it.

But, God, how stupid she would have felt—and looked— later, when the cameras came back all by themselves! A lot of people were already convinced she was crazy, and that would have just given them more ammunition to shoot full of holes anything she said.

It had reached the point where she never knew which way to turn or what to do, and whatever she did always seemed to be wrong. She could feel herself becoming more paranoid by the hour, but as far as she was concerned, her paranoia was amply justified. She had taken Gordon Shanklin's warning to heart and hadn't breathed so much as a word to anyone about her suspicions concerning LBJ, but her problems seemed to go on and on and keep getting bigger. And Shanklin and company was certainly no comfort to her; it was as much an enemy as ever, as the incident with the cameras proved. In her entire life, she had never felt so angry or frustrated, so helpless or vulnerable.

She was still in this mood when she put in a call to the Dallas field office of the FBI during her free period at school the next morning.

"Gordon Shanklin, please," she told the voice that answered.

"Special Agent Shanklin has someone with him at the moment. I'd be glad to try to help you, or I can take your number and ask him to call you."

"No," she snapped. "Just tell him this is Jean Hill and it's very urgent. I have to talk to him now."

There was a long pause, and then she heard Shanklin's voice on the line.

"Jean," he said, "what can I do for you?" He sounded elated to hear from her, but that wouldn't last long, she thought. "I hope everything's all right."

"No, it's not all right," she barked, "and you can tell your damned agents to stay out of my house and keep their hands off my personal property." She wasn't sure if it was possible to sue the FBI or not, but she was seriously considering finding out.

"I don't understand, Jean," he said. "Has something been taken from your home? Is something missing?"

"Not anymore," she said. "Somebody took my cameras, but they brought them back. No run-of-the-mill burglar'd do anything like that. It has to have been the FBI."

"I don't have the slightest idea what you're talking about," Shanklin said quietly, "but I assure you that nobody from this office has ever been inside your home while you weren't there, and nobody from this office has ever touched your cameras. I'd swear to it."

Jean suddenly felt confused and outflanked.

"I don't care what you swear to," she blurted. "Your people sit in front of my house all day and all night. They follow me everywhere I go. I know they have my phone tapped and they're probably opening my mail. God knows what else they're doing. Why can't you just leave me alone?"

"We're trying to protect you, Jean," Shanklin said calmly. "As I told you the other day, we have reason to believe you're putting yourself in serious danger."

She felt an icicle of fear stab through her chest. "But why should I be?" she demanded. "I'm a nothing, a nobody. Why should anyone care about me or what I think?"

"Unfortunately, you're a 'nobody' who talks too much," Shanklin said bluntly. "You should've listened when all those people—myself included—were telling you to keep quiet and forget about what happened in Dallas last November."

"I wish to Christ I *could* forget it," she assured him, "but I can't. Besides, I haven't said anything to anyone about it since the last time we talked. And what does that have to do with the FBI invading my privacy anyway?"

"Even if you never say another word, it looks to me like some serious damage has already been done," Shanklin said gravely. "Unless you cooperate fully with us, Jean, I'm afraid you may have a lot more than just your privacy to worry about."

The strident ringing of the telephone jerked Jean rudely from a deep sleep and she sat up with a start in the darkness of her bedroom. The luminous dial on the bedside clock told her it was 1:48 A.M. Who in God's name could be calling at this hour?

She groped in the gloom until she found the nightstand, then the phone. She lifted the receiver and stifled a yawn as she spoke into the mouthpiece.

"Hello?"

"Is this Jean Hill?" a harsh, slurring male voice asked.

"Yes, it is. Who's this?"

"Never mind about that. I just wanted to tell you what a low-life, good-for-nothing little bitch you are. I know all about you running around with a married man and making up lies about who shot President Kennedy. It wouldn't surprise me none if you and that cop boyfriend of yours was in on the assassination your ownself . . ."

The caller was obviously very drunk, and his voice became steadily more strident and out of control.

". . . trying to make people believe that bastard Oswald didn't have nothing to do with it and just got framed. You'd like that, wouldn't you? You'd like to make everybody think the FBI or somebody killed JFK, instead of that no-count commie sombitch. Well, I just hope they turn ol' Jack Ruby loose pretty soon. I'd like to see him take care of you like he took care of Oswald. And if ol' Jack can't get the job done, maybe I will . . ."

Jean dropped the telephone back into its cradle, mercifully breaking the connection. Crank calls were nothing new, but, dear God, she thought, none of the others had ever been as vicious as this one. How could the caller possibly know about her and J. B. unless he was a cop himself or closely connected to someone on the police force? How could he possibly believe that she and J. B. were somehow mixed up in the assassination?

What if he should call again? And, worse yet, what if he should follow up on his threat? She would have gotten an unlisted number if her principal hadn't believed so firmly that teachers should always be accessible to parents by phone. Now it was probably too late. This was the third nasty call this month, and if whoever it was knew her phone number, they obviously knew her address too. She wasn't sure just how much more of this she could stand.

She lay in the dark, dabbing a tissue at the tears streaming down her face until she heard the soft sound of the bedroom door opening.

"Mom, are you okay?" It was Jeanne, her voice husky with concern.

"Yes, baby, I'm all right. You'd better go on back to bed."

"Who was that on the phone?" Jeanne asked.

"Just some nut," Jean said. "It's nothing for you to worry about."

"But it's worrying *you*, isn't it, Mom?"

"A little, I guess," Jean admitted, wiping her eyes. "But I'll get over it."

"Sometimes I think we ought to just move, Mom," Jeanne said. "I mean just get away from here and go live someplace else. Do you ever feel that way?"

"I don't know," Jean said. "I guess I do sometimes."

After Jeanne had padded back down the hall to her own room, Jean got quietly out of bed. Without turning on the light, she tiptoed her way to the dresser and pulled open the heavy bottom drawer.

There, buried under some sweaters that she seldom wore was the heavy .38-caliber revolver that her father had given her years before during a prowler scare in Oklahoma City. Thanks to her dad, Jean had grown up with guns and was as comfortable with them as any man. Despite its weight and recoil, she had learned to handle the .38 with considerable skill, and during outings to the wilderness along the East Fork of the Trinity River with J. B., she had banged away at enough cans, logs and turtles to become a respectable shot with it.

Now she took the revolver out of the dresser and carried it gingerly back to the bed. At first, she slipped it into the top drawer of the night stand, then removed it again and shoved it under the extra pillow, where it would be right at her fingertips if she should need it.

But when she sank back on the mattress, she found her insides as tight as piano wire, her palms damp with sweat and her heart pounding loudly in her ears, and even with the reassuring bulk of the .38 beside her, sleep refused to come.

When the first pale light of dawn filtered through the windows of her bedroom, Jean still lay wide awake, staring at the ceiling and wondering what she was going to do.

The weeks that followed brought no improvement in the situation. If anything, Jean's personal life deteriorated still further. The crank calls continued sporadically, most of them coming late at night. Often, the callers wouldn't say anything at all; other times, they would mutter brief threats, usually punctuated with expletives, then hang up. Even when there were no calls, Jean often caught herself waiting in tense anticipation for the phone to ring and unable to fall asleep. And likely as not, if she did manage to drift off into an uneasy slumber, she was tormented by bad dreams in which she was pursued by a shadowy figure with a rifle.

For obvious reasons, J. B. still didn't contact her at home very often these days. Instead, they met at least two or three times a week at pre-arranged locations, and if she needed to get a message to him in the meantime, she usually went to a pay phone and called either the police dispatcher or a mutual friend. But toward the end of June, several weeks after school was out, she received a rare and unexpected daytime call from J. B.

It was plain from his tone that he was worried about something.

"Meet me at the usual place at the usual time," he said, not bothering with small talk or pleasantries, "but make it tonight instead of tomorrow night, and be extra careful on the way. Something's come up and I need to talk to you."

Almost before she could mumble a response, the line was dead in her hand. As she replaced the receiver, it came as no great surprise when she noticed that her hand was shaking.

The "usual" time and place to which J. B. referred was 7:00 P.M. at a certain secluded picnic area beside Lawther Drive, a winding road which meandered along the shore of White Rock Lake. Fearful of leaving the kids at home, even for an hour or so, Jean dropped them off at a theater en route to the lake and promised to pick them up when the movie was over. Only then did she go through the irritating but necessary process of eluding the FBI car that had followed her from home.

J. B.'s white GMC pickup was already parked under some

trees a few yards from the water's edge when Jean got there. It was still broad daylight as she pulled up and stopped the VW next to the pickup, and the blue waters of the lake were studded with graceful, white sailboats. The sounds of frolicking children were clearly audible from an adjacent grove. Someone was grilling hot dogs not far away, and a steady stream of slow-moving traffic was drifting past on the road. Despite all this nearby activity, however, Jean had always felt isolated and secure in this spot, and she felt no less so today.

J. B. didn't look happy as she opened the door of the pickup and slid in beside him. He had parked so that they were facing the lake and none of the passersby on the road could have identified them, even if they bothered to stare in their direction.

He reached out, caught her hand and squeezed it.

"Sorry to have to change plans on you," he said.

"It's okay," she assured him. "What's the matter? Is something wrong?"

He gazed out through the windshield toward the sailboats for a moment before he answered.

"Yeah," he said then, "it sure looks like it is. It looks like something's bad wrong."

For some reason, Jean didn't immediately connect J. B.'s words with any kind of physical threat or danger. In fact, the first thought that crossed her mind was that he was going to tell her he couldn't see her anymore. She could hardly stand the thought, but somehow the suspense was even harder to bear.

"Well, come on, what is it?" she pressed.

He turned to face her and the uneasiness was evident in his eyes. "I don't know how to tell you this except to just spit it out," he said. "The department's gotten word there's a contract out on you, Norma Jean, and there's a good possibility it's on the level. That means you've got to be extra careful until we can check it all out."

She sagged back against the seat, feeling as if someone had just hit her between the eyes with a sledgehammer. Her head was swimming and her heart had jumped up into her throat. She had read about contract killings in the newspapers and heard allusions to them on the TV cop shows, but she had never once dreamed—even with all the recent upheaval in her life—that she would become the object of one. Even at this moment, the idea that someone would pay a hit man to murder her seemed utterly inconceivable; yet here was a veteran police officer telling her that this very thing could be happening.

"But how . . . ?" she stammered. "Who? Why?"

"Look," he said, "stuff like this comes through the grapevine all the time and it's hard to tell how authentic it is until police intelligence has a chance to run down the sources and come up with some solid information. It may be nothing but bullshit, and on the other hand it could be something serious. But until we find out more, I want you to watch yourself, okay? I don't want to scare you; I just want you to know what the situation is and be on your toes. Right now, it's in the nature of an unsubstantiated rumor, and I wouldn't even tell some women about it, but I figure you're tough enough to handle it."

"I don't feel tough," Jean said, trembling. "I don't feel tough at all."

"Just don't get all panicky," J. B. urged. "The best thing to do right now is keep your head and not take any unnecessary chances. Stay close to home as much as you can, especially at night. Keep your doors and windows locked and your curtains drawn. Keep your car doors locked when you're driving around. Don't open any doors for anybody until you're 100 percent sure who they are. Are you still keeping that pistol beside your bed?"

"Not exactly," Jean said. "More like *in* the bed."

"That's good. Keep it handy and if somebody tries to get in your house, don't hesitate to use it."

"I don't know if I could actually shoot a real live person or not," Jean said.

"You could if your life depended on it. Think about it that way."

"How long is it going to take to find out if this thing's for real or not?" she asked.

"There's no way to tell," he said. "We might come across something in the next 24 hours or we may never find out any more than we already know."

"Oh, great," she sighed. "How does information like this originate anyway?"

"All kinds of ways," he said, "but it usually happens when the homicide or robbery bureau starts questioning suspects in a particular case. Sometimes a suspect offers to trade information if the detectives'll agree to let him walk. Sometimes the information's good; sometimes it's not."

Jean's mind flashed abruptly back to the last conversation she had had with Gordon Shanklin. A tingling sensation rushed up her backbone as she recalled his exact words: "We have reason to believe you've put yourself in serious danger."

"Do you think the FBI knows about this . . . 'contract'?" she asked, forcing herself to speak the dreadful term aloud.

"I wouldn't be one damned bit surprised," J. B. said, with unmistakable rancor in his voice. "It wouldn't surprise me if they knew a whole helluva lot about it—a lot more than they'd ever admit."

"Do you think I ought to ask them and see what happens?"

"I wouldn't waste my breath if I were you," he replied coldly. "I don't trust those bastards as far as I could throw them. I think the less you say to them about anything, the better off you'll be."

As it turned out, there was no need for Jean to broach the subject of contract killers with the FBI. When Shanklin came to her home three or four days later, it was the very first thing he brought up, and it quickly became apparent that it was the main reason for his visit.

"Jean, there's no point in beating around the bush," the agent said. "I'm extremely worried about you. As your friend J. B. Marshall may already have told you by now, we suspect someone may have been hired to kill you, and I strongly recommend additional steps to ensure your safety."

"What kind of steps?" she asked.

"I think you should get out of this house and stay somewhere else for awhile," he said, looking intently at her. "I'd feel much better if you did."

"But this is my home," she protested, "and I don't want to leave it. Besides, I don't have anywhere else to go."

Shanklin sat down beside her on the living room couch. "If you're interested, I could work something out, Jean," he said softly, leaning toward her. "I could arrange for an apartment on the other side of town. It could be leased under an assumed name and nobody would need to know about it except you and me. You'd be perfectly safe and comfortable there . . ."

"What about my job? I've got to earn a living somehow."

"You could take a leave of absence from your job," he said, putting his hand on her shoulder. "I could, uh, cover your expenses for the time being."

"What about my children?"

"You could send them to stay with relatives until this blows over."

"Suppose it doesn't blow over."

"If we decide there's an ongoing threat to your safety, the FBI has a very efficient witness relocation program," Shanklin said. "We can move you across the country, equip you with a whole new identity, and help you start over in a new life. I don't think it ever has to come to that, but . . ."

Jean smiled wryly. "You mean after a few months of 'playing house' with you in some North Dallas apartment, you think everything will be just fine. Is that what you're trying to say, Gordon?"

"Now, Jean," he protested, "I don't want you to get the wrong idea . . ."

"I'm not," she said, standing up from the couch. "Believe me, I understand exactly what you're suggesting. Now let's just forget it. I'm not interested."

"There no need to make a hasty decision, Jean," he said evenly. "Why don't you just think about it for a while. It could be a very beneficial arrangement. Very safe and secure."

She walked to the front door and opened it, biting her tongue to keep from saying something that she might have reason to regret later.

"Goodbye, Gordon," she said.

Jean didn't recount her conversation with Shanklin to J. B. for a period of several weeks. When she eventually did, she understood her reasons for the long delay and only wished she had postponed it even longer. Ordinarily, J. B. was one of the quietest, most undemonstrative men she had ever known, and she hadn't expected him to react nearly as angrily as he did. He was easily as furious as she had ever seen him.

"Goddamn!" he roared, hurling a glass into her kitchen sink and smashing it into a million fragments.

"Take it easy," she said. "You don't have to wreck the place. I let him know what he could do with his apartment."

"I can't believe this guy," he thundered. "I can't believe he'd pull something that cheap and sleazy. I feel like calling him up and telling him to meet me someplace and settle this man-to-man."

"Oh, J. B., don't be silly," Jean said, trying to soothe him. "Shanklin's not my type and there's no way I'd ever get personally involved with him. But I'll tell you the truth: This witness relocation program he talked about might be something I ought to find out more about. If worse comes to worst, I may need it."

"To hell with that!" J. B. snapped. "The last thing in the world you want to do is let the FBI take you off someplace and hide you from everybody who knows you and cares about you. If that ever happened, you could just as easily disappear permanently and nobody would ever know what happened to you. You talk about jumping out of the frying pan into the fire! God, that's exactly what you'd be doing."

Sometimes Jean was stunned at how naive she could still be occasionally—and this was definitely one of those times. Up until J. B.'s outburst, she had never once considered that, as a "protected," relocated witness, she would be totally under the control of the FBI. Not only would she never be able to call her life her own again, but if something *did* happen to her . . .

"I see what you mean," she said in a soft, subdued tone. "I guess that's not a very good idea, after all, is it?"

"No, it's not," he said. "You've got to remember, the Feds could be right in the middle of this whole Kennedy mess—some of them anyway. If not somebody in the FBI, then maybe in the CIA or military intelligence or the Secret Service. Christ, honey, they could all be in it, and the point is, you can't trust any of them."

Jean felt the tears coming and she couldn't stop them.

"But what am I going to do, J. B.?" she pleaded. "As far as I can tell, I've never committed a single crime in my life, but I feel like the worst criminal that ever lived. I feel like a hunted animal, and I don't think I can stand it much longer. The whole thing's driving me crazy."

"Listen to me, Norma Jean," J. B. said, putting his arms around her. "I know we can ride this thing out if we just keep our wits about us and don't go off the deep end. We can beat this thing together. There may not be anybody else in the whole world we can trust, but we've got to trust each other."

"I know," she cried, burying her face in his shirt, "and I do trust you. I couldn't make it without you."

But even as Jean spoke, a small, insistent doubt kept chipping away at her trust. Did J. B. genuinely think she had something to fear from Gordon Shanklin and the FBI, or was he actually motivated only by personal jealousy and selfishness? Did J. B. honestly believe they were both the targets of some intricate, interwoven federal conspiracy—one that likely reached all the way to the LBJ White House—or was he merely trying to keep her as close to him and dependent on him as possible?

She tried to dismiss the doubt, but like all her other troubles, it refused to go away.

CHAPTER EIGHT

"Accidents" Will Happen

Somehow, a year had passed—a year in which, on the surface at least, Jean's life had taken a decided turn back toward stability. Her divorce had become final in August 1964, and she had allowed her relationship with J. B. to emerge more and more from the shadows, although he was still married to someone else—a "someone" who continued to come and go in his life. And while he often seemed no closer than ever to obtaining his full freedom, he and Jean felt few restrictions on being together, except for the fact that, other than the two or three times a month when the kids were gone, J. B. always went home at night.

That fall, Jean had started her first full semester of teaching in the Dallas school system, and the job had since become a comfortable, reassuring part of her routine. She was a good teacher, one who truly enjoyed teaching, and she had missed the classroom sorely during her nearly two years away from it. With most of her waking hours now solidly filled, she made a concerted effort to push the assassination and its aftermath as far into the back of her mind as possible. And although she knew she could never forget those events, she almost never talked to anyone about what she had seen and heard on November 22, 1963. Jeanne and Billy made it abundantly clear that they would just as soon not be reminded of her role as an eyewitness, and that they found the whole idea disturbing. J. B., of course, had long ago made his feelings known on the subject, and even family members and old friends in Oklahoma seemed to cast perplexed glances in her direction whenever the topic came up. And so Jean grudgingly took Gordon Shanklin's advice and kept quiet about it.

Sometime in the spring of 1965, after more than 15 months of constant 24-hour-a-day surveillance, the FBI quietly dropped its vigil outside Jean's home. One day, the nondescript car containing the two conservatively dressed agents simply wasn't there anymore. The car and its occupants turned up at sporadic intervals after that, but by the end of the school term, they appeared to have departed for good. Oddly enough, as many times as she had wished for them to leave her alone, Jean almost missed them once the realization sank in that they probably would not be back. She no longer feared the Dallas FBI as she once had; it was the nameless, faceless "those people" in Washington or somewhere else, to whom J. B. had so often referred, who still unnerved her.

Even after calling off his men, Shanklin still called Jean every few weeks to inquire about how she was doing, express his concern and offer none-too-subtle hints that his offers of putting her up in a protective hideaway were still open anytime she chose to accept.

"As a sign of my good faith and friendship, and just to prove to you that you can trust me," he told her at one point, "I'm going to have your whole local file destroyed. I have no control over anything they might have in Washington, but I can see to it that all your records in the Dallas office are shredded. That way, they won't be able to cause you any future problems."

Jean took Shanklin's offer with a grain of salt. She didn't really dislike the man, but she didn't trust him either. She did nothing to actively encourage him, but she also made an effort not to offend him. As for his promise to destroy her records, she had no way of knowing whether he would keep his word or not.

The intensive media coverage of the months immediately following the assassination had dwindled considerably by now, but there were still occasional calls from writers and reporters who were working on speculative articles about JFK's death and the lingering hints of a conspiracy. One such call came just a few days after the summer break had begun. It was from a man who identified himself as a free-lance journalist working on assignment for a national magazine. Jean had become increasingly reticent about talking to anyone from the press and she tried politely several times to cut the man off, without success. She was on the point of simply hanging up when the caller mentioned something that sent an icy stab of panic through her and froze the receiver to her ear.

"I really think you ought to take advantage of this opportunity to talk to someone, Mrs. Hill," the journalist said. "Are you aware that at least a dozen people—witnesses and others with close ties to the assassination—have died under very mysterious circumstances over the past year and a half?"

Jean's throat was suddenly as dry as powder. "No," she said softly, "I didn't know that."

"Oh, yeah, it's the God's truth," he said. "They're literally dropping like flies, Mrs. Hill. For instance, did you hear about the two reporters who went to Jack Ruby's apartment a few hours after he shot Oswald? Both of them were killed within a few months. One of the lawyers who went to the apartment with them died too. Then there were those two girls who worked for Ruby. One of them supposedly hanged herself in jail with her toreador pants, and the other one was shot to death—and that's just the beginning."

Until that very moment, Jean had never realized that the list of "assassination victims" was so extensive or that it was continuing to grow almost monthly. Not even the countless vile and threatening phone calls, the hundreds of unsettling letters that had come in the mail, or the repeated warnings of "contracts" and impending danger relayed to her by FBI and police sources had filled her with such terror as this sudden knowledge.

"I hear you claim to have seen Ruby in Dealey Plaza when the shots were fired," the journalist pressed. "I also hear you heard up to six shots and saw at least one of them come from the grassy knoll area. That goes against the whole Warren Commission Report, and I'd really like to talk to you about it before . . . well, before anything else happens."

"I'm sorry, but I can't talk about it anymore," Jean mumbled in a quavering voice. "I've said way too much already."

As she replaced the receiver, Jean could feel her whole body trembling.

"I didn't see any sense in talking about it, so I didn't," J. B. said. "All it would have done is get you upset—just like you are now—so what was the point?"

Several hours had passed since Jean had talked to the journalist, but there was still a tightness in her chest and a fluttery feeling in her stomach. J. B. had responded to her urgent summons by hurrying straight to the house as soon as his shift was over, and he sat beside her now on the couch in the den, still wearing his dark-blue uniform and trying to calm her. He wasn't doing a very good job, however, especially after admitting he had known about most of the assassination-related deaths.

"The point was, I had a right to know," she told him testily. "I can't believe you knew all along that so many people were being killed and you didn't say a word about it."

"I didn't think much about it at first," he said. "In fact, I didn't really start hooking it all together until a couple of months ago when that lawyer of Ruby's, Tom Howard, dropped dead all of a sudden. They said it was a heart attack, but they didn't do an autopsy, and he sure as hell looked healthy enough to me the last time I saw him."

"You mean you knew him?"

"Sure. Practically everybody knew Tom Howard. He was as wild and woolly as any lawyer in town, and he damned sure wasn't the kind of guy you'd expect to keel over with a heart attack. Hell, he was only forty-something."

J. B. told her how Howard, along with several other attorneys and two newsmen, had visited Ruby's apartment on the evening after Oswald's murder and before police had had an opportunity to search the premises. One of the newsmen, Bill Hunter, a reporter for the Long Beach *Press-Telegram* in California who had been in Dallas covering the assassination, had been fatally shot on the early morning of April 23, 1964, when a detective's gun discharged, apparently by accident, at the Long Beach police station. The other reporter, Jim Koethe of the *Dallas Times Herald*, had been found dead in his East Dallas apartment five months later. His neck had been broken by a karate chop.

(Once she heard the details, Jean dimly recalled reading about the Koethe case. Since the victim was a staff writer for a major newspaper, the slaying received prominent play in the press, but she didn't remember any references at the time to the link with Ruby, and she had no recollection at all of any of the other cases J. B. outlined to her that day.)

"A week or so later, homicide picked up a young ex-con named Larry Reno who had some of Koethe's personal stuff in his possession and looked like he was good for the murder," J. B. said. "But the grand jury no-billed Reno, and I heard rumors that the prosecution didn't really want him indicted anyway. Now he's back in jail on a robbery charge, but I don't think they can make a case on him in the Koethe killing."

J. B. also told Jean that someone was apparently targeting witnesses to the murder of Off. J. D. Tippit. One witness, a used-car salesman named Warren Reynolds, had been shot in the head in January 1964 just two days after telling the FBI that he could not positively identify Oswald as the killer. After a miraculous recovery from his wound, however, Reynolds had decided that Oswald *was* the man he had seen fleeing the scene, after all. The second victim was Edward Benavides, the look-alike brother of another Tippit slaying witness, Domingo Benavides, who had given police a distinctly un-Oswaldlike description of the murderer. Eddy Benavides had been fatally shot in the back of the head in a South Dallas beer joint in February 1964.

"The Benavides killing's still officially unsolved—just like the Koethe killing," J. B. said, "but there's a strange twist to it. A couple of weeks after it happened, somebody took a couple of shots at Domingo Benavides's father-in-law, a guy named Jackson, who'd been doing a little investigating on his own. There's something weird about the Reynolds shooting too. We picked up a guy for attempted murder in that case, but he had an alibi. He claimed he was with a gal named Nancy Jane Mooney, who used to be a stripper at Ruby's Carousel Club, at the time Reynolds was shot. She corroborated his story, so we had to turn him loose.

"Then, just about a week later, this same Nancy Jane got picked up herself for getting in a fight and disturbing the peace. They put her in a private cell at the city jail and when they went in to check on her a few hours later, they found her dead. It looked like the damned broad had hanged herself, but . . ."

"Yeah," Jean interjected. "She supposedly hanged herself with her own toreador pants, right?"

"That's right. How'd you know?"

"The guy on the phone told me. He said there was another girl who used to work for Ruby who got killed too. Only this second one was shot."

"I don't remember hearing anything about another one," J. B. said. "It must not have happened in Dallas. There've been several people killed somewhere else. I heard about one guy that they say was connected to Ruby and Oswald both; he got his throat cut and bled to death when he was thrown through a plate-glass window down in Florida someplace."

(As a matter of record, the Florida victim was Hank Killam, whose wife, Wanda, had worked for Ruby as a waitress and cigarette girl for 15 years. The Killams had been close friends with one John Carter, who had worked with Hank as a house-painter and who had lived for a time in the same rooming house with Oswald. After the assassination, Wanda Killam claimed her husband came home "white as a sheet" and that he was harassed for months by "agents" and "federal police" to the extent that he was fired from several jobs in Dallas. The harassment allegedly continued even after he moved to Florida around Christmastime of 1963. On St. Patrick's Day 1964, Killam received a phone call at his mother's home in Tampa and left immediately. A short time later, he was found on a sidewalk in front of a broken window with his jugular vein severed, and he bled to death en route to a hospital. His wallet and a diamond ring were missing. No mention of Killam appears in the Warren Commission Report.)

"My God, let's stop talking about it," Jean said. "I don't think I can stand to hear any more."

J. B. put his arm around her and drew her close to him, so close that she was sure he could feel her shaking and her heart pounding.

"That's the reason I never brought it up before, Norma Jean," he said gently. "I just didn't want to worry you with stuff like this."

"But what if this is some kind of systematic thing?" she said. "How do we know there's not some grand scheme to wipe out everybody with any 'inconvenient' knowledge about the assassination?"

"We don't," he said simply. "That's why I keep preaching at you to be careful and not take any unnecessary chances. If all these other people had been careful enough, they might still be alive."

Jean didn't sleep much that night, or the next night, or the next. She lay awake, her hand touching the reassuring bulk of the .38 revolver under the pillow next to her, wondering how many seemingly ordinary people across the country would eventually die as part of the grotesque aftermath of the Kennedy assassination.

How many would die simply because they had happened to be in the wrong place at the wrong time? Or because of a casual association, a chance meeting or an innocent remark? Who would be next? Would Jean Hill or someone she loved be among them?

By later in the week, she had decided her most sensible course of action was to take the children and get out of town for a while. They had made a habit each year since moving to Dallas of going to Oklahoma soon after school dismissed for the summer for an extended visit with Jean's parents (who, although divorced for some 30 years, still lived in close proximity to each other). This year, Jean had purposely delayed the trip in order to have a few days to relax and be with J. B. But under present circumstances, relaxation seemed out of the question in Dallas, and even the chance to spend time with J. B. each day had become of secondary importance. Her first priority right now was simply to get away from Dallas, to escape its constant reminders of the assassination, and to wrap the quiet and solitude of rural Oklahoma around her like a protective shield.

On Friday morning, Billy went on ahead to visit his dad and stepmother, but before Jean and Jeanne could leave, it was necessary to outfit themselves with some new summer clothes. So, early that afternoon, under gloomy, overcast skies, the two of them set out in Jean's almost-new 1964 Plymouth Barracuda (which she had bought a few months earlier to replace her banged-up old VW). Their destination was the Wynnewood Village Shopping Center in the Oak Cliff section of Dallas.

By the time they finished their shopping and started back across town, the skies had opened up and a steady rain was falling. It wasn't one of the lightning-studded, flash flood-producing type of thunderstorms that so frequently occur in North Texas in the spring, but the raindrops were coming down hard enough to keep the car's windshield wipers busy and to make the streets treacherously slick.

After the serious accident in which Jean had been involved a year and a half earlier, she had grown much more safety conscious than she had once been—particularly in the rain, and especially when one or both of her children were in the car. Partly because of this newfound caution and partly because of the downpour, she was traveling at a relatively low speed— only about 45 miles per hour—as the Plymouth started into a long, sloped cloverleaf intersection where Illinois Avenue emptied into South Central Expressway.

Dallas Police Department accident investigators would later tell Jean how fortunate it was that she was going as slow as she was, and how lucky it was that the ground beside the highway was soft and muddy from the rain.

Otherwise, they said, it was highly unlikely that either she or her 11-year-old daughter would have survived the events of the next few seconds.

Suddenly, inexplicably, Jean felt the steering wheel go slack. She pulled it frantically to the right, then back to the left, but nothing happened. It was as though the circular object in her hands was no longer connected to the rest of the car. Instead of continuing into the curve as it should have, the car refused to respond. As the steering wheel spun loosely in her hands, the Plymouth kept plunging straight ahead—directly toward a huge tree some 20 feet from the roadway.

"Mom! Look out!" Jeanne screamed.

"I can't steer!" Jean shouted. "Hold on!"

She hit the brakes with all the force she could muster, but it was too late. The car skidded and went barrelling over the curb, while Jean stared through the windshield in helpless, horrified fascination at the massive trunk of the tree hurtling straight at them.

Instinctively, she reached out for Jeanne, a desperate prayer on her lips.

"Please, God, please . . ."

She closed her eyes and felt her head jerked forward as the front bumper of the Barracuda struck the tree with a sharp bump, but the fierce impact and grinding crash that Jean had expected never came. Miraculously, the car bounced against the tree trunk a time or two and then came to a standstill.

Jean reached out and threw her arms around Jeanne, who was breathless and wide-eyed, but unhurt.

"Mom," Jeanne gasped. "What . . . what happened? Why didn't we crash?"

"I don't know," Jean said, feeling lightheaded and somewhat winded herself. "Something stopped us, but I'm not sure what."

Slowly, she pushed open the car door and peered out at the tires and wheels on the driver's side of the Plymouth. They were buried all the way to the hubs in a thick, oozy quagmire.

As the realization of what had happened slowly dawned on

her, Jean almost laughed in spite of her frayed nerves. She had never imagined that anyone could feel such a surge of sheer thankfulness at getting stuck in the mud.

When the patrolman in the yellow slicker had completed his report and the tow truck had dragged the Plymouth from the bog in which it had come to rest and hauled it slowly away, Jean and Jeanne—both thoroughly drenched from standing in the rain—clamored gratefully into the seat of J. B.'s pickup and let him drive them home.

On reaching the scene, J. B., too, had at first been tremendously relieved that they were all right. But as he slogged around in the mud, looking under the car and testing the flapping steering wheel, he seemed to grow more upset by the moment, although he didn't say much of anything until they were back at the house and Jeanne was in her room.

"There's something very fishy about this accident of yours," he said finally. "The steering doesn't just suddenly fail on a car with less than 10,000 miles on it, unless . . ." He paused and stared at her. "Unless somebody *wants* it to fail."

Jean felt a tingling sensation on the back of her neck. "You mean you think somebody did something to my car?"

"I think it's completely possible," he said, "but I'm not sure yet. How long were you at the shopping center?"

She shrugged. "A couple of hours, I guess. I wasn't really keeping track of the time."

"Have you been putting the car in the garage at night or leaving it out?"

"Leaving it out mostly. You know what a junkpile that garage is."

As an experienced "backyard mechanic" who did most of his own automotive repairs, J. B. was concerned enough that he wanted to go to the repair shop where the Barracuda had been taken and examine it himself. Jean insisted on going along, and they left as soon as she and Jeanne could shed their muddy clothes and change into fresh ones.

Once they reached the shop, which was only about three

miles from the house, Jean and Jeanne were left to sit in a waiting area while J. B. and one of the mechanics jacked the car up and checked it over. The first thing they had to do was clean off the thick, drying mud that covered the entire underside of the car, and even after that was done, the examination seemed to take forever.

Finally, after almost an hour, during which the two men alternately crawled under the raised front end of the Barracuda and conferred in hushed tones while pointing at various unidentifiable mechanisms, they both walked slowly over to where Jean and Jeanne were waiting. While J. B. was still 50 feet away, Jean could tell by his expression that something was seriously wrong.

"You better sit down and brace yourself," he told her gravely. "We've got something to tell you, and I don't think you're going to like it."

She looked silently from J. B. to the grim-faced mechanic and back again. Then she sank back down in the same chair where she had been sitting and waited, almost sensing what they were going to say before either of them spoke.

"I'm afraid there was nothing accidental about this 'accident,'" J. B. said quietly, putting his hands on her shoulders. "What happened was deliberately caused by somebody."

Along with the disbelief that swept through her mind, Jean felt a slight chill and she placed her arm around Jeanne in a protective hug. "How can you tell that?" she asked. "How can you be so sure?"

"Let me try to explain, ma'am," the mechanic said. "There's only one way to make the steering fail suddenly on a car like yours. To do that, you have to take the nuts off the tie-rods so they'll come loose and drop down. When that happens, you completely lose control of the car, and as I understand it, that's exactly what happened to you."

"Well, yes, it is," she said, "but couldn't the nuts have just worked loose on their own somehow?"

"No way," he said. "If your car was 15 years old and hadn't ever been near a repair shop, it might be an outside possibility, but on a car this new, it just couldn't happen by itself. I'd bet my last nickel on it."

"You might as well face it, Norma Jean," J. B. said gravely. "There's just no doubt about it. Somebody deliberately loosened those nuts—somebody who knew exactly what he was doing—until they were just hanging there by about one thread. Then, after you'd driven a few miles, the nuts just fell off. The likeliest time for it to happen was when you were making a sharp turn and putting a strain on the tie-rods, but it also could've happened on the expressway while you were zipping along at 65 miles an hour. I'd say you and Jeanne are pretty damned lucky to be alive right now."

The mechanic nodded. "I'd have to agree, Mrs. Hill," he said. "It looks like a definite case of tampering to me, and you could've had a really bad smashup because of it."

"How long would it have taken somebody to loosen the nuts?" Jean asked.

The mechanic frowned thoughtfully. "Probably no more than five or ten minutes if the guy knew his stuff and had the right tools," he said.

"Then it could have happened while we were shopping today," Jean said. "Somebody could've done it right there in the parking lot."

"They could've done it anywhere," J. B. said. "In the parking lot, in your driveway, or someplace we left the car when you rode with me. You remember what I told you about being careful? Well, we just haven't been careful enough."

Jeanne had been listening to the conversation without comment, but now she suddenly injected a very pointed question.

"What does this all mean, Mom?" she asked, her eyes wide with innocent wonder. "I mean, why would anybody want to mess around with our car and make us have a wreck?"

Jean shuddered at the question, momentarily unable to reply and wondering how she could possibly give her 11-year-old daughter an honest answer. The last thing in the world she wanted to do was frighten or traumatize Jeanne, but it was also obvious that keeping her daughter ignorant of the danger facing them could only increase the risk.

Should she lie or tell the truth? Jean wondered. How do you explain to your own child that somebody wants you dead?

A stay of slightly less than three weeks in Oklahoma proved to be highly effective therapy for the various symptoms of Jean's anxiety. After a few days, her jangled nerves settled down, her insomnia went away, and her constant indigestion and stomach aches (which she feared might be the start of an ulcer) also eased. She missed J. B., but she was able to talk to him by phone every day, sometimes two or three times, and he urged her to stay until she felt fully rested and ready to come home.

She had sense enough to know that, if someone was truly determined to kill her, she would never be totally safe anywhere. And yet, simply being this far removed from the scene of the assassination gave her an enhanced feeling of security. Even so, she made a point of keeping her car parked as close as possible to the house of whichever relative she might be visiting, and preferably out of the sight of passersby. During quiet moments in the evenings or early mornings, she reflected a great deal on the list of people who had died under questionable circumstances, and she knew beyond the shadow of a doubt that she didn't want to be one of them. Even now, when she could think about it calmly and with a certain degree of detachment, she remained as convinced as ever that the list was real, and that it would inevitably continue to grow.

Unfortunately, she was not able to take any of the "good medicine" of Oklahoma back to Dallas with her, and as she drove south on U.S. 75 toward the Red River on her return trip, she could almost feel the tension returning. It seemed to tighten a notch each time another mile clicked off the odometer, but she didn't mention her feelings to Billy or Jeanne.

In the final analysis, Jean had told Jeanne neither an out-and-out lie nor the whole truth about the incident with the car. Instead, she had said something about someone "playing a prank" and not realizing how much harm they could have caused. But she also re-emphasized her past warnings to Jeanne to be careful at all times, to avoid walking alone outside her own yard, and to steer clear of strangers. Meanwhile, Jean said nothing to Billy about the "accident" and assumed that, unless Jeanne had told him what happened, he had no knowledge of it. Billy was almost 14 now, she told herself, and big enough to take care of himself in most ways. And besides, it was hard for her to conceive of anyone deliberately targeting her children for harm. The primary danger to Billy and Jeanne, she believed, was being caught in some "line of fire" aimed at their mother.

An incident that occurred only a week or so after their return home caused Jean to have strong second thoughts about this conclusion, however.

She was in the kitchen on that particular midsummer afternoon, preparing dinner and waiting for J. B. to get there. Jeanne was at a girlfriend's house and Billy was out riding the motorbike he had recently bought with his paper route earnings. With all the doors and windows closed and the central air conditioner running, it was next to impossible to hear outside noises unless they were exceptionally loud, and Jean was blissfully unaware of what was going on in the street just a few yards from her own driveway, until she heard the front doorbell ring.

Since she had been peeling carrots and potatoes, she took time to wash and dry her hands before starting toward the door and was surprised to hear the bell ring insistently again before she got there.

"All right," she muttered under her breath, feeling a little irritated, "I'm coming!"

A second or two later, she turned the lock, pulled the door open, and shrank back in horror at the sight confronting her.

J. B. was standing on the front porch, holding Billy in his arms as effortlessly as if Billy had been a five-year-old. Billy's shirt was torn and dirty, his hair was powdered with dirt and gravel dust, and the left leg of his blue jeans was mangled. His left arm and the whole left side of his face were covered with blood.

"My God, Billy," she gasped. "What happened to you?"

"A car ran me off the road," he groaned, making an obvious effort not to cry. "I don't know where it came from. All of a sudden, it was just there."

"He fell and skidded about 10 feet," J. B. said, brushing past her and carrying Billy into the bathroom, "and the car just peeled out and left him lying there. I saw it happen from about a block away, but I wasn't close enough to see the license number. I started to chase 'em, but then I thought I'd better stop to see if he was okay. You think anything's broken, champ?"

"I don't know," Billy said. "My arm sure does hurt."

From the looks of him, Jean was ready to rush him to the nearest emergency room, but when they got some of the blood and dirt wiped away, she was relieved to see that Billy apparently wasn't badly hurt. He was able to move all his limbs, which meant there were no broken bones, and he seemed to be more skinned-up than anything.

While Jean finished doctoring Billy, J. B. went out to the street and retrieved the motorbike. The front wheel was badly bent, he reported, and would have to be replaced.

"That's the least of my worries," Jean sighed after she had given Billy some aspirin and helped him to bed, and she and J. B. were alone in the kitchen. "As far as I'm concerned, the wheel can stay bent. I never wanted him to have that damned bike anyway."

"From what I saw, the car just came right at him," J. B. said. "It sure looked like they did it on purpose."

"What kind of car was it?"

"It was a two- or three-year-old Chevy sedan," he said. "Kind of an off-white or real light tan color. I hate to say it, Norma Jean, but it looked a helluva lot like one of those FBI cars to me."

"Oh, come on, J. B.," she said. "The FBI may've harassed me unmercifully for 15 months, but I can't believe they'd stoop to running down little boys on motorbikes."

"Yeah, probably not," he said with a shrug, "but sometimes I don't know what to believe anymore. Whoever it was, it damned sure looked deliberate and they took off like a bat out of hell once they'd done it; that's all I'm saying. And I'll tell you something else as long as we're on the subject."

"The subject of 'accidents,' you mean?"

"That's right," J. B. said. "Ever since that thing with the steering on your car, I've been thinking about that other wreck you had. You know, the one winter before last. Maybe it wasn't a real accident either. Maybe . . ."

"Oh, no," she said. "There's no way I can blame anybody else for that one. It was my fault, pure and simple. I was just going too fast on a dark, wet road."

"Well, maybe so," he said. "I probably never would've thought anything about it if all this other stuff hadn't happened, but I just got to wondering and worrying about it. I still wish I'd had enough sense to check over that VW after the wreck."

"I don't think there's any connection," she said. "I'm sure the other one was just bad driving on my part. But these things with the kids . . ."

Now that the emergency was past and Jean was no longer buoyed by the rush of her own adrenalin, she sagged limply against the kitchen counter, feeling her knees turn suddenly to rubber and her eyes fill with tears.

"Oh, God, J. B.," she whispered, "I can face up to the idea of somebody trying to kill me. I guess they think they've got a reason to kill me. But if they start going after my kids, I just don't think I can stand it."

He came and closed his arms around her, wiping at the wetness on her cheeks with his fingers.

"Easy, honey," he said. "Just try to take it easy. Maybe this deal with Billy was just some punk showing off. Maybe it doesn't mean anything at all."

"I hope not," she wept, "because if anything ever happened to Billy or Jeanne, I wouldn't want to live. I really wouldn't, J. B. I'd just want to be dead."

CHAPTER NINE

The Breaking Point

The weeks turned into months and the months into years, and slowly, almost imperceptibly, the stark horror of the assassination faded slightly and began to recede into the fabric of history. That was true for most of the rest of the country, at least, but for Jean, the passage of time seemed to offer no real respite. Whenever it seemed that the furor and trauma might die down enough to allow her to resume a normal, secure life, something happened to touch off a new wave of notoriety.

In mid-1966, for example, Mark Lane's book, *Rush to Judgment*, made its long-awaited appearance as the first authoritative nationwide best-seller to attack the Warren Commission's investigations and conclusions—and Jean Hill's most sensational claims and observations were liberally scattered throughout it.

From the entire 19-page transcript of her Warren Commission testimony, author Lane judiciously picked out just two complete sentences of Jean's to quote verbatim. They were, of course, sentences that flew in the face of every official Warren Commission finding: "I frankly thought they (the shots) were coming from the knoll. . . . I thought it was just people shooting from the knoll—I did think there was more than one person shooting."

Since Jean herself had charged that the vast majority of her alleged "testimony" appearing in the Warren Commission Report was either a gross distortion of what she actually said or a complete fabrication, it was understandable for Lane to pick one of the few passages that was a true representation of her words. But in building his own case against the commission, Lane also attributed to Jean a lengthy series of controversial and combative remarks, some of which she had repeatedly asked him not to publish.

On page 262, Lane described Jean as one of the persons closest to the president's car when he was shot and quoted her as saying she had seen a man running from the vicinity of the school book depository just after the shots. Lane noted Jean's description of the man's hat and brown raincoat and mentioned that, although she believed that she knew the man's identity, she was reluctant to tell the Warren Commission who he was, since the government claimed that he was known to have been somewhere else at the time. The author made it clear that Jean believed the man to be Jack Ruby and that, in her opinion, the man's physical appearance was virtually identical to Ruby's.

On page 285, Lane mentioned his original conversation with Jean in February 1964 and her comment that after she had talked to Lane, the FBI kept her under surveillance for days. He quoted Jean as saying, "They practically lived here. They just didn't like what I told them I saw and heard when the president was assassinated." Lane also made it clear that Jean had declined to permit a filmed interview, and quoted her further as saying, "For two years I have told the truth, but I have two children to support and I am a public school teacher. My principal said it would be best not to talk about the assassination, and I just can't go through it all again. I can't believe the Warren Report. I know it's all a lie, because I was there when it happened, but I can't talk about it anymore."

On page 389, again calling Jean an "important eyewitness" to the assassination, Lane told of her being encouraged by Secret Service agents to alter her testimony about the number of shots she had heard to conform with the official government position that there were only three. Lane pointed out that Jean had told the Secret Service and later a Warren Commission counsel that she had heard more than three shots. He also quoted a Secret Service agent as telling her that he had also heard more than three shots, but since the authorities had three wounds and three bullets, that was all they were "willing to say right now."

In reproducing these very statements and sentiments in his book, Lane had effectively defied Jean's emotional appeal to be left in peace. The book dragged the whole bloody mess right back into the public eye: The "shooter" atop the grassy knoll; the elusive Jack Ruby look-alike; the prying persistence of the FBI; the duplicity of the Secret Service. About the only thing Jean could find to be grateful for was that Lane hadn't mentioned the "damned dog."

Predictably, the book also touched off another storm of controversy, particularly in Dallas, and Jean found herself caught up in the maelstrom all over again. Once more, the abusive phone calls began to pour in, along with a new flood of letters from all parts of the country, and another round of requests for fresh media interviews. By now, however, in desperation, Jean had become totally reclusive. She refused to answer or even acknowledge letters, and hung up on would-be interviewers when they called.

"I was trying very hard to withdraw from it," Jean says today, "but it seemed totally impossible. In the very beginning, maybe I had been flattered by the attention I was getting and the idea that my name and my face were being seen by countless people from coast to coast. But if I had ever felt that way, I definitely didn't anymore. All I wanted was to hide someplace for about 10 years, until it all blew over. I prayed to be left alone, but there just didn't seem to be any escape for me. It was as though all the exits were blocked."

By now, worries about her children haunted her constantly. Although there were no further injuries or near injuries to either Billy or Jeanne, the possibility was never far from Jean's mind, and it was reinforced by at least one other "accident-in-the-making," which was luckily defused by J. B. before it could turn into a disaster.

Following the obvious tampering with the tie-rods on Jean's car, J. B. had begun making almost weekly inspections of the vehicle. During one of these, in the late fall of 1965, he discovered a clean, fresh cut in a line carrying brake fluid from the master cylinder to one of the front wheel cylinders. At the time of his discovery, more than 90 percent of the fluid had leaked out of the car's brake system, creating a condition under which the brakes could have failed completely at any moment.

From that point on, the car was never left in the driveway, even for a few minutes. Jean made it a practice to pull into the garage immediately on arriving home and to make sure that the garage door was closed and locked before going into the house. She also asked the custodians at her school to keep a close watch on the car while it was parked in the teacher parking lot, and she and J. B. permanently discontinued the practice of meeting each other in separate cars, then leaving one of them behind somewhere.

And yet, despite the fact that all these precautions made perfect sense, they did virtually nothing to stop the insistent, nagging worries that gnawed at Jean's mind almost constantly. It was as though she could never be careful enough, no matter how hard she tried. No matter how well she planned or how much caution she exercised, there was always the feeling that she was still vulnerable to the shadowy "those people" whose presence—whether real or imagined—hung over her like a black cloud.

She seldom had an appetite and she lost weight steadily until her cheeks were hollow and her sunken eyes developed dark circles under them. Her frail, emaciated appearance alarmed her friends, who feared that she might have some serious illness. The insomnia which she had experienced since shortly after the assassination grew worse, and even when she managed to sleep for a few hours at night, she awoke with the same exhausted, apprehensive feeling the next morning. She frequently heard strange noises, and sometimes she was too frightened by them even to investigate their source. When she was alone in her car, she could scarcely drive for watching the rear view mirror, although what she expected to see there, she couldn't explain, even to herself.

She was becoming paranoid, and she knew it.

On Wednesday, March 1, 1967, perhaps the biggest post-assassination furor of them all exploded. It was one that would refocus public attention on the murder of JFK for many months to come, but one that was also destined to inflict severe damage to the credibility of those who disputed the "one man-one gun" scenario. Claiming to have uncovered a complex plot to kill Kennedy, New Orleans district attorney Jim Garrison arrested Clay L. Shaw, director of the New Orleans International Trade Mart, that day and charged him with conspiring to assassinate the president.

From the very beginning, Garrison and his investigation were lampooned and lambasted by both the media and the federal government. U.S. attorney general Ramsey Clark, a Texan hand-picked by Lyndon Johnson to replace Bobby Kennedy, launched an immediate attack on Garrison. Clark proclaimed loftily that federal authorities had already exonerated Shaw of any wrongdoing, but was soon forced to concede that his pronouncement had been "erroneous." The FBI had never checked out Shaw at all, a Justice Department spokesman later admitted, because "nothing arose indicating a need to investigate Mr. Shaw."

Several months later, Chief Justice Earl Warren himself, the man who had headed the Warren Commission, announced from Tokyo that Garrison had produced "absolutely nothing" that would contradict the findings of the commission that Lee Harvey Oswald acted alone. Despite the fact that Clay Shaw's trial was still more than a year away, the nation's highest-ranking jurist apparently had already reached his own verdict in the case.

Meanwhile, almost every major newspaper and magazine in the country castigated Garrison and his investigation in heavily slanted news articles and scathing editorials. They accused the New Orleans prosecutor of being a power-mad, un-principled opportunist, whose only objectives were self-promotion and the prospect of higher political office, and who didn't care whom he hurt in achieving these goals. They called his investigation a sham, a circus and a mockery.

It quickly became obvious to Jean that, however well inten-tioned he might be, Garrison was engaged in a lonely and most likely futile effort, and that both the government and the media were far more interested in discrediting the Garrison investigation than in pursuing new leads or examining new evidence in the murder of a president.

Although she didn't know enough about the particulars of the case to have a definite opinion as to Shaw's innocence or guilt, Jean felt deep sympathy for Garrison because, in a sense, he was going through much the same type of ordeal she had faced when she disagreed with the "official" version of the assassination—only more so. But the fact that a formerly re-spected district attorney of a major American city could be hounded and discredited, just as she had been, clearly showed how little chance a private citizen like herself had of suc-cessfully disputing the powers that be.

Her sympathy was not enough, however, to make her eager to volunteer any kind of direct assistance to Garrison's cause, certainly not in her present fragile psychological state. J. B.'s warning that Garrison might try to subpoena her as a witness unnerved her terribly. The thought of being called upon ever again to testify to anything relating to the assassination was al-most more than she could bear—especially when J. B. told her how fruitless he thought it would be.

"I think the guy may really be onto something," he said, "but you'd be smart to stay as far away from him as possible, because he's never going to be able to make it stand up. They're not going to let him. If he's lucky, all they'll do is make him look like the world's biggest fool. If he's not, they'll proba-bly end up killing him."

"I don't want to have any part of it," she said in a strained whisper. "If they subpoena me, I just won't go. They can't make me go down there if I don't want to, can they?"

"I don't know," he said, "but don't worry about it. I'm sure Garrison's smart enough to know that dragging in a scared, reluctant witness isn't going to do his case any good."

"I'm so jumpy, J. B.," she moaned. "Just talking about this is making me a bundle of nerves. I'm shaking so bad right now I'm surprised you can't hear my bones rattling. Sometimes I think I may just go to pieces."

His concern was evident as he studied her for several seconds. "I'm really worried about you, Norma Jean," he said. "You don't eat and you don't sleep and you don't look well. I think you ought to go to the doctor. Maybe he could give you a prescription for something to . . . you know, help calm you down."

She tried to laugh, but all that came out was a hoarse croak. "You think I need tranquilizers?" she said, trying to sound sarcastic.

"I think you need something, hon," he told her quietly.

"Are you afraid I'm going to flip out on you?" she demanded in the same tone. "Is that what you think?"

"If you don't get hold of yourself," he said bluntly, "I think you just might."

Her blood pressure was somewhat low, Jean's doctor said, which was surprising in itself, since the stress under which she was living would tend to make it high. But the explanation, he added, might lie in the fact that she was anemic, suffering from malnutrition and probably had a "good start" on a peptic ulcer. He told her to stop smoking so much (she was up to three packs or more in an average day by this time), start eating right and generally take better care of herself. He prescribed high-potency vitamins to help build up her strength and two different kinds of sedatives to relax her and help her sleep.

The sleeping pills prescribed by Jean's physician seemed to help quite a bit at first. They at least enabled her to get a few hours' rest at night, but the pills intended to keep her calm during the daytime also left her groggy and unable to concentrate. They seriously hampered her effectiveness in the classroom, and she soon decided she had no choice but to quit taking them on days when she had to teach. Although she tried to force herself to eat more, she still had very little appetite, and her lunch frequently consisted of a Dr Pepper and four or five cigarettes.

Still, as the fall semester wore on, she had begun to feel slightly better overall, when she received another unexpected jolt from the media.

In November 1967, to commemorate the fourth anniversary of the assassination, the *Saturday Evening Post* published a blockbuster cover story based on excerpts from a new book entitled *Six Seconds in Dallas* by Josiah Thompson. Dominating the front cover of the magazine was a pensive profile picture of President Kennedy. A photograph of the motorcade at the instant of the fatal shot—with Jean clearly visible in it—was superimposed over the side of JFK's face, along with a blaring headline which read:

THREE ASSASSINS KILLED KENNEDY

Inside the magazine, spread across the tops of two facing pages, were four color photographs in which Jean's red-clad figure stood out like a flare against the pale green backdrop of the grassy knoll in Dealey Plaza. The sequence of pictures began with Jean as an innocent bystander, standing beside Mary Moorman, who was still sighting through the viewfinder of her camera, a split-second after JFK was struck in the head. They then continued as Jean pulled away from Mary and followed Dallas police officer Bobby Hargis up the knoll in pursuit of the "shooter" and the man in the brown overcoat.

The caption beneath the photos described how Jean had a "perfect view" of the presidential limousine just before the firing started, how Hargis was hit by a shower of Kennedy's blood as he rode his motorcycle at the left rear of the president's car, and how Hargis ran up the knoll in search of the assassin because he was convinced that the shot came from the right front. The caption mentions Jean's red coat, which made her stand out plainly, and the fact that she, too, rushed up the knoll, certain that at least one shot had come from there. It also noted that three of the pictures in the set had never been published before.

Jean was aghast when she happened to pick up the magazine at a news stand. She remembered being contacted by Thompson at some point during one of the six trips he had made to Dallas while researching the book, but she had had no idea that a condensation of the book was to be published in a major magazine—much less that she would be prominently featured in it. The point was, she had told the author virtually nothing, except that she didn't want to be interviewed, and yet here she was, spread all over one of the largest-selling periodicals in the English language.

Her message to Thompson had been the same as her message to Mark Lane, only it had been even more strongly stated: She had nothing further to add to her previous statements about the assassination. She did not want and could not stand any more publicity. She wanted only to be left alone.

The absence of fresh comments from Jean was readily apparent in the article, since the only Jean Hill quotes it contained were taken directly from the unreliable Warren Commission transcript and said only that she had heard two distinct sequences of shots. Yet she was very much the "star" of the accompanying photographs, and she cringed at the idea.

The worst part was that her continuing notoriety now seemed totally beyond her control. It no longer seemed to matter whether she actually submitted to interviews and made statements or not. The thing had taken on a life of its own, and she felt powerless to stop it.

Now the letters would start again. So, probably, would the phone calls. With them would come more worries about the children, more pressure, more tension. There was no end to it. No relief.

She wanted to scream, but she scarcely had the strength.

As the new year of 1968 began, Jean found herself even more despondent. She had always suffered from the post-holiday blahs during the weeks after Christmas, but this time the feeling was different, more oppressive, harder to shake off. Everything about her life seemed to have taken on dark, tragic overtones, and none of her problems seemed to have any solutions anymore.

On top of her nervousness and anxiety—or possibly because of it—even her relationship with J. B. seemed to be deteriorating. For well over four years now, she had been the "other woman" in a triangle that seemed permanent and indestructible. At times, J. B.'s wife would be gone for months at a time and his marital situation would seem on the very verge of resolving itself. But then, everything would change, and Jean would find herself back at "square one" again.

The problem was, much as he professed to want to make the final break, J. B. simply couldn't bring himself to do it. If his wife had taken the initiative and divorced him, Jean sincerely believed that he would have been grateful and relieved, but he was unable to force the issue himself. Part of his reluctance related to his children, Jean knew, but part of it also stemmed from his belief that his wife was too dependent on him to survive on her own. And so, the impasse dragged on, and it became a recurring source of friction between them.

The off-again, on-again state of J. B.'s marriage grated on her already raw nerves and made her harder and harder to get along with. She wanted reassurance and a sense of permanence and stability in her life, she thought, and all that she got from the man she loved was excuses and endless rationalizations.

"You need to make up your mind one way or another," she flared on more than one occasion. "How long am I supposed to wait? If you think I'm going to go on like this forever, you're crazy!"

At which times, he would usually apologize and ask her once more to be patient. But her patience was in short supply these days, and it seemed to shorten his, as well. More than once, these confrontations had ended with shouting matches and J. B. angrily storming away. Usually, they managed to patch things up and get back together within a day or two, but the heat and frequency of the blowups had undeniably increased over the past year.

And so, with J. B. too—as with every other aspect of her life—she sensed herself losing control. She wasn't sure what to do about it, but she knew that if she ever lost him she might as well be dead.

As the spring of 1968 wore on, Jean was moody and detached. The only halfway positive thought in her mind was that the school term would soon be over, thank God. She was convinced that, because of the worries and distractions that kept closing in on her, she was turning in a thoroughly rotten performance as a teacher. There had been several days when she simply couldn't drag herself out of bed in the morning, and consequently she had been absent from school more often than usual. She was afraid that her principal was mad at her—he had certainly *seemed* mad the last time she had seen him—and she wondered how she would possibly manage if she should lose her job. Maybe when summer came, she could somehow regroup and let her batteries recharge.

The third weekend in May 1968 found Jean floundering in the depths of desolation and despair. Despite the fact that Mother's Day was that Sunday, her ex-husband had prevailed on her to let him take the kids on a trip to San Antonio. A few days later, J. B. reluctantly broke the news to her that his wife was at home and he felt obligated to spend Mother's Day with her and the children. Until then, it hadn't occurred to Jean that she would be left completely alone, and when the realization hit home, it devastated her.

Suddenly, all the black feelings of gloom and doom that she had been trying to hold at bay descended on her en masse. She was a tragic failure as a mother, she told herself morosely. All she had ever done was embarrass and endanger her children, and they would be far better off without her. If she were out of the picture, they could find a good home—a safe, secure home—with Jean's mother, and their dad was perfectly capable of taking care of them financially.

She was a failure as a teacher too, she thought, and it was probably only a matter of time until she was fired from her job and disgraced in her profession. But it was as a woman and a human being that she was the greatest failure of all. If not for her, J. B. could go back to his family with a clear conscience and be the kind of husband and father he was capable of being. How could she have ever thought that J. B. could love her, as foolish, unstable and messed up as she was?

The solution came to her in such a flash of clarity and brilliance that she couldn't believe she had never thought of it before. There *was* a solution to her insolvable, entangled problems, after all. There *was* an escape from the unmerciful anxieties that assailed her. There *was* a hiding place where no lurid publicity could ever reach her.

It was all so simple. The ultimate answer to all her concerns was contained in the little brown bottle of sleeping pills in the bathroom medicine chest. All she had to do was swallow enough of them and everything else would take care of itself. All her fears and worries would vanish. She would never be troubled by insomnia again.

The one way left open to her to take control of her life, she realized, was to end it.

"'Bye, Mom," Jeanne yelled, as she started for the front door. "We'll see you tomorrow night." Then she paused abruptly and turned back to her mother. "Are you okay, Mom?" she asked. "Are you sure you don't mind us going off this weekend?"

Jean smiled at her bubbly 14-year-old daughter, thinking how pretty she was and wondering how she had managed to gain so many of both parents' good features and so few of the bad ones. She was proud of Billy too, but at 16 he often seemed more of a man than a boy and, like most adolescents his age, he tended to put a certain amount of distance between himself and his mother. Jeanne, on the other hand, although she was rapidly growing up too, still showed a desire to be close to Jean emotionally.

"I'm fine," Jean said. "Just come here and give me a hug before you go."

Jeanne ran over and threw both arms around her mother. "Somehow I just don't want to go," she said. "I mean, tomorrow *is* Mother's Day."

"You just go and have a good time, and don't worry about it," Jean said, biting her lower lip to keep it from trembling.

"Well, okay," Jeanne said, pulling slowly away and turning again toward the door. "I love you, Mom."

"I love you too, baby," Jean said. "I always will."

"'Bye, Mom."

"Goodbye, Jeanne. Be a sweet girl."

She sat on the sofa in the living room until she heard the car start and pull out into the street. Gradually, the sound of the engine faded away, and when it was completely gone, Jean put her head on one of the sofa pillows and cried for a while.

She thought about writing a note, but she didn't know what to say and she was too tired to think about it, so she decided it wasn't necessary.

It was about 11:30 on Saturday morning and Jeanne, Billy and their father had been gone for perhaps 20 minutes when Jean took a glass from the kitchen, walked into the bathroom and removed the bottle of sleeping pills from the medicine chest. She filled the glass with water and washed down three or four of the pills experimentally with a gulp of water, just to see how it felt.

The pills were quite easy to swallow, she found, so she refilled the glass four or five times and took the whole bottle.

By the time she reached her bedroom, she was already feeling drowsy. Perhaps it was only her imagination, but she knew it wouldn't take her long to go to sleep.

As she lay down on the bed, she was disappointed that she didn't feel at peace—at least not yet. She hated to think about Jeanne and Billy coming home the next evening and finding her there. They would be grief-stricken for a little while, but they were young and resilient, and they would get over it.

"I'm sorry," she murmured, "but I didn't know any other way."

She felt a strange, floating sensation. Then she closed her eyes, expecting never to open them again.

She seemed to be on a boat of some kind, rolling and tossing on gentle swells in a pitch-black sea. The movement made her slightly dizzy, and it was very difficult to focus her eyes, but somewhere far away, across the swells, she thought she saw a light. It was only a faint spark at first, but as she watched, the light came nearer and nearer until it became a shaft of sunlight coming through an opening in a heavily draped window above her head.

She was lying on her back in a bed, but it wasn't the same bed in which she had lost consciousness. There was a burning feeling in her throat, but except for that, she felt nothing and for a while she had no sense of time or place.

Then she started remembering what she had done. It took quite a while, with the details coming to her slowly, one at a time, but she eventually remembered it all.

She had tried to commit suicide, but she had the distinct feeling that she hadn't succeeded. She felt extremely peculiar, but she also felt alive. How could this be?

When she tried to sit up, she discovered J. B.'s head and shoulders lying across her mid-section and the rest of him seated in a chair close beside the bed. Surely, she thought, her mind was playing tricks on her. How could this be either?

At that moment, J. B. raised his head and she could see his red eyes and tear-streaked face.

"You scared me to death, Norma Jean," he whispered brokenly. "For God's sake, don't ever do anything like that again. I think I'll die myself if you do."

"I thought it'd be the best thing for all of us," she said vaguely. "And then, right at the end, I was sorry, but it was too late to do anything about it. How come I'm not dead?"

"You've got Jeanne to thank for that," he said. "She nagged her daddy until he turned around and came back to your house. She kept telling him she'd forgotten something, but she was really worried about you. Female intuition, I guess you'd say. Anyway, they got you here in the nick of time and got your stomach pumped."

He leaned down and kissed her. "Tell me the truth," he said. "You didn't do this because of me, did you?"

She shook her head. "I did it because I couldn't stop worrying and being scared and feeling everything closing in on me. I just couldn't stand it any longer, and I thought everybody'd be better off without me around."

"I knew you were on edge," he said. "I should've watched out after you better than I did."

"It's not your fault," she said. "How did you find out about it anyway?"

"Jeanne called me at work," he said. "You may not realize it, Norma Jean, but you've got two damned fine kids there. You've also got an old boy sitting here who cares a helluva lot about you."

"I know," she said and started to cry.

"If you'd gotten away with what you tried to do, don't you see it would've just meant you'd let the bastards beat you? They couldn't get rid of you by messing with your car, or harassing you and spying on you all those months, or stealing your personal belongings, or threatening you and calling you names. But they finally got you to the point where you just gave up and damned near did their job for them."

"I'm sorry," she said. "I'll never do anything like this again."

"You promise?"

"I promise," she said. "And I promise you something else too. Somehow, I'm going to put this whole ugly mess behind me. Somehow, I'm going to forget it and get myself to where I can live a normal life without thinking about it all the time. I've spent four and a half years tormenting myself with it, and I'm not going to do it anymore."

"I'm glad," he said, "but you know there'll still be people

who want you to talk about it. There'll always be people like that."

"It doesn't matter," she vowed. "That part of my life is over and I've finally learned my lesson. I don't care who asks me, I'm not ever going to talk about it again—not to anybody."

CHAPTER TEN

Searching for Normalcy

Jean was as good as her word. She knew that she could never stop thinking and wondering about the assassination and everything that had happened to her since. Vague fears and worries would continue to lurk in the back of her mind, and sometimes when they were left unguarded at night, they would emerge to assail her in the form of bad dreams, but even then, she steadfastly refused to express them aloud. For years to come she would cling resolutely to the vow she had made in the hospital that day, and even when the subject tried to creep into her private conversations with J. B., she would cut it off the instant she realized what was happening.

"Let's talk about something else," she would say. "I don't want to talk about that."

She now avoided assassination-related books, magazine articles, newspaper stories and TV reports as fervently as she once had sought them. She refused to read any of the probing, questioning letters that still arrived in the mail almost weekly, usually discarding them unread for the most part as soon as she saw what they were about. Although it went against her better nature, she also started hanging up on telephone callers who persisted after being told once or twice that she had nothing to say on the subject.

At first, she managed to maintain her silence only through grim determination. But after a few months, she was pleasantly surprised to find that (a) it gradually grew easier not to talk, and (b) not talking actually *did* make her feel more normal and less stressed-out. She had reached a point long ago, she realized, where she had said everything there was to say. Verbalizations no longer provided any effective outlet for her tensions, but merely exacerbated them.

Still, one of the most difficult tests of Jean's commitment to her oath of silence came in the late summer of 1968. Not only was the approach of the fifth anniversary of the tragedy in Dallas touching off a new round of speculation and finger-pointing at this time, but this also happened to be when Jim Garrison's New Orleans investigators finally came calling—just as J. B. had predicted months earlier that they would.

On a Thursday afternoon in August, not quite three months after her suicide attempt, Jean received a telephone call from a man who identified himself as Alvin Oser, an assistant district attorney on Garrison's staff. When Oser told her that he and another investigator wanted to interview her at 4:00 P.M. the following day, she could feel a tight, choking sensation form immediately in her throat.

"I'm sorry," she said, "but I have nothing further to add to what I've already said about the assassination. If you want to know anything, you can read my testimony in the Warren Commission Report."

"And could we be sure that this was what you actually said, Mrs. Hill?" Oser asked pointedly. "Could we be sure that your words and meaning hadn't been altered?"

Jean's hesitation grew into a long, awkward pause while the choking sensation grew more pronounced.

"No," she said finally, "you couldn't."

"Then please give us a few minutes of your time tomorrow, Mrs. Hill. We've traveled a long way to talk to you, and it's very important."

"You can come if you want to," she said, "but I don't have anything else to say, and I won't even promise I'll be here."

After she hung up, Jean paced the floor in the den, feeling her heart pounding and wondering what to do. She had no ill feeling toward Garrison and his investigation; on the contrary, she admired his efforts to get at the truth and she wished him well. But at the same time, she would not—*could* not—allow herself to become involved. She was just now beginning to recover her physical and emotional health, and she couldn't run the risk of being thrown back to where she had been on Mother's Day weekend. Her greatest fear was being forced to go to New Orleans, take the witness stand in an internationally publicized trial, and tell again the damning story that had almost cost her her sanity and her life.

What she needed was a lawyer, she thought, but she didn't have one and there was really no time to look for one now. As it was, she had no idea what her legal rights were in refusing to answer questions or defying a subpoena in a criminal case of this type. She had gotten off with an official reprimand and an off-the-record tongue-lashing when she had stood up the Warren Commission, but for all she knew, she might face criminal charges herself if she refused to cooperate with the New Orleans prosecutors.

If this had happened a few months ago, she would have already been on the phone to J. B. But now, as she thought about it, something made her hesitate. In the first place, J. B. was a cop, not a lawyer, and he couldn't advise her about the legalities of the situation. In the second place, J. B. would tell her to run and hide somewhere, to shut up like a clam, and to hell with the consequences. That's what J. B. always said. And besides, for reasons that she couldn't quite define, she just didn't want to talk to him about it, not this time.

On an impulse, she called Gordon Shanklin instead. Most FBI agents were lawyers themselves, she thought. Shanklin could tell her what to do—if he would.

"Hello, Jean," he said cordially when she finally got him on the line. "It's been a long time since I've heard from you. To what do I owe the pleasure?"

"I need some legal advice, Gordon," she said tightly, "and I was hoping you could help me."

"What's the problem?"

"Two men from Jim Garrison's office in New Orleans are in

town and wanting to talk to me about the assassination," she said. "I told them I didn't have anything to say, but they insisted. They're coming to my house at four o'clock tomorrow afternoon, and I don't know what to do."

She could hear Shanklin chuckle over the line. "That's easy," he said. "Just refer them to the Warren Commission transcript and tell them both to get lost."

"But can they *make* me talk to them? I mean, what if I refuse and they subpoena me for this trial of theirs?"

"Officially, the FBI isn't allowed to give legal advice in a matter like this," Shanklin said. "But unofficially, I'll tell you this: First off, these guys have no jurisdiction whatsoever in Texas or Dallas County, so, no, you don't have to give them an interview if you don't want to; it's totally your prerogative. Secondly, I don't think they'd ever try to subpoena you if they thought you were going to be an uncooperative, hostile witness who might do their case more harm than good. Now I know from past experience that you're very good at being hostile and uncooperative—so just be yourself, Jean, and I expect they'll leave you alone."

Later, Jean felt stupid and angry at herself for calling Shanklin, of all people. How could she possibly have expected a straight answer from the special agent in charge of the Dallas FBI office? After all, the FBI was almost certainly doing everything in its power to derail the Garrison investigation, and the only thing she had really done was help them to achieve this goal by tipping the New Orleans investigators' hand to the Feds. But it was also a time for self-preservation. If she could persuade the FBI that she wasn't going to cooperate with Garrison, maybe they would never bother her anymore. Maybe they would even find it to their advantage to protect her. At any rate, Jean had to admit she was immensely relieved by what Shanklin had told her.

Garrison's men couldn't force her to talk to them, and consequently she wasn't going to tell them a thing.

Assistant district attorney Al Oser, accompanied by an investigator named Tom Bethel from the Orleans Parish, Louisiana, district attorney's office, arrived at Jean's home promptly at 4:00 P.M. the next afternoon. As she ushered them into the living room and motioned for them sit down on the sofa, she was experiencing the effects of two tranquilizers she had swallowed a half-hour earlier, and she was, by her own recollection, feeling "a little nutty."

"We appreciate the opportunity to talk with you, Mrs. Hill," Oser began. "Mr. Garrison regrets that he was unable to come here and meet you in person, but he asked me to convey to you that he considers you very important to our investigation."

Oser was a tall, pleasant-looking young man with clear blue eyes, blond hair, a warm smile, and a voice softened by the dialect of the Louisiana bayou country. (Jean would not learn until some two decades later, on reading Garrison's book, *On the Trail of the Assassins*, that Oser was also a crack prosecutor, whom Garrison described as having "snapping-turtle tenacity" in cross-examining witnesses. Fortunately for her, Oser did not employ this talent on this particular day.)

"I'm sorry to hear that, Mr. Oser," she said, smiling at him, "because, as I told you on the phone, I really can't tell you anything."

"I can imagine what you may have gone through at the hands of the FBI and the Secret Service, Mrs. Hill," Oser said, "but I want to assure you of one thing: You have absolutely nothing to fear from us."

"Oh, yes, I do," she said. "I have something to fear from anyone who wants me to talk about the assassination. I've been through almost five years of hell, Mr. Oser. I've been called every dirty name you can think of. I've had my words twisted and used against me. I've had my life and the lives of my children threatened. I've had my health wrecked and my nerves shattered. And it was all because I tried to do my duty as a citizen. I'm not going through that again—not for Jim Garrison or anybody else."

"I can readily understand your feelings, ma'am," he said. "Do you still believe you're in some kind of danger even now?"

"I don't know," she said. "I think. . . . I mean, I *hope* the danger may be less now than it was for a while. It's hard to say, but I've decided the best way to protect myself, my kids, my job, and my sanity is to keep my mouth shut from now on. That's why I can't talk to you."

"But we're on your side, Mrs. Hill. We're trying to prove that a group of people conspired to kill President Kennedy, and that would bear out many of the things you say you saw and heard on the day of the assassination. Things like hearing up to six shots fired. Things like seeing others besides Lee Harvey Oswald involved in the shooting."

"I don't know anything about Clay Shaw or your case against him," she said. "How could I be so important?"

"The first thing we have to do is establish the fact that there *was* a conspiracy, that there *were* multiple assassins. Only you and a handful of other eyewitnesses who were actually there that day are capable of doing that."

"Okay," she said, "let's say you prove your case and get your conviction. That'll be the end of it for you, but what about me? What happens to me when it's all over? You and Mr. Garrison can't protect me from New Orleans—can you?"

"No," he admitted, "but if we can put the conspirators behind bars . . ."

"But you can't!" she shouted. "There's too many of them and they go too high up in the government. I wish you could make a case against them all, but you can't. Some of them will always be running around loose, and I'll never have a minute's peace again if I talk to you. Don't subpoena me, Mr. Oser. If you do, I'll only be a detriment to your investigation, because I can't ever again say the things you want me to say—not for any kind of official record."

"We'd never subpoena you against your will, Mrs. Hill," he said. "We don't operate that way, but you could be a tremendous help to us if you'd agree to testify."

She laughed bitterly. "What do you want me to do? Get on the stand and say I saw Jack Ruby running across Dealey Plaza that day? They'd say, 'There's that crazy Jean Hill again,' and there your case would go—right up in smoke."

Oser's blue eyes looked unblinkingly into hers. "The FBI may have told you that was a crazy idea, Mrs. Hill," he said, "but it doesn't sound a bit crazy to me."

"It doesn't?" she said, genuinely surprised.

"Not at all," he said. "You see, we've located another witness—a woman who lives right here in Dallas—whose story gives your own account a lot of credence. She was never called by the Warren Commission, but she saw Ruby in Dealey Plaza that day too."

"She did?" Jean asked, stunned. "What was he doing when she saw him?"

"Unloading one of the riflemen from a truck," Oser said, "just about an hour before the president was murdered."

When Clay Shaw finally went to trial in January 1969, J. B. Marshall and Mary Moorman were among the witnesses appearing for the prosecution, but Jean Hill was not. Neither was Julia Ann Mercer, the other witness mentioned by Oser who could place Ruby at the assassination scene. Like Jean, Ms. Mercer was in fear of her life, and Garrison's investigators refused to reveal her married name or present address either to the media or the federal government. Although both women could have greatly strengthened the case for conspiracy, Garrison chose in the end not to endanger their lives, even at the expense of the prosecution, and neither was subpoenaed. The decision was made, according to Garrison, after taking into consideration "the number of witnesses who had been murdered or otherwise disposed of by 'accidents.'"

Jean was fascinated by Julia Ann Mercer's story and reassured by the credence given to it by Garrison and his staff. It not only supported Jean's own story, but bore uncanny resemblances to it in several ways. Ms. Mercer had been driving west on Elm Street past the grassy knoll at about 11:30 A.M. on November 22, 1963, when she had become stalled in traffic and noticed a pickup truck pulled up over the curb at the side of the street. About that time, she saw a young man get out of the truck and climb up the knoll, carrying what appeared to be a rifle case in his hands. She paid particular attention to the driver of the truck, a dark-haired, heavy-set man who was only a few feet away from her at the time.

On November 23—the day *before* Ruby shot Lee Harvey Oswald—Ms. Mercer had positively identified Ruby as the driver of the truck from photographs shown her by FBI agents. Garrison concluded from this that the FBI must have known by this time that Ruby might be involved in a conspiracy, and yet the bureau apparently made no attempt to locate or question Ruby. (One reason for this, as Garrison further deduced, may have been the fact that Ruby enjoyed a "special relationship" with the Dallas FBI office, having met at least nine times with one of its agents during 1959.)

In an experience almost identical to Jean's, Ms. Mercer had been watching TV on November 24 at the moment Ruby gunned down Oswald and she had instantly recognized him as the man who was driving the truck. She promptly notified the FBI, but later found that both the statement she gave to federal authorities that day identifying Ruby as the truck driver and an earlier statement given to the Dallas County sheriff's office had been significantly altered—just as Jean's had been.

In some ways, Jean deeply regretted her decision not to go to New Orleans and testify for Garrison, and would continue to regret it for years to come. The debate had raged inside her for weeks before she had finally settled it, and at times she had leaned strongly toward going. Although the case he was trying to build against Shaw was complex and tenuous, she sincerely believed that Garrison was on the right track, one that could eventually expose the entire mechanism of the conspiracy. And, she thought guiltily, it was also the first time that she had ever shunned what she still thought of as her "patriotic duty." But in the end, her personal resolve not to talk publicly about the case anymore proved stronger than anything else, so she stayed at home while Mary and J. B. flew to New Orleans.

In mid-February 1969, a parade of witnesses subpoenaed from Dallas was brought to the witness stand by Garrison. In addition to Mary and J. B., they included former Dallas County deputy sheriff Roger Craig, who had seen a light-colored Rambler station wagon pick up Oswald outside the school book depository minutes after the assassination, and Phil Willis, a Dallas amateur photographer who had taken a series of 35-millimeter slides of the motorcade. (One of Willis's slides, taken seconds before the shots, had shown a man standing near the depository whom many observers said closely resembled Jack Ruby. Among those who identified the figure as Ruby, Willis told this author in June 1991, was Lt. George Butler of the Dallas Police Department, who was in charge of security arrangements when Oswald was killed. If Butler didn't know what Ruby looked like by the time he saw Willis's photo, it seems safe to assume that nobody did. Unlike the running figure seen by Jean, however, the man in Willis's picture was hatless and wore sunglasses.)

The New Orleans *Times-Picayune* of Saturday, February 15, 1969, carried a detailed account of much of these Dallas witnesses' testimony. The article included J. B.'s statement that he had found "red splotches" and "gray matter" on the windshield and front fender of his motorcycle, as well as on his helmet and uniform, after arriving at Parkland Hospital with the president's car. This testimony strongly indicated that the fatal head shot had come from some point at the right front of the limousine, rather than from the school book depository behind him, since J. B. had been riding at the left rear of the car when he had been showered with Kennedy's blood and brain tissue.

Unfortunately, though, none of the witnesses—including J. B. —had had as close or clear a view of Kennedy at the time of the fatal shots or enjoyed as unrestricted a vantage point to observe activity in the grassy knoll area as Jean had had.

Under questioning by Assistant District Attorney Oser, for example, Phil Willis was asked if he had actually seen the shots strike the president.

"Honestly, no sir, I didn't," Willis replied. "I was using my lens finder and I was more interested in getting the whole car and not any one person in focus."

Willis also testified that he heard only three shots and that all seemed to come from his right, the direction of the school book depository.

Exactly two weeks later, on the early morning of March 1, 1969, Clay Shaw was acquitted by a jury that remained unconvinced that Shaw had sufficient motive to conspire to kill the president. Garrison himself expressed no surprise at the verdict, saying, "I had known from the outset that we would be unable to make Shaw's motivation clear." That motivation, in Garrison's view, stemmed from Shaw's connections to the CIA and his desire, shared by many hardliners in the intelligence community, to keep Kennedy from drastically altering U.S. foreign policy. At the time, Garrison was unable to prove such connections, although they were subsequently revealed in another trial 10 years later by former CIA deputy director Richard Helms.

As Garrison would tell Jean when they met face to face for the first time some 22 years later: "The Cold War was a life-support system for the CIA. They couldn't afford to let Jack Kennedy live."

Would the testimony of such witnesses as Jean Hill and Julia Ann Mercer have changed the outcome of the Clay Shaw trial? Probably not, since their testimony supporting a conspiracy would have been only peripheral to the case against Shaw, who represented only a small part of that conspiracy.

Still, Jean would have serious second thoughts about her decision not to testify for a long time to come. By refusing to speak up, she would sometimes tell herself accusingly, she had turned her back on the one real chance she might have had to help make the truth known about conspiracy and coverup within the federal government.

Now, like it or not, the window of opportunity was closed. It was not likely to reopen again, she told herself, and neither was Jean Hill's mouth. Despite her misgivings, she had survived the ultimate challenge to her vow of silence. In the process, she had convinced herself that she could keep the vow as long as necessary, and in the years ahead, she would prove and re-prove that contention over and over again.

Long-time friends and associates scratched their heads in wonder as they encountered the "new" Jean these days. Gone was the emotional, outspoken, high-spirited Jean of a few years ago; in her place was a quieter, more serious, more introspective Jean, whom many of her old acquaintances found difficult to recognize or relate to. As for those whom she had only recently met, few, if any, would have dreamed that the elementary school teacher they knew as Mrs. Hill was the same notorious "lady in red" of Kennedy assassination lore.

She cherished her newly discovered anonymity far too much to enlighten them. The fewer people who knew, the better, she thought, and the fewer who talked about it, the better yet. And toward this end, she would not utter another word about the assassination and related events, not even in casual conversation, much less for publication or any sort of official record, for more than a decade and a half.

Meanwhile, within two years of that spring day in 1968 when she had sought the only escape that seemed left open to her, Jean's life had changed profoundly in many ways. Suddenly, it was a new decade and, although she still lived in the same house on the same street in the same city, everything was somehow different. Jeanne had blossomed into a rapidly maturing young woman who would turn 17 in the summer of 1970, and Billy was almost 19 and an honor student at the University of Oklahoma. Sometimes it depressed Jean to see how rapidly her children were turning into adults right before her eyes, but more often she was grateful that they had lived to grow up at all; there had been innumerable times when she had feared they might not.

Her relationship with J. B. was no longer the same either. In a very real sense, she still loved him and needed him every bit as much as she had seven years ago, but somewhere along the way, she had discarded the fanciful, fairy-tale idea that they would someday marry and live happily ever after. Common sense told her that, in all probability, that would never happen now, and it was just one more thing not to talk about anymore. He still came to the house once or twice a week and she met him for dinner somewhere at least that often, and yet they had no more of a real life together than they had when they had first met in that now-distant summer of '63. Jean couldn't conceive of life without him, but the torrid flame that had once burned between them had gradually settled into embers.

All told, Jean no longer expected as much out of life as she once had. Part of it, she supposed, was simply part of the price of maturity, part of the fact of being seven or eight years older. But the flip side of that coin was that both her physical health and her mental outlook had shown marked improvement. She no longer looked like a walking skeleton. In fact, she could have stood to shed a couple of pounds.

Win some, lose some, she thought.

Although she maintained her pledge never to speak of it aloud, soft but insistent voices inside Jean's head continued to whisper to her about the assassination. She spent a great deal of time lost in her own thoughts about everything she had seen, heard and learned over the better part of a decade. Often, she questioned her own senses, particularly her eyesight. Could she have really seen what she thought she saw in Dealey Plaza that day? Had the dim form of the "shooter" really been there behind the wooden fence? Had she actually seen the shot that exploded JFK's skull? Had she truly glimpsed Jack Ruby or his identical twin running across the grassy knoll? Or had she simply dreamed or hallucinated the whole thing?

Why had she merited so much negative attention from federal authorities? Why had they tried so hard to shake her, to intimidate her, to make her change her story? Why had they spied on her and invaded her privacy for months on end? How many other innocent bystanders had been subjected to the same kind of treatment? Who had been behind the death threats, the warnings, the "contracts"?

Sometimes it all seemed terribly long ago and far away. At

times she could almost convince herself that it hadn't happened to her at all, but to someone with the same face and name. But then, once in a great while, the nightmares would still come, and when they did, she would still wake up screaming.

She had not been able to resist reading a recent newspaper article pointing out that the list of witnesses and others with close ties to the assassination and its principal cast of characters who had now died had reached unbelievable lengths. And each time she read about that list, she was inevitably struck by the similarities between some of the victims' stories and her own.

Catching her eye this last time, for example, had been Lee Bowers, a railroad supervisor stationed in a 14-foot tower just north of the grassy knoll on the day of the assassination, who might have spotted the same "shooter" that Jean had seen. Bowers told of observing two suspicious men behind the wooden fence atop the knoll and a "commotion" that might have been a flash of light and smoke just as the shots were fired. Bowers's descriptions of the men were remarkably similar to those given by Julia Ann Mercer of the two men she had seen at the grassy knoll earlier.

To Jean, the most chillingly fascinating part of the Bowers story was the manner of his death in August 1966—in a mysterious one-vehicle accident in which his brand-new car veered suddenly off a highway near Midlothian, Texas, and crashed into a bridge abutment. No skid marks were found, indicating that Bowers never hit the brakes. Despite the statement of a doctor who rode in the ambulance with Bowers en route to a hospital that he seemed to be in a "strange state of shock," there was no autopsy, and Bowers's body was cremated soon afterward. "They told him not to talk," his grieving wife reportedly mumbled to an assassination investigator.

Bowers's "accident" was too much like Jean's own near disaster at the wheel of a sabotaged car to allow her to forget it. But for the grace of God and a fortuitously placed sea of mud, she, too, might have already been on the ever-expanding list of fatalities.

One by one, the doors that could lead to the truth were being permanently and irrevocably closed.

And Jean could only watch in silence as it happened.

CHAPTER ELEVEN

The End
of the Affair

In the months preceding Jeanne's graduation from Samuell High School in Dallas in the spring of 1971, Jean began to be assailed by the worst fits of restlessness and dissatisfaction she had ever experienced. She turned 40 that February, and the psychological impact of crossing the threshold of middle age hit harder than she had expected. The abrupt realization that she was as close to 60 as she was to 20, coupled with a stifling feeling of tedium and uselessness, often made her fidgety, impatient and short-tempered. It was as though her life were somehow "stuck in neutral," and she didn't know how to get it back into forward gear.

Her children were now grown and didn't require her mothering anymore, at least not in the ways they had once required it. Although Jean still kept his room ready for him anytime he wanted it, Billy had been gone for eons, it seemed. Now he was away at the University of Oklahoma from September through May, and was also spending the bulk of his summer vacations and other time off in Oklahoma. Soon it was inevitable that Jeanne would be out on her own too, and then Jean would have only a big, empty house to remind her of her son and daughter.

She hated the impending sense of loneliness and gloom that descended on her when she thought about living by herself. It wasn't that she was afraid; the lingering sense of danger that she had carried inside her for years after the assassination was all but gone now and played only a slight role in her feelings. It was just that the prospect of aloneness was so utterly depressing. She hated it, but she had to admit that, at present, it matched up well with the other major facets of her existence. They were all depressing.

Even her career seemed to be at a standstill. The challenge she had always found in teaching children now sometimes deteriorated into boredom and drudgery, and she worried that she was losing the dedication she had always felt for her work. After 16 years in the classroom, during which she had taken only one relatively brief break, she was feeling the effects of "teacher burnout" and had begun to think seriously about trying her hand at something else for a while.

But by far the most depressing and distressing part of her life right now—the greatest symbol of disappointment and failure—was her relationship with J. B. As the first months of 1971 crept by, that relationship and the limitations it had been forced to endure for almost eight years became the main focal point of Jean's restlessness and discontentment. It loomed over her as the ultimate dead end on a road that seemed to be leading nowhere.

Her feelings were like a snowball, which grew and gathered momentum as it rolled downhill, and before many weeks had passed, she had reached the grim conclusion that, one way or another, major changes had to start taking place in her life. Most of all, her relationship with J. B. had to take on more meaning and solidity. She had never loved anyone as intensely as she loved this man, and she knew she never would again. There had been times when that love had carried her to immeasurable heights, but there had also been times when it had plunged her to the most abysmal, unfathomable depths of despair. Now, the inescapable fact was that, for nearly one-quarter of her life, her whole being had revolved around a man who was someone else's husband. A man whose every moment with her had been furtive, stolen and tainted with deceit.

For a long time, she had been patient and accepting, but no

one could stay that way forever. She had waited long enough. Now it had reached the point that she simply couldn't go on like this, not even for another year, much less another eight years.

She didn't know what she would do or how she would cope if she lost him. All she knew was that she had to do something to take the dead-end sign off their relationship. Something that would let it grow into what she had always wanted it to be.

The relationship had to change—or it had to die.

When she was able to think about it objectively later, Jean could trace the beginning of the end to one particular Saturday evening in the late spring of 1971. Jeanne was out of town and Jean had made a point of asking J. B. to spend the whole weekend with her. He had agreed, or at least had seemed to agree, and she had fixed an extra-special dinner for the two of them that night.

But even before they finished eating, Jean noticed distinct warning signs that something was wrong. J. B. seemed tense and on edge and he kept glancing at his watch, although it wasn't quite nine o'clock yet when she picked up the dinner plates and started preparing the dessert.

"What's the matter with you?" she asked half-teasingly, as she set a piece of homemade pie in front of him. "You're acting as jumpy as a cat on a hot tin roof."

He looked down at the tablecloth for a few seconds before he answered. "I don't want to spoil the evening," he said, "but there's something I've got to tell you, and I might as well get it over with."

She eased herself into the chair across from him and looked into his face. She could actually feel the tension building between them.

"Well," she said, "I'm listening."

"I'm sorry," he said, "but I can't stay the night. I've got to go home."

"But I thought . . ." she started, then stopped herself. "Why?" she asked. "Why do you have to go home?"

"Well, my kids are there. I have to take care of them."

As Jean well knew, J. B. had a boy and a girl who were about two years younger than Billy and Jeanne respectively, but she also knew they were plenty old enough to survive very nicely on a Saturday night without their father's presence. Unless she missed her guess, J. B.'s kids weren't even home; it was someone else he was worried about.

"Don't play games with me, J. B.," she said, trying to keep a tight rein on the anger in her voice. "Your wife's in town and expecting you home, isn't she? You probably told her you were just going out to meet McGuire for a beer and you'd be back by ten o'clock, right?"

"Something like that," he said lamely. "I'm sorry, Norma Jean."

She could feel herself losing control and she scarcely even cared. "I can't stand this anymore," she said, her voice rising and her eyes blazing at him. "I can't stand just being with you when it's 'convenient'—when you don't have anything better to do, or anyplace more important to be. I'm sick of being treated like somebody's old shoe, J. B. I'm so damned sick of it that if it has to keep on being this way, I think I'd just as soon not see you anymore at all."

He looked as defeated and defenseless as she had ever seen him. "I wish you wouldn't say that," he said. "You know I want to be with you."

"I wish I didn't have to say it," she told him, "but it looks like I do. *When* do you want to be with me, J. B.?"

"Whenever I can. As often as I can."

"I don't believe you," she snapped. "I got a divorce almost seven years ago, with the understanding that you were getting one too. Since then, all I've done is wait and hope we'd be together permanently someday, but the only thing I've gotten from you is seven years worth of promises and excuses. I'm not listening to that anymore. As far as I'm concerned, you can either go down and file for a divorce on Monday morning, or you don't need to come back here again—ever!"

He shook his head miserably. "I can't divorce her," he said.

"Lord knows, I've wanted to a thousand times, but I just can't. And I might as well face facts. I'll *never* be able to do it. I'm too afraid of what she might do to herself if I did."

"Then go home to her," Jean cried, her eyes blurring with tears, "and at least try to be a husband to *somebody* for a change."

The weeks that followed were one of the most dismal periods of Jean's life. Despite the feeling that someone had ripped her heart out and left her empty and lifeless, she swore an oath to herself that she wouldn't call J. B. and that she would hang up on him if he called her. She was able to keep the first part of that oath, but when the telephone rang three days after the blowup between them and she heard his voice on the line, she simply couldn't make herself break the connection.

"I want to see you, Norma Jean," he said. "I need to talk to you."

"Have you done anything about a divorce?" she asked coldly.

"Not yet. That's what I want to talk to you about. I want to come over there right now and talk. What do you say?"

"I don't think we have anything left to talk about, J. B.," she said. "I think we've said it all, and until something changes, we might as well leave things where they are."

"But I love you," he protested. "I need you."

"I love you too," she said desolately, "but I'm not going to give in and say, 'Okay, let's just forget it and go back like we were.' Damn it, I'm not, J. B., and you might as well get it through your head."

The stalemate dragged on for a month or more. Several times, she relented slightly when he called and told him to come over, but when he got there, things simply weren't the same anymore. Within a week or two, his wife left town again on another of her endless back-and-forth trips to California to "visit" her sister, and Jean could tell that J. B. was achingly lonely. He was hopelessly trapped in an impasse between love and obligation, and while she could sympathize to a degree, it was an impasse of his own making, and she could never allow herself to go back to where they had been.

In the three years since she had placed the Kennedy assassination verbally off-limits, Jean had grown adept at introspection, at withdrawing into herself to escape outward unpleasantness, and this ability served her well during this period of withdrawal.

It was odd, she thought, but it had actually been the assassination that had formed the foundation for her long-running love affair with J. B. Their gnawing need to talk openly and frankly to someone about the horror they had witnessed, to express the fears and suspicions they each felt, to offer moral support to each other in the face of official harassment and oppression—these had been the catalyst that drew them to each other in the first place and the glue that held them together later on. She had never realized it before, but without the murder of JFK and the ugly enigma that followed, their affair might not have lasted six months.

If that were the case, she admitted ruefully, then her decision to stop talking about the assassination may have itself triggered the real undoing of their relationship. She didn't like to think of it in those terms, but it could very well be true.

Oh, but what a consuming combustion of a romance it had been in the beginning, before they had been saddled with the curse of the assassination. Even now, she could often lose herself for hours at a time in the bittersweet memories of those giddy early days with J. B. Of their first sparring advances, followed by shy lunch dates and brief meetings for coffee; of the rampant passions that had swept them far beyond shyness to breathless midnight liaisons in some parking lot; of their picnics at White Rock Lake and their adventurous excursions to the Trinity River bottoms . . .

Often, as she drifted in one of these reveries, Jean's hand would move instinctively to the little silver turtle on the chain around her neck, the one J. B. had given her for Christmas in 1963. He had given her at least two dozen other turtles of various sizes and shapes since then, but she had never been as attached to any single object as she was to the little silver turtle. She had worn it constantly since that first day she had put it on, and at least a million times she had reached down to touch it for reassurance.

She knew they could never go back to the river bank or the lakeshore, or to any of the other times and places that had faded into memory.

But as long as she had the turtle, she would have a tangible reminder of everything that had passed between them. As long as she could reach up and touch its tiny shape, she would have something left to hold on to.

Shortly before Jeanne's commencement exercises that May, Jean received an unexpected, out-of-the-blue job offer from Children's Press, a large publisher and distributor of educational books. It was the first non-teaching employment opportunity that had come her way in years, and at first she wasn't particularly interested. But as she thought about it during the next few days, she began to wonder if the job offer, coming so suddenly at this tenuous juncture in her life, wasn't actually some sort of message delivered by fate. The job was as a traveling sales representative for the publishing company, covering a three-state area, and it would keep her on the road an average of 20 or more days per month. In many respects, it would be gruelling, lonely work, but the pay wasn't bad and the more she turned the idea over in her mind, the more potentially attractive she found it.

Jeanne would be leaving within a few weeks to join Billy at OU, and, if nothing else, the job would get Jean away from the echoing rooms of a house that was soon to become an "empty nest." But that was really only the first consideration. In addition, it would remove her physically from the dead-end stalemate with J. B. and force her to meet new people and confront new situations, to travel on toward whatever the future might hold, instead of clinging to the past. It would give her a sense of freedom and movement that could be truly rejuvenating after being restricted and tied to one spot and one situation for so long. And finally, it would provide the professional "breather" that she knew she needed, the chance to get out of the classroom for a while and explore new horizons.

More than anything else, she needed time to think through this period of undeniable transition in which she found herself, and the hours alone in her car as she drove from town to town across Texas, Oklahoma and Arkansas would certainly give her that.

Less than a week after watching Jeanne walk across the stage in her cap and gown to receive her high school diploma, Jean accepted the job with the book company, effective July 1.

J. B. was clearly upset when she told him what she had done.

"But you'll be gone all week long every week," he lamented. "I'll never get to see you."

"I'll be home most weekends," she said, not really meaning to taunt him, but knowing full well that weekends were when he had the hardest time getting away from home.

"I don't like this at all," he said. "I mean, what's going to happen to us if you take this job, Norma Jean?"

"I don't know," she said. "But as long as you're married to someone else, I don't think there really is an 'us,' J. B. And I can't afford to spend the rest of my life waiting to find out."

The snowball was rolling faster and faster downhill.

And even if she were to try to stop it now—to turn it around and send it back up the slope in defiance of the law of gravity—she doubted that she could.

Over the next five years, the snowball became an avalanche that cascaded over and obliterated every vestige of Jean's former life. It picked her up and carried her far away, both geographically and philosophically, from J. B. Marshall and Blanton Elementary School, from the house on Bluff Creek and the grassy knoll in Dealey Plaza. It swept her across endless miles of highway to an infinite number of vague destinations, into various brief relationships with other men, through a half-dozen temporary homes and a series of jobs with no particular significance.

None of it brought her either security or satisfaction, however, and there were innumerable times when she would have turned back the clock if only she could have.

For the first few months, she made an effort to call J. B. at least once a week from wherever she happened to be, and most of the time she managed to reach him. They would usually talk for at least 20 or 30 minutes and she would tell him about all the jerkwater towns in which she had stopped that week and give him a description of the bleak motel room in which she sat. He would tell her how much he missed her and promise to try to see her the following weekend.

A handful of times, they did get together on Friday or Saturday nights, but their conversations had developed a noticeable hollowness about them. After he got past the usual anecdotes about Len McGuire and the other cops he worked with, and they talked for a few minutes about old times, their conversations tended to lag. She no longer brought up the subject of divorce, because she knew it was pointless and she didn't want to make him uncomfortable or to hear him apologize. Occasionally, she got the feeling that he was right on the verge of telling her something important, but it never quite seemed to come out.

One night in mid-1972, he inadvertently brought up the subject of the assassination, and she was touched by how embarrassed and upset he seemed when he realized what he had done.

"It's okay," she said. "I can handle it now. I can handle a lot of things that I couldn't handle a few years ago."

"That was a helluva tough time for you, Norma Jean," he said. "I guess maybe I didn't understand just how tough it really was."

"I'd have never made it without you," she said. "If I hadn't had you to pull me through it, I would've ended up on that fatality list for sure, one way or another."

He grinned. "I know I helped talk you into staying home, but I sure wish you'd have been with me in New Orleans when I went down there for the Garrison thing. We could've had a blast."

"I didn't know how to have fun back then," she said. "I was too uptight."

"Well, maybe the two of us can go back there one of these days," he suggested.

"Sure," she said, "that'd be great."

As it turned out, it was one of the last evenings they ever spent together.

By the fall of 1972, Jean had grown weary of the road, so she quit the book company, moved back home and decided to start her own business. With a partner, Mary Strebeck, she opened a women's and children's apparel shop, which she nostalgically named "Owl and the Turtle," in the Dallas suburb of Mesquite. The shop struggled at first, then did fairly well, profit-wise, but it demanded huge amounts of time and Jean hardly had a minute she could call her own.

It was on the chilly morning of January 23, 1973, about three months after the store had opened, when Jean paused to pick up her newspaper on her way to work and stared in mild fixation at the headline across the top of the front page:

FORMER PRESIDENT JOHNSON DEAD AT 64

She read the first nine or ten paragraphs of the obituary of Lyndon Baines Johnson, 36th president of the United States, with no particular emotion. She felt neither regret nor vindication, neither remorse nor relief.

She thought of how convinced she had once become that Johnson was the chief instigator and key culprit behind the assassination, but that had been a long time ago, and it no longer seemed as earthshakingly important as it had in 1964 and 1965. Life had moved on; the world had changed; so had a lot of priorities and perspectives. The job as chief executive that Johnson had coveted so fiercely had ended up consuming him in the end. The debilitating war in Southeast Asia, which the military and the CIA had pursued with equal vigor and to which JFK had stood as a major obstacle in the mid-1960s, had driven Johnson out of the White House and left him a sick old man. Now President Nixon was pulling the troops out and abandoning it all.

Now that he was dead, Jean didn't know what she thought about LBJ. Based on everything she had learned through Dallas police sources, she still felt that he had to have taken part in the coverup, at the very least. But had he known in advance that an ambush had been laid in Dealey Plaza? Had he looked the other way or actually given his approval to the assassination?

These were moot questions now, and Jean didn't pretend to know anymore. All she knew now was that, if Johnson *had* engineered the assassination, he had had plenty of help afterward in obscuring the facts. Someone was undoubtedly continuing the job today, even though Johnson no longer had any reason to care. Even though none of it seemed to make any sense or have any further purpose.

The only aspect of LBJ's death that she found genuinely upsetting was that it meant another door had been slammed shut forever. Another pair of lips sealed for all time to come.

She had had the same thoughts when J. Edgar Hoover had died some eight months earlier. No sorrow, no joy, but a strange, undeniable sense of loss.

Another door had been closed, and no power on earth could reopen it.

Jean was not really happy as a shopkeeper and she wasn't destined to remain one for very long. In some ways, she enjoyed spending her weeks back in familiar surroundings and not fighting some endless highway, but her restlessness had not subsided. She still yearned to be somewhere else— someplace far enough away from J. B. Marshall that she could get him out of her mind for a few hours at a stretch, instead of constantly wondering what he was doing and where he was and whether he might be driving past her house at that very moment. Someplace where the fact that she almost never saw him anymore would seem more normal somehow.

The avalanche in which Jean was caught up was far from spent, as it turned out, and it would roar on through the first half of the 1970s, dragging her along with it. Before it was through, life would become little more than a series of fleeting images, a journey without a destination, a mission without purpose.

In her travels for the book company, she had met a man in Amarillo, an older man who seemed nice enough, and whose company was pleasant, if not particularly stimulating. She had scarcely thought of the man in the months since she had been back in Dallas, until she heard about a position that was open at the Amarillo office of the State Welfare Department. On an impulse, she applied for the job and got it. And suddenly, incredibly, she found herself turning the shop over to her partner, packing up a few essentials, and moving to Amarillo, of all places. Behind her, she left the business she had spent most of a year building, as well as her house and 90 percent of everything she owned. She simply asked a neighbor to look after things, and left.

At the time, she didn't think of it as running away. It was just that she felt the irresistible urge to move on. Somewhere out there, there had to be a place where Jean Hill could feel satisfied and fulfilled again, a place where she would rediscover a comfortable sense of belonging.

The place wasn't Amarillo, though, and it wasn't in the company of the nice, older man, who had always seemed so docile and harmless.

She learned that quite suddenly one morning, when she awoke to find him holding the barrel of a loaded .38 revolver against her head and calmly telling her he was going to blow her head off.

She closed her eyes, held her breath and waited. Had the execution squad for the Kennedy conspirators finally caught up with her? Was this man her personal messenger of death? She felt so foolish and futile that she hardly cared anymore, one way or the other.

"Go ahead and shoot if you're going to, Charlie," she told him. "Just get it over with."

He held the gun barrel motionless against her skull for another few seconds, then mumbled something under his breath and ambled off across the room.

She learned a few days later that the man was dying of an inoperable brain tumor.

"It makes him do funny things sometimes," his sister said.

Jean packed up her things again and moved again, this time to a nondescript apartment in the neighboring town of Canyon, and as far away from the nice, older man as she could get and still be able to hold a job in the Amarillo area. Miraculously, within a few weeks, she was offered a chance to transfer to the State Welfare Department office in Dallas, and she jumped at it.

By January 1974, she was back home again. The house on Bluff Creek had never looked so good to her. This time, she hoped to God she would be smart enough to stay there, but she couldn't be sure.

Sometimes she thought about returning to teaching, but she didn't. Even if she didn't go back to the Dallas Independent School District, there were plenty of teacher-short school systems within driving range that would have hired her in a minute. But there was so little stability in her life right now that she couldn't bring herself to sign the required one-year contract. So she continued to drift from job to job. She worked as a nursing home supervisor, a credit clerk for a wholesale food distributor, an office manager for a sporting goods company.

And somehow life went on. Billy was about to finish law school at the University of Texas in Austin. Jeanne was finishing her studies in the drama school at Oklahoma University and planning to be married. And J. B. Marshall was still riding his motorcycle for the Dallas Police Department. He had written her several times in Amarillo, and she had called him once or twice since her return, but she hadn't talked to him in weeks when he surprised her one Friday evening in March 1974 by calling and asking if he could come over the next day.

The very sound of his voice made her heart ache, and she wished she had the fortitude to say no, but, of course, she didn't.

That night, as she was preparing for bed, a most peculiar thing happened. As she pulled her blouse over her head, she reached automatically for the silver turtle on its chain so that it wouldn't get caught in the garment, but to her horrified amazement, it was missing. The chain was still there around her neck, but the turtle was gone.

Innumerable times in the past, the turtle had slipped to the back of the chain, so when she got the blouse off, she quickly pulled the chain around to see if this had happened again. She examined the chain from one end to the other, but the turtle simply wasn't there. Next, she looked carefully through the folds of the blouse, then through all the other clothes she had taken off. The turtle was nowhere to be found.

If the link that held it on the chain had somehow broken, perhaps she had dropped it somewhere. Possibly it had slipped under a cushion on the couch or fallen on the carpet beside the bed. For the next hour and a half, she combed every inch of the house, looking every place she could think of where it might possibly be, but she still couldn't locate it. After more than 10 years of constant togetherness, the turtle had utterly vanished.

She searched some more the following morning. She looked under the beds, behind the dresser and in the floor of every closet in the house. She even went through every piece of dirty laundry in the hamper and dug through the filth and lint in the vacuum cleaner bag, thinking she might have inadvertently vacuumed it up from the carpet. But nothing did any good. The turtle seemed to have literally disappeared from the face of the earth.

It was like some kind of ill omen, she thought.

When she answered his knock on her front door, J. B. looked trim and fit and his smile was the same as always, but there was sadness in his eyes.

"I've bought a farm about 50 miles east of town," he said.

"Looks like I'll be spending just about all my free time out there from now on."

She smiled. "It'll be good for you," she said. "You know what they say. 'You can take the boy out of the country, but you can't take the country out of the boy.'"

He laughed uneasily. "Yeah, that's true," he said. He hesitated for a moment, then added: "I wanted to let you know because . . . because I guess it means we won't be seeing each other anymore."

"Oh," she said. "Sounds like you're planning to go in for farming in a big way."

"It's just that I'd like for it to be kind of a new beginning for me and my family," he said. "I think I owe them that."

"Maybe you do," she said.

"You've meant a lot to me, Norma Jean," he said, "and you still do. But we both know that for the past few years, all we've been doing is hurting each other. I think it's time for us to go our separate ways, for you to live your life and me to live mine. We'll both be better off."

"I hope so," she said. She thought about telling him about the turtle, but she knew she would end up crying if she did, so she kept quiet about it.

"Goodbye, Norma Jean," he said, hugging her.

She bit her lip and turned away. "Goodbye," she said.

It was the last word she ever spoke to him. And she never saw the little silver turtle again.

The shock of knowing it was finally, irrevocably over took a long time to wear off. Jean still felt like a rudderless ship drifting in a heavy sea, but the avalanche had finally run its course.

She barely noticed at first, but in other places, the highest political drama since the assassination was being played out. The government in Washington was convulsed by the ongoing Watergate scandal. Spiro Agnew resigned in disgrace as vice president, and Richard Nixon followed him into political exile within a few months. Suddenly, the new president of the United States was a former Republican congressman from

Michigan named Gerald Ford. He was the first man in history to reach that exalted office without his name ever appearing on a national ballot.

Even in her more settled, down-to-earth days, Jean had never been much for keeping up with politics, but the name of the latest occupant of the White House sounded strangely familiar. Who was this Gerald Ford anyway? Why did that name start ringing bells in her head? Why did she get the feeling that he had some tenuous, indirect connection with something in her past?

Then she remembered. A week after the assassination of John Kennedy, Gerald Ford had been appointed by Lyndon Johnson as one of the seven members of the Warren Commission. He was the one some people had called the CIA's "best friend" in Congress.

Love blooms and love dies; children grow up and parents grow old, and much of human existence is of the here-today, gone-tomorrow variety. But there *are* certain exceptions to that rule.

Some things never change, Jean thought. Some things just go on and on.

CHAPTER TWELVE

Emerging from Obscurity

By mid-1984, everything about Jean had changed to such a remarkable extent that sometimes she hardly recognized herself as the same person she had been in the 1960s. For one thing, Jeanne and Billy had children of their own by now, and she was a grandmother several times over. Both Billy and Jeanne's husband, Kevin Poorman, were successful attorneys practicing in Dallas, and Jean was justifiably proud of how well her offspring were faring as adults. She was also comforted by the strong sense of family that continued to exist between herself and her grown children. That was the pleasant, rewarding side of the transformation of Jean Hill, but there were other, less happy sides to it as well.

She had now been away from teaching for more than a dozen years, an absence that once would have seemed totally out of the question to her, and although she sorely missed it at times, she had grave doubts about her ability ever to return to the classroom. Time and again, she thought of applying with the Dallas Independent School District, but nagging worries that she might not be accepted, or that she might not be up to the challenge, kept her from actually doing so.

For more than five years, Jean had been trying to regain not only her emotional equilibrium, but also her physical health, which had dealt her almost constant misery during the period following her final breakup with J. B. By 1978, she had been seriously ill, but her doctors had had a hard time pinpointing the cause. One told her he feared she had terminal cancer, but the source of her problem was eventually diagnosed as an extremely rare blood disorder known as "RH mozaic," only a handful of cases of which had been identified worldwide at that time. The disorder caused her to gain weight sharply and severely sapped her energy, and for months that stretched into years she was unable to work at all. If Jeanne and Billy hadn't come to her aid with liberal financial support, she didn't know how she would have survived.

Now, although she was back on her feet again physically and only 53 years old, Jean had never recaptured her confidence, her zest for living or her psychological focus, and for the most part, she still seemed to be drifting in limbo. Sometimes, it was as though the end of her relationship with J. B. had also marked the end of everything meaningful for her. There was no point in denying the sense of loss that had been inflicted on her by the breakup. It was still an emotional boulder that weighted her down, and all her attempts to throw it off and walk away from it had so far been unsuccessful.

As for the assassination and the years of torment following it, they might as well have happened to someone else in another life. It was only because they were so inseparably linked with J. B. that she ever thought of them at all, and then they were nothing more than fleeting, phantom images which she brushed from her mind as quickly as possible. There was enough unpleasantness in her life as it was, she told herself, without dredging up that lingering curse from the distant past.

(It had been at the height of her illness in 1978, incidentally, that the House Select Committee on Assassinations had conducted its hearings and staged a re-enactment of the JFK assassination in Dealey Plaza. Even if Jean had been perfectly well, she would have made no attempt to contact the committee, but it seemed peculiar, in retrospect, that the committee apparently made no real effort to contact her. The committee's only reference to Jean was that it had been "unable to locate" her, although she lived at the very same address as she had in November 1963, and her whereabouts was no secret to anyone. It is also interesting to note that, despite a letter to the committee from Jim Garrison, in which he offered to reveal the whereabouts of Jean's fellow witness, Julia Ann Mercer— who, like Jean, professed to have seen Jack Ruby in Dealey Plaza on November 22, 1963—the committee also was "unable to locate" Ms. Mercer.)

Meanwhile, Jean never once violated the vow she had made more than 15 years ago to "hear no evil, speak no evil" about the assassination. Not one word about it ever crossed her lips in conversation and if someone else made some passing reference to it, she simply didn't respond. In November 1983, as newspapers, magazines and television concentrated on the 20th anniversary of John F. Kennedy's death, Jean had bought a half-dozen paperback romance novels, withdrawn into a sort of shell and spent a week or more reading them until the worst of the hubbub died down.

Surely, she thought when it was over, this would be the last big media blitz on the subject. Surely, there was nothing further to say until that far-distant day, still 55 years into the future, when the federal government's secret files on the assassination would be declassified. By then, all concerned— both the guilty and the innocent—would be long dead and beyond the reach of justice or retribution. In the meantime, both the public and the press had to be tired of rehashing the same set of distorted, fabricated, inconclusive "facts."

Who cared anymore anyway? And if anyone *did* care, what was the point of caring? What had once been the nation's most important unsolved murder case was nothing but ancient history now—no more than a musty museum piece, like a relic from some pharaoh's tomb or a chunk of fossilized dinosaur bone.

Or so Jean told herself in bitterness and resignation. She repeated it to herself so often that sometimes she almost believed it.

On a fall day in 1984, the telephone rang and the caller

identified himself as Jim Marrs, a free-lance writer and researcher who taught a course on the assassination at the University of Texas at Arlington. He told Jean he would like very
much to meet her. But even more, he said, he would like to
persuade her to come and talk to his class sometime.

Along with the familiar uneasiness which his request
aroused in her, she also felt surprise and mild curiosity. "How
did you know about me?" she asked. "It's been so long . . ."

"Good Lord, every serious JFK investigator knows about
Jean Hill," Marrs said, sounding amazed at her question.
"You're probably the most important assassination eyewitness
still living. Surely, you realize that."

A slight but unmistakable chill crept up her spine. "The
most important assassination eyewitness still living?" She had
had no inkling that she had achieved such stature. The knowledge brought a trace of the old apprehension seeping back
over her.

"I'm sorry," she said, "but I don't talk about it anymore, especially not to investigators. Do you work for the government,
Mr. Marrs?"

The caller laughed. "Absolutely not," he said. "When I say
'investigators,' I mean the independent variety—just private
citizens who know the truth's never been told and have been
moved to do some research on their own. There are a quite a
few of us, believe me."

Jean frowned at the phone. In all these years, she had never
heard the term "independent investigators" or realized that
such a group existed. Except for a few opportunistic authors
who had exploited the subject for their own benefit, she had
never known anyone in a non-official capacity to devote serious effort to investigating the case.

She liked the sound of Marrs's voice—he sounded friendly
and keenly interested—and for some reason she found herself wanting to know more about these "independent investigators." For a moment, she felt her grip weakening slightly on
the resolve that had kept her silent for 15 years, but then she
managed to regain it.

"No," she said firmly, "I just can't talk about it. I tried too many times when nobody would listen, when all they wanted to do was call me a liar or a fool and try to make me change my story. I kept trying even when my children and I were being threatened and harassed. Finally, I had to quit talking or lose my mind or die. Those were the only three choices I had. So it's nothing personal, but I made a rule a long time ago that I'd never discuss it again, and I simply refuse to break that rule."

Marrs seemed understanding enough, and like scores of previous callers, he left his name and phone number "in case you change your mind." As it had been with all the others, Jean had no intention of ever calling him back, but unlike most of the others, Marrs didn't allow the matter to drop after one or two tries.

He wasn't insistent or intrusive, but for the next year, he phoned on the average of once every month or so, "just to keep in touch." Each time, the urge to agree to his request grew a little stronger, but each time she somehow managed to fight it off—until one day almost a year after Marrs's initial call.

"Listen," he said, "a small group of us are getting together in a very informal session to talk about the assassination. Several other witnesses involved in some aspect of the Kennedy case are going to be there, and I think you'd find their stories very interesting. You don't have to say a word if you don't want to, but you've got something in common with every one of these people, because none of them believe we've ever been told the truth about what happened either. If you'll agree to just come and listen, I'll be glad to drive out and pick you up."

She hesitated, intrigued by the idea of hearing the subject batted around openly in a roomful of people with the same doubts and unanswered questions as she had. She yearned to take advantage of the opportunity more than she had yearned for anything in years. And yet she was restrained by her own threadbare pledge, her uneasiness at venturing into something so new and different—and the vague but all-too-real fear that she might again open a Pandora's box of troubles for herself if she gave in.

"Oh, I don't think so," she said, grasping for an excuse that wouldn't sound too stupid or lame. "Maybe some other time, when I feel a little more . . ."

"Please think it over before you say no, Jean," Marrs urged. "I think you'll be pleasantly surprised to learn how many people there are who believe your story 100 percent. People who think the same way you do and want to do everything possible to set the record straight."

"You mean they believe there was a . . . conspiracy?" she asked, hardly daring to utter the word aloud. "They think there was someone besides Lee Harvey Oswald shooting at the motorcade?"

"Certainly," he said. "We *know* there was a conspiracy, Jean. We *know* Oswald wasn't acting alone. There's absolutely no doubt about that anymore, if there ever was. It's when we try to move beyond that, to piece together the means and motives involved in the conspiracy, that we get into the real debate. There are a lot of different theories and viewpoints, but most of them have some merit."

"But what difference does it really make, Jim?" she asked in a voice heavy with pessimism. "I mean, who are we kidding? Who really cares about any of this anymore?"

"Millions of Americans care, Jean," he told her, "and don't make any mistake about that. Millions and millions of Americans are sick and tired of being lied to by their government. Did you know that roughly nine out of ten adults in this country don't think the truth's ever been told about what happened that day?"

"No," she said, awed at the idea, "I never would have guessed it was that many. I thought most people lost interest in it a long time ago."

"No way!" he said. "It's only three years until the 25th anniversary, and the momentum's already building. A whole new generation of Americans has discovered the assassination, and they're not willing to accept the same old worn-out myths anymore. Come help us dispel those myths, Jean."

She felt a sudden burst of exhilaration that was like nothing she could remember feeling before. It was as though all the years of accumulated darkness in her soul had been swept away by a sudden, penetrating light.

"Okay," she said simply. "I'll be there."

The events of the next few weeks constituted the beginning of a miraculous kind of rebirth for Jean. At her first meeting with Marrs's group, in a classroom at the University of Texas at Arlington, she ignored her sweating palms and pounding heart to speak briefly about her role as a witness, then listened in fascination while others revealed their own eye-opening experiences relating to the assassination and evidence of a cover-up. For Jean, there was so much hitherto unknown information floating around in that classroom that it was impossible to assimilate it all. But even more important was her discovery that there was a small army of dedicated people working with quiet determination to unravel the interwoven fabric of mystery surrounding the deaths of JFK, J. D. Tippit, Lee Harvey Oswald and Jack Ruby.

Through Jim Marrs, Jean met Larry Howard, head of an organization called the JFK Assassination Information Center, which was in the process of opening its headquarters in Dallas's West End Historic District. Over the past decade or more, in addition to their own original research, Howard and his co-workers had been painstakingly collecting and organizing photographs, publications, historic documents and personal eyewitness accounts. Now they were making all these materials available to the public, many of them for the first time. Their headquarters included a shop offering numerous books, tapes, photos and documents for sale.

She also was introduced to Gary Mack, a television producer and veteran assassination researcher, who had helped locate and piece together countless feet of rare film footage pertaining to the assassination. Among this footage was the original NBC-TV news coverage of the event as it had appeared "live" on the afternoon of November 22, 1963, and on which Jean was now able to see herself for the first time as she had appeared to a nationwide television audience some 22 years earlier. In addition, she met more than a dozen persons with direct links to principal figures in the Kennedy case. Some were former employees at Ruby's nightclubs, some were acquaintances of Oswald, some were one-time law enforcement officers, some were people who had chanced across links between the assassination and organized crime.

On her second visit to the group, Jean was encouraged enough to tell her story in its entirety. It was the first time she had done so at one sitting in close to 20 years, and this time, she was able to incorporate details and insights that she had not even known about two decades earlier. Her audience listened with rapt attention as she recounted her glimpse of the "shooter" behind the wooden fence, the running figure of a Ruby look-alike in Dealey Plaza, her abuse at the hands of alleged Secret Service agents, her months of harassment by the FBI, the attempts to discredit and intimidate her by a Warren Commission counsel, the threats and attempts on her life, and even the rare perspectives gained through her relationship with J. B. Marshall.

The longer she talked, the more apparent it became that there were no doubters or naysayers among her listeners. When she was finished, they asked her numerous questions, but not a single one of them called her a liar or cast doubt on her senses or her morals. Jean felt a warm rush of appreciation for this audience, plus a great surge of relief just at being able to unleash all the thoughts and memories, all the suspicions and misgivings, that had been bottled up inside her for so terribly long. She could actually feel her spirits being lifted and her confidence being restored.

For the first time in many years, she felt like a complete human being again, not some drifting nonentity or meaningless fragment of historic debris. For an incredibly long time, she had been reduced to a barren, sleepwalking, zombie-like existence, but now, thanks to Marrs and the others, she was a living, functioning person again.

Later, as Jean thought back over what had happened to her, she was struck by one of the most amazing realizations of her life. As she phrases it today:

"It was just as J. B. had told me once not long after the assassination—there was more than one way to neutralize a witness. By the time I met Jim Marrs, well over 100 persons associated with the Kennedy case in one way or another had died or been killed under mysterious, or at least questionable, circumstances. I had managed to avoid being one of them, but what I had never understood before was that I had been neutralized just as effectively as if I *had* been killed. I had been bullied and frightened into total silence and submission, and I couldn't have said any less for the past 17 years if I had been dead and buried all that time."

It was also as her newfound friend, Jim Marrs, had told her in convincing her, finally, to open her mouth and her heart:

"None of us has all the answers, Jean, and maybe we never will. But as we seek out those answers, we can draw comfort and support from all the other people helping in our search. There definitely *is* strength in numbers, and more people are being attracted to this cause every day. So just remember, you're not alone. You never have to feel alone again."

With these thoughts in mind, Jean was able to develop an even stronger resolve than the one that had committed her to silence for so long. She now swore that, from this point on, she would seize every opportunity to expand public knowledge of the assassination by telling her story. She would tell it and re-tell it for as long as God gave her breath, in the hope that someday the whole truth would be known.

She would never again let fear make her a prisoner of her own silence.

Over the next year or so, Jean's emergence from obscurity seemed to gain momentum by the month. Planning for the 25th anniversary of the assassination two years hence was hitting full stride. A number of authors were working feverishly to complete new books on the subject in time for the anniversary—Jim Marrs's own monumental work, *Crossfire: The Plot That Killed Kennedy*, being one of the most important—and several film projects also were in the works.

Once again, requests for interviews, personal appearances and assistance of one type or another were beginning to roll in, and this time Jean was determined to honor as many of them as possible.

In the early stages of this new outpouring of interest, Jean encountered a peculiar and perplexing disappointment, for which she has never been able to find any logical explanation.

Early in 1986, she was contacted by a British movie company and asked if she would consider coming to London to participate as a consultant in the production of a new made-for-TV movie to be entitled *The Trial of Lee Harvey Oswald.*

The idea of traveling so far from home, going to a foreign country where she had never been before, and remaining there for an extended period of filming was slightly scary, even for the "new" Jean. But representatives of the production company called so frequently and were so adamant about how vital her assistance was to the film that Jean couldn't quite bring herself to refuse.

"We want your story to be an integral part of the movie," said the woman who did most of the intercontinental telephoning, often forgetting the seven-hour time difference between Dallas and London and awakening Jean at four or five o'clock in the morning. "We want to portray Jean Hill as one of the most important defense witnesses in our simulated trial of Oswald, and we'll need to rely heavily on your expertise and intimate knowledge of the assassination."

"How long would I have to be there?" Jean asked.

"Oh, I'd suggest allowing about two weeks, including travel time," the woman said. "Of course, you won't be working every minute. You'll have a chance to enjoy yourself and do some sightseeing too."

The more Jean thought about it, the more attractive the idea became. The filmmaker was offering to pay a significant fee, plus all travel expenses, and assured Jean that the filming could be scheduled with her convenience in mind. She was actively encouraged in her decision by Marrs, Howard and other new friends, and even Jeanne and Billy thought it would be a wonderful opportunity for Jean to see Britain and Europe for the first time.

"You can take Granny with you for company," Billy said, referring to Jean's mother, "and when you're through in London, you can go on to France and Germany and make a real grand tour out of it. We'll help you with the extra expenses."

"All right, you talked me into it," Jean said. "I guess I'd be silly to turn down a chance like this. I'll go."

The next few weeks were filled with preparations for a late spring departure date. A contractual agreement was signed with the film company, passports obtained, new clothes and travel accessories purchased, reservations made, and a complete trip itinerary planned.

Then, slightly more than a week before they were to leave, another call came from London, and everything suddenly fell apart.

"I'm terribly sorry, Jean, but there's been a change in plans," the woman said. "I'm afraid we won't be using you for the film after all."

"What do you mean?" Jean asked. "We're all ready to fly over there. I don't understand."

"I'm really very sorry," the woman repeated, "but the fact is, the producer has decided to write your character completely out of the script. It's regrettable, but there's nothing any of the rest of us can do about it."

Although she demanded, and received, a call directly from the producer himself, a Mr. Redhead, Jean never obtained an adequate explanation for this abrupt reversal of course. The producer blamed the film company lawyers, who were unavailable for comment.

Jean was able to salvage her fee and trip expenses out of the deal only after her attorney son-in-law, Kevin Poorman, wrote the film company threatening legal action to prevent the showing of the movie on American television unless the company honored its contract with Jean. In the end, she and her mother did, indeed, fly to Britain for two weeks, but she was ordered by the filmmaker to stay completely away from the studios where the movie was being made, and as a result, much of the joy and all of the sense of purpose attached to the trip were lost.

To this day, Jean can only wonder what caused this odd and perplexing turn of events. Had pressure again been applied from some covert source to stifle her story once more? Had that pressure somehow reached all the way across the Atlantic Ocean to thwart a filmmaking effort that had offered sensational possibilities?

Jean candidly admits that she still doesn't know the answers to these questions. But the fact that, when it finally reached American TV, *The Trial of Lee Harvey Oswald* was generally dismissed as a punchless, inconclusive flop by critics and the public alike, leads Jean to wonder if the film was not purposely "gutted" by someone before its release.

The "old" Jean might have crumbled under this disappointment and crawled back into her shell, but the "new" Jean was bolstered by the moral support of her friends, and she scarcely let it slow her down.

"There'll be other opportunities," Jim Marrs assured her. "The movie industry has barely scratched the surface of this subject."

Soon after her return home, Larry Howard consoled Jean by taking her to meet a man revered as the "granddaddy" of all assassination researchers and the greatest "independent investigator" of them all—the legendary Penn Jones.

Like virtually everyone else who had lived in the Dallas area during the mid-1960s, Jean had encountered numerous references to Penn Jones in the local media. As editor of the *Midlothian Mirror*, a weekly newspaper in a small town southwest of Dallas, Jones had gained national attention as one of the few members of the media to denounce the official version of the assassination and publicly charge that JFK's death was the result of a giant conspiracy. Jones had subsequently become the object of derision and ridicule by the rest of the press and the target for hatemongers of every description. As a lonely questioning voice in a sea of arrogant closemindedness, his cutting editorials in the *Mirror* and other writings on the assassination earned him even worse vilification than Jim Garrison had suffered. He was the object of innumerable threats from extremists of the far right, and the target of actual physical attacks on more than one occasion.

Despite all this opposition, however, the country publisher and retired army officer had devoted most of his time during the two years following the assassination to compiling and writing a five-volume set of books entitled *Forgive My Grief*, based largely on his own exhaustive investigations and research. Although he was forced to publish the volumes at his own expense, they are recognized today as a truly monumental work that has formed a crucial part of the foundation of virtually every major assassination-related book published since.

Like Jean, Jones had eventually been driven into anonymity and obscurity by the scope and savagery of the attacks against him, and he and his wife now lived in almost total isolation in a small house surrounded by cotton fields in the rural hinterlands 40 miles south of Dallas. Understandably suspicious and mistrustful of outsiders, they rarely received guests and never opened their door to strangers, but they welcomed Jean with open arms.

Jean was amazed to discover that Jones was familiar with her role as an eyewitness down to the last detail, and she was even more surprised at his greeting.

"It's a privilege and an honor to meet you," Jones said, throwing his arms around her. "In my opinion, you have to be the bravest woman in the world to stick to your story after everything you've gone through."

"I'm the one who's honored, Mr. Jones," she replied. "If a few more Americans had your courage, the mystery of the assassination would've been solved a long time ago. I only wish I had met you 20 years ago."

"It's most likely a good thing you didn't," he told her sadly. "So many of the people I talked to in the 1960s are dead now, and I would've hated for you to be one of them."

They spent the rest of the afternoon talking and comparing notes. Jean recounted her post-assassination ordeal with a willingness—even eagerness—that she would have found impossible a short time earlier, but she was far more interested in what Jones had to say. He was a veritable "walking encyclopedia" of information on the whole Kennedy case, and the afternoon was one of the most educational she had ever spent.

She learned for the first time, for example, of yet another reliable—one might justifiably say "expert"—witness who claimed to have seen Jack Ruby in Dealey Plaza immediately after the assassination, yet was never even contacted by the Warren Commission. Jean was especially intrigued because this witness was Dallas police officer Tom G. Tilson, Jr., a close friend of slain patrolman J. D. Tippit, who had served as a pallbearer at Tippit's funeral. She was surprised that she had never heard about Tilson from J. B, since they had been fellow officers, and she couldn't help but wonder if Tilson's story was just one more detail that J. B. had known about but decided to "spare" her from hearing.

Tilson had been off the day of the assassination, but had happened to be driving east on Commerce Street with his daughter, Judy, on his way downtown from the Oak Cliff section of the city, when he heard over the police radio in his car that Kennedy had been shot. As Tilson approached Dealey Plaza from the west, he saw the presidential limousine streak past on its way to Parkland Hospital. Seconds later, he saw a man run down the grassy slope on the west side of the triple underpass, from the direction of the railroad tracks, throw something into the rear seat of a black car parked on the shoulder of Elm Street, then jump into the car and speed away.

Thinking it was "suspicious as hell" for one person to be running away when everyone else seemed to be converging toward the scene of the shooting, Tilson quickly reversed his direction, turning left on Houston Street, then back west on Elm. He caught up with the black car and followed it as it turned left (or south) on Industrial Boulevard. Instructing his daughter to write down the license number of the car, Tilson got a close look at the driver. Like many other Dallas policemen, he was well acquainted at the time with Ruby, and as he later recalled: "If that wasn't Jack Ruby, it was someone who was his twin brother."

Tilson, whose account was supported by his now-grown daughter, claimed to have turned the man's description and the license number of the black car over to Dallas homicide detectives by phone a short time afterward. He had later discarded the scrap of paper on which the number was written, thinking he had no further use for it. He had no way of knowing that, from that point on, his information would be totally and steadfastly ignored.

Jean also learned that the very same Arlen Specter who had treated her so rudely as an assistant counsel for the Warren Commission, then butchered the transcript of her testimony, had been the originator of the so-called single-bullet concept. This preposterous thesis, which became the basis of the Warren Commission conclusion that only three shots were fired at the motorcade, contended that the same bullet which struck JFK in the throat also tore through John Connally's body, wrist and thigh, then emerged virtually unmarred after doing all this damage. Ballistic experts dismissed the "immaculate bullet" idea as a total impossibility, yet it was accepted as indisputable fact by the commission.

Small wonder Specter had tried to intimidate her and destroy her credibility as a witness when she talked about six shots, Jean thought.

The afternoon marked the beginning of an instant and abiding friendship as Penn Jones and his wife became two more strong links in a growing personal support system for Jean.

With such support, she knew she would never again sink into the depths of depression and self-doubt in which she had floundered for so long.

In the fall of 1987, Jean passed another monumental milestone in her return to a full and productive life. After an absence of many years, she was rehired as a teacher in the Dallas Independent School District and assigned to one of its showcase elementary schools, the H. S. Thompson Learning Center in South Dallas.

Her decision to apply to the DISD came only after many hours of inner debate. Much as she wanted to go back to the classroom, she might never have taken the step except for the wholehearted encouragement of Billie Cox, an old friend from her days at Blanton Elementary School and one of the few former fellow teachers with whom she had stayed in close touch. Billie persuaded Jean that she still had what it took to do the job, and she soon discovered that Billie was right.

Once again, Jean had concrete proof that, far from being lost and alone, she was surrounded by friends and allies. And as the 25th anniversary of the assassination drew near, she found herself elevated to a level of respect and recognition that she had never dreamed possible. As the closest and most important surviving eyewitness—and the only major witness yet willing to state her dissenting beliefs openly before any forum—Jean was about to step to the front of the class in more ways than one.

After the *Boston Herald* interviewed her and ran a major feature article on her role as an eyewitness, containing details of her story that had never been published anywhere before, she was invited to appear on two national television talk shows— "Geraldo" and "The Oprah Winfrey Show."

In keeping with the controversial adversary format of "Geraldo," she was confronted before a "live" audience by former Warren Commission counsel David W. Belin, one of the staunchest defenders of the commission and most vitriolic critics of its detractors.

Although a quarter-century had passed, Belin was all too familiar with Jean's unfortunate initial references to the nonexistent "damned dog."

"You don't know what you're talking about," Belin chided her tauntingly. "Anybody who thought they saw a dog in the presidential limousine couldn't be a reliable witness."

The "old" Jean might have capitulated and run for cover under such a vicious assault, especially in front of the whole country, but it was the "new" Jean who responded.

"You can't shut me up, you —!" she yelled. "I may not be infallible, but neither are you, so don't try to keep me from telling the truth."

To Jean's delight, the audience roared its approval.

It was just one heady moment among many, but the most memorable experience of all was yet to come.

CHAPTER THIRTEEN

Memories
and the Movies

In August 1990, a call came from Jim Marrs that was to open up a whole new world to Jean Hill. Marrs told her that Academy Award-winning director Oliver Stone was in Dallas and wanted to talk with her. At the time, Jean was still recuperating from injuries sustained when she had fallen during a teacher training activity, in which she was pretending to be a deer, the previous spring, breaking her shoulder and knee and spraining her ankle.

Despite her aches and pains and the casts she was still wearing, Jean agreed to meet with Stone and producers Clayton Townsend and Alex Ho at Dallas's Stoneleigh Hotel. "Oliver asked me what I thought about doing a movie about JFK," Jean recalls. "I told him I thought it was a wonderful idea if someone could bring out the truth. He had just bought *Crossfire* from Jim Marrs, and I asked him how in-depth he planned to go, but all he would say at the time was that he hadn't finished his research yet."

Stone also asked Jean to tell him her story. "He was making notes so furiously," she says, "that it was almost as if I was watching his brain work. He was completely focused on what I was saying, hanging on every word. I was truly impressed with him. I really had the feeling that I was in the presence of greatness."

Her reaction, it should be noted, was not that of a starstruck movie fan either. Jean was not an avid moviegoer and actually didn't know who Oliver Stone was at the time of Marrs's call. Her daughter, Jeanne, had filled her in with a list of Stone's accomplishments and also reminded her to get his autograph for a collection of memorabilia that Jean was saving for her grandchildren.

"I'd heard from someone that Oliver Stone didn't give autographs," Jean says, "but I knew I had to get that autograph, and I was looking around for a piece of paper when Oliver deftly pulled one out of his own notebook and wrote, 'Jean, you're cute. Oliver Stone.'"

Jean was so appreciative that she invited Stone to her house for dinner. It was an invitation that she never really expected him to accept—more of a gesture of friendship than anything else—but to her surprise, Stone took it very seriously, as he would later demonstrate.

She heard nothing further for several months, but then received an urgent call one day from Clayton Townsend, asking if Jean would permit the production company to photograph her house for consideration as a possible movie location site.

"Sure, if it's for Oliver," Jean said.

Townsend told her that Jeff Flach, head of Camelot Productions, would be in contact with her, and no more than 15 minutes later, Flach called and made an appointment for 4:00 P.M. the next day. Slightly rattled by the speed with which things were moving all of a sudden, Jean agreed to the meeting without remembering that she had to attend a teacher training session at school at exactly the same time. So she was forced to postpone the appointment for 24 hours, then was embarrassed to arrive home 30 minutes late and find Flach waiting for her.

Nervously and apologetically, she invited him in, and after a long talk, he began photographing the interior of the house, taking 20 or 30 shots in every room, and suddenly Jean grew even more nervous.

"You're not going to do the bedroom and bathroom, are you?" she asked uneasily as he started down the hall.

"Oh, yes," he said, "I'm going to take pictures of everything."

Jean dashed ahead of Flach to the bedroom, where she had dumped piles of dirty clothes and other unsightly odds and ends the night before while rushing to straighten up her messy house. She grabbed them up in a panic and crammed them into the only hiding place she could think of—the bathroom shower stall.

"Fortunately, he didn't open the shower door," she says, "or all those dirty clothes would have fallen out right on top of him."

Flach also photographed the backyard, which was overgrown with high grass and weeds at the time. As he did, Jean kept assuring him: "It looks much better when it's mowed; it's really not always such a jungle."

When it was eventually decided not to use Jean's house in the movie, after all, Jean didn't know whether to be glad or disappointed. There was another long time lapse after the photo session, but Flach did stay in touch with her, and on a Monday in December, just before school dismissed for winter break, he called to say that Stone would be in town that Wednesday and could accept the invitation she had given him for dinner four months earlier.

Once again, Jean found herself thrown into a state of near hysteria as she wondered how she could possibly get ready to entertain a Hollywood movie mogul in less than 48 hours. These moviemakers were a lot like the army, she thought. Hurry up, wait, then hurry up again.

To complicate matters, Jean was planning to leave that Friday for Chicago to spend the holidays with Jeanne and her family, who had recently moved there from Dallas, and none of the preparations for her trip were made. On top of that, she had scarcely started her Christmas shopping, and didn't even have the obligatory holiday party ready for her kids at school on Friday. For the moment, though, all other considerations had to be pushed out of the way and into the background in much the same way that Jean had piled her dirty laundry in the shower stall.

All she could think of was, What do you feed a bunch of

movie big shots? Do Oscar-winners eat real food like ordinary mortals, or do they have caviar and champagne for every meal?

Jean knew she didn't know how to cook Hollywood-style, and she had no intention of trying. She would cook her own kind of down-home meal, and if they didn't like it . . . well, they just didn't have to eat it.

She rushed out to the grocery store on Monday night immediately after Jeff's call, then spent Tuesday evening washing and polishing the crystal and dusting off the linens, and faced the monumental task of getting everything ready and in place on Wednesday. Jean had never been more grateful for the help of her friends and co-workers in this emergency. Her fellow teachers agreed to take over her classes at noon so she could leave early to prepare the meal—roast beef, potatoes and gravy, candied yams, green bean casserole, salad, hot rolls and double-fudge cake for dessert.

"I've never cooked and slung food so fast in my life," says Jean.

That afternoon, Jean's son, Billy, sent her a gorgeous centerpiece for the dining room table and banks of poinsettias to decorate the house. He also asked what she was serving to drink.

"Iced tea, I guess," she answered.

"Mother, you need to serve wine," Billy said.

"Son, I don't even know how to open it," she responded.

Jean hurriedly placed the centerpiece on the table, which it almost covered, and not knowing what else to do with them, deposited the poinsettias outside on the front porch. Fortunately, two teacher friends, Billie Cox and Vee Williams, arrived about this time to assist with the last-minute preparations.

"Do you want them to think you're having a funeral?" Billie asked when she saw the poinsettias on the porch, and then proceeded to arrange them attractively throughout the house. Meanwhile, several bottles of wine were dispatched by Billy, along with Jean's teenaged grandson, Andrew, who supposedly knew how to open and serve it.

In the midst of this frantic scene, Flach called and said the guests needed to come early because they had another meeting after dinner. A short time later, however, Jean breathed a sigh of relief when he called back and said they would be late, instead. Finally, about 7:30, Stone and his party arrived.

"Oliver swirled through the front door wearing a black jacket with a 'red baron' scarf flung over his shoulder," Jean recalls.

When Jean asked if she could take his jacket, Stone replied brusquely: "You may not—and I'm not eating a bite until you get me some pictures of you in 1963."

Jean brought out her disorganized box of pictures, and Stone proceeded to go through them until he found the pictures he wanted.

"Well," Jean said, taking charge, "I guess we can all have a glass of wine and admire the centerpiece, or we can move it, and eat dinner."

As the centerpiece was moved from the table, Stone said, "Oh, let's see. Where do I want to sit?"

"You're the director in Hollywood, Oliver," Jean told him crisply, "but I'm the director here." As she pointed to a chair, he grinned and sat down.

Despite all the problems and palpitations, it was a memorable meal, one worth all the effort that went into it, and one that Stone would rave about for months to come.

In Chicago, Jean was in much demand to tell every last detail of her evening with Oliver Stone. When she returned home on January 2, a huge bouquet of flowers came to her door. The card read: "Wishing you a happy new year. Looking forward to working with you. Thank you for all you have done so far. Oliver Stone, Alex Ho, Clayton Townsend and Co."

In February, Jeff Flach called to invite Jean to meet Kevin Costner, who was to star in *JFK* as New Orleans district attorney Jim Garrison, and Ellen McElduff, who was to play Jean in the movie. Eagerly, she agreed to meet Stone and the actors on the grassy knoll in Dealey Plaza.

Earlier in the month, however, on the eve of her 60th birthday, Jean had suffered what was diagnosed as a mild stroke at school. And as the Dealey Plaza meeting began, both Stone and Flach seemed deeply concerned over the state of her health.

"The minute they saw me, Oliver and Jeff both started asking if I was feeling all right," she says.

When Oliver said, "I'd like you to meet Kevin Costner," Jean glanced around in confusion. As she recalls the moment:

"I was looking straight at him, but I kept asking, 'Where?' Finally, he took off his sunglasses and said, 'Hi, Jean. I'm Kevin Costner.' I felt like such a dunce."

"I'm glad to meet you," Jean responded. "I'm glad you're going to play Jim Garrison."

"So am I," Costner said. "You know, I was in New Orleans a few days ago, talking to Jim, and he told me he thought you were the 'one constant factor' in this whole assassination story. I've been wanting to meet you ever since."

Jean could hardly believe her ears. She had never laid eyes on Jim Garrison, but here was one of the most famous actors in the world relaying a compliment to her from him. It seemed unbelievable.

As she basked in the thrill of the moment, she heard herself inviting Costner to come to her school to speak to the students.

"I'd like that," Costner said. "I'll let you know if I can make it."

Jean also met another assassination witness she had never met before that day. She was Beverly Oliver, known as "the babushka lady" for the scarf she had worn around her head on the day of the assassination. A friend of Jack Ruby, who she claimed had once introduced her to "Lee Oswald of the CIA," Ms. Oliver had filmed the entire assassination, only to have her film confiscated and never returned by federal agents who then claimed to have "lost" her. Since her identity had been established only recently by independent assassination investigators, she had never had a chance to testify before the Warren Commission or any other official body. And despite her fascinating story, Jean doubted that it would have done any good if she had.

During the day, Jean and Ellen McElduff also went over the script to make sure the scene portraying Jean's interrogation by Secret Service agents shortly after the assassination was correct. Stone also asked that Ellen read through the script with Jean present, so that she could catch any inaccuracies.

Jean later accompanied Stone and the actors to the Criminal Courts Building, where she had been interrogated so long and abusively on November 22, 1963. On the elevator, Stone jestingly showed Jean a brass calling card case given to him by Beverly Oliver.

"Look here what Beverly Oliver gave me," Stone said teasingly. "What have you done for me, Jean?"

"Listen, Oliver, I fed you the best meal of your life," Jean replied in the same tone. "The question is, what have you done for me?"

Jean recalls how Oliver burst out laughing and Flach whispered to her, "Oliver likes you, Jean. Hardly anyone talks back to him."

"I like him too," Jean replied.

At the Criminal Courts Building, there was no air conditioning, and it was stiflingly hot, but Oliver refused to remove his black jacket, even while he was sitting on a window ledge with the sun beaming directly in on him. Seemingly oblivious to the unpleasant working conditions, he pressed Jean for information.

"Tell me what went on, Jean," he urged. "Does it look the same as it did then? Tell me everything you remember."

At that point, Stone was distracted by something in the corridor outside the room. "Close that door," he instructed someone curtly. "I want us to be alone. I don't want anyone else in here."

Then he looked back at Jean and said, "Jean, just start talking."

She started retelling the story, recounting every detail she could remember. As she talked, Jean notes, "Oliver was writing furiously, and he was dripping with sweat. He kept saying, 'I like that; I like that, Jean. I knew we needed the flare you could give it in your own style.'"

In April, Stone staged the long and tedious—and to Jean often traumatic—re-enactment of the assassination scene in downtown Dallas. She was told to report to the set on a Saturday, arrived there at 9:30 in the morning and remained all day. It was her first experience with the intensity of Stone as a director and the exhaustive schedule through which he put those under his direction.

That day, Jean not only learned about the business of moviemaking but she also came to realize that she was a something of a celebrity in her own right. "I was surprised at how many movie people wanted to meet me," she says. "It made me feel really good when someone would yell, 'Get the *real* Jean Hill in here.'"

As a technical advisor to the film, Jean could visit the production offices at the Stoneleigh Hotel or the movie set whenever she wished. Often, she took cookies and cakes to the actors and production staff just to help them feel more at home in Dallas. (She was overwhelmed by their gratitude and by the way they devoured her treats. "I don't think any of those Hollywood types ever gets any home cooking," she says.) Despite this access, however, she still didn't feel really secure about her newfound status.

One afternoon in April, after a hard day at school, Jean decided to take some teacher friends to the Dealey Plaza set to watch the filming of a scene involving three "tramps" who were briefly detained by authorities after the assassination, then allowed to vanish without a trace, and to meet Kevin Costner.

"What if they don't let us in?" Jean wondered aloud. "What if they say, 'Who's this Jean Hill? We never heard of her.'"

Jean soon found that her fears were groundless. She approached the security guard beside the school book depository and said, "I'm Jean Hill, and I need to get on the set."

The guard just stepped aside and let her through.

"Is Kevin Costner here?" Jean asked another guard carrying a walkie-talkie. "I'm Jean Hill, and I'd like to see him."

"So would everybody else," the guard said. "See that black screen over there? He's behind it."

Moving freely past the security guard and Costner's own bodyguard, Jean unceremoniously plopped herself down onto the curb beside Costner and proceeded to strike up a brisk conversation with the actor and his wife, Cindy.

Jean told Costner she wanted him to meet her friends, and each time she would stand up to call them, he would politely stand up too. As a result, almost everyone in the vicinity soon knew he was behind the screen, and he was swamped by autograph seekers and people trying to take his picture. Somehow, in the midst of this confusion, Jean managed to make the introductions, and Costner graciously posed with her for a picture for the school newspaper.

At school, Jean was the center of attention as she told the story to her fellow teachers. She recounted how one of her friends, Billie Cox, had gone to her school the next day and put a note on the faculty sign-in sheet that said proudly: "Come to Room ___ if you want to shake the hand that shook Kevin Costner's hand."

Not only had Jean gained "celebrity status" on the movie set, she was becoming a celebrity at school too. And it was spilling over onto her friends.

Outside a run-down apartment house in East Dallas, a crowd of Dallasites had gathered to watch the filming of yet another scene for *JFK*. Oliver Stone was inside the house, which was almost totally shrouded with black tarps. None of the onlookers could see anything of what was going on inside, but they waited anyway, some patiently, some not so patiently. The scene, which demanded absolute silence, was being held up by some birds that were chirping persistently in the trees nearby.

"Kill the birds," someone shouted irritably, and crew members armed with noisemakers that produced sounds closely resembling gunshots finally managed to drive the birds away briefly.

After several hours of this activity, Stone came out of the house, wearing his ever-present jacket despite the heat, and when he saw Jean, he came over to talk to her. At the same moment, however, two female onlookers who had been standing on the periphery also spotted Stone and moved quickly toward him, approaching him from the rear.

"Be still, my heart," sighed one of them, a frail-looking, fiftyish woman, who furtively sidled up behind the handsome director and signaled a male friend to take her picture with Stone. "Take it!" she hissed in a loud stage-whisper. "Hurry!"

"Walk along with me, Jean, and let's talk," Stone said, still blissfully unaware of the women's presence.

But as he moved away, he noticed that a whole crowd of people had now gathered and was following him. Stone turned around to acknowledge the smiling faces of his fans, made polite conversation for a few moments, and allowed himself to be photographed again and again.

When he excused himself to return to the exacting task of making a movie, it was obvious that Oliver Stone had also made his fans' day.

As he gave Jean a parting hug, she could feel every other woman in the crowd looking on with envy.

After Stone had disappeared back into the house, Jean found herself face to face with the frail woman who had tried so hard to sneak into a photo with Stone. The woman was clearly curious about how Jean rated such special attention.

"Are you anybody?" she asked guilelessly.

Jean smiled. "I'm Jean Hill," she said, "and I sure *feel* like somebody."

For two weeks, Jean had been in contact with Stone's assistant, Christina Hare, in quest of a special favor. She knew that Stone rarely, if ever, gave interviews on the set, but she had asked him to try to find a few minutes to talk to the editor of her school newspaper, and was hoping that he would comply.

On the afternoon of May 14, Christina called to tell Jean to come to a studio at Las Colinas in the Dallas suburb of Irving. Stone was ready to do the interview, she said, but she cautioned Jean that she might have to wait.

The cavernous studio was scorchingly hot, and when Jean arrived, Stone was hard at work on a scene with actor Tom Howard, who portrays Lyndon Johnson in the film. They were inside an enclosed replica of the Oval Office doing a scene in which Johnson was meeting with his key advisors prior to the 1964 elections.

Howard was having problems with LBJ's Southern accent, and he kept having to repeat the lines, ". . . till they know we mean business in Asia. . . . Just get me elected, and I'll get you your damned war."

Someone placed two chairs for Jean and her friend beside the small door of the set only a few feet from where Stone was working, and several times, he raced past them without even noticing they were there. Jean had learned long before that when Stone was concentrating on a scene, he seemed to be wearing blinders and was oblivious to everything else.

Sometime during the evening, actor John Larroquette walked by and entered the small doorway to talk to Stone. Jean was familiar with Larroquette from his role on the TV series, "Night Court," but she wouldn't let her friend persuade her that this was actually him. When Jean learned from a crew member after he was gone that it had, indeed, been Larroquette, she immediately wanted his autograph for her collection, but the opportunity was lost.

"Come back tomorrow," the crew member said. "Larroquette and Kevin Costner will be doing a big scene at the University of Texas at Arlington. You can get his autograph there."

Between takes, Tom Howard came off the set and introduced himself to Jean and her friend and fellow teacher, Lana Sloan, editor of the school newspaper. When he found out who Jean was, he gave her a kiss. Howard seemed perplexed with his difficulty in mastering LBJ's Southern drawl, explaining that, like Jean, he was originally from Oklahoma, but that he had worked to lose his drawl when he became an actor. Now he was struggling to get it back again.

Finally, after about three hours, Stone came out of the Oval Office, looked Jean squarely in the eye and boomed, "Jean, you must learn to announce yourself. Someone told me you'd been here for hours. Is that right?"

Jean nodded, as Stone told her with simulated grumpiness, "I'm tired. Get up and give me your seat."

Then he turned to the school newspaper editor seated next to him, and asked politely: "Now what can I help you with?"

"I want to know what you think about this lady," Lana said, nodding at Jean.

"Jean, you get out of here," Stone said. "I can't talk about this with you watching me. You make me nervous."

As totally focused as he had been on the movie, Stone now became equally focused on the interview he was about to give.

And that was how Jean's elementary school newspaper, *The Thompson Tiger*, obtained perhaps the only "media" interview granted on the set of *JFK*.

Having missed John Larroquette's autograph the night before, Jean was determined to try again the next day. She received permission to leave school at noon and headed for the campus theater at UTA where filming was taking place.

In the parking lot, she was stopped by a young security guard named Mike Bain. "You can't go any farther than the corner," he said.

"I'm in the movie, and I need to get on the set," Jean told him.

"Who are you?" Bain asked.

When Jean explained, Bain not only let her past; he also asked for her autograph as though she were a star in her own right. It was only one of many such requests she would receive during the course of the filming. Bain was impressed not only with the fact that Jean was a real-life eyewitness to history, but that she would portray the stenographer who took the statement of the Jean Hill character in the movie.

"Be sure to write on there that you played the secretary to yourself," the young man urged. (Unfortunately, moviegoers do not see the real Jean Hill in the film. In order to hold the movie down to its official running time of three hours and eight minutes—which still makes it an extremely long movie by current Hollywood standards—Jean's highly dramatic scene was one of many that were cut from the final version. Even John Larroquette's part was completely deleted. Perhaps in an effort to soothe Jean's feelings about the omission, Stone has Costner prominently mention the name "Jean Hill" twice during his emotional final argument to the jury, which forms the climax of the film.)

On the set, Larroquette and Costner were already hard at work taping a talk show segment before an audience of extras. The crew politely moved Jean from one side of the theater to the other, depending on the camera angle, allowing her to watch the entire afternoon's filming.

She was joined at lunch by another new friend, Robert Groden, author of the book, *High Treason*, and also a technical advisor for the movie.

"Did you get that interview with Oliver?" he asked.

"Sure did," Jean replied.

"Wow!" he said, obviously impressed. "I'm sure that's one of the very few he's given."

Before the day was over, Jean not only got Larroquette's autograph, but a pleasant surprise from Costner, as well. As she was asking the star of *JFK* to autograph a picture of himself taken with her and actress Ellen McElduff on the grassy knoll, Costner told Jean matter-of-factly:

"I think I'll be able to come to your school this week."

"Really? When?" Jean asked tremulously. Costner's remark was so unexpected that it left her practically speechless.

"Oh, Thursday or Friday," he said.

Jean felt a thrill of anticipation surge through her. She had never allowed herself to believe that Kevin Costner would actually agree to come all the way across the city—a normally composed city that had gone slightly ga-ga with "Kevin fever" over the past few weeks—to talk to a bunch of grade school kids. But now she realized that it was true. The leading man and director of *Dances With Wolves*, the star of the soon-to-be-released *Robin Hood, Prince of Thieves*—the absolute biggest name in all of show business—was really coming to her school! Unbelievable!

This was going to be a day that no one at H. S. Thompson Learning Center would ever forget, she thought.

But even Jean didn't realize until later what a once-in-a-lifetime experience lay just ahead for several hundred South Dallas youngsters.

H. S. Thompson principal Don Williams arrived at school early on the morning of Friday, May 17, just as he always does. But at first he gave no indication that he was expecting anything more dramatic to happen that day than the usual series of small crises that were part of his daily routine.

"Are you ready for today?" a teacher asked him, as he got out of his car.

"Kevin Costner's not coming," he told the teacher.

"Oh, yes, he is," the teacher argued.

"No, he's not," said Williams skeptically.

"Okay, just keep saying that, but he's going to be walking into this building pretty soon."

Sure enough, at 9:15 that morning, the Camelot Productions office called Jean to say that Costner and Jeff Flach were on their way to the school and would be there around 9:30. The news resounded through the school like a shock wave, touching off a pandemonium of preparations.

In the auditorium, a group of teachers and administrators worked frantically to welcome the most famous visitor in the school's history. Teacher John DeLaRosa was on a ladder hanging a welcome sign; assistant principal Judith Zimny and community liaisons Frances Murchison and Bruce Williams were placing plants on the stage; head custodian Arthur Clark was vacuuming.

At 9:30 on the dot, Costner and Flach drove up by themselves in a very ordinary-looking car. There was no vast entourage, no bodyguards, no chauffeur-driven limousines, no hype. As they walked through the front entrance, Jean greeted them with a plate of her homemade brownies, which they ate while they talked with Williams and the other administrators. Meanwhile, a group of very awed teachers queued up at the auditorium door, as eager as teenagers for a glimpse of the world's number one matinee idol, but managing to show remarkable restraint. A smiling, accommodating Costner spent several minutes signing autographs and posing for pictures.

The actor was clearly grateful that there were no TV cameras or flashing strobes, no pushy reporters demanding quotes, and no crush of boisterous outsiders. Costner had been the object of relentless pursuit by the public ever since his arrival in Dallas, a pursuit that was magnified by a daily "Kevin Watch" feature in a local newspaper, in which readers were urged to call in and describe where and how they had spotted the actor. Because such attention had forced Costner to "hide out" for much of his stay in the city, Jean had insisted that his visit to the school be kept totally confidential, with no alert given to the press, and her demand had been honored.

"This is especially nice because it's just us, and we can talk like friends with nobody watching us," Costner told his audience of 325 Thompson students after he was introduced by Williams. "I appreciate that."

Then, in an hour-long talk that somehow managed to be friendly, down-to-earth and gripping, all at the same time, Costner held his young audience spellbound with comments like these:

"If you follow your own path as a person, you have a chance to be very successful. Don't try to be something you're not. If you want to be a carpenter in your life, be the best carpenter you can be, the best architect, the best musician, the best teacher. That will be your job for the rest of your life, trying to find out who you are. Every one of you is very special. There's no difference between you and me, except age . . .

"I wasn't a very good student, but I went to school. I liked recess more than other stuff, but I learned . . . I tried. I kept going forward and in college I realized that the world is a very big place, and it doesn't wait for people. It won't wait for you either. The world moves very quickly, and you have to move with it. Your opportunity to move begins here. You have to learn how to read. You have to learn your math. You have to know if someone is cheating you . . .

"Drugs are unnatural. They aren't meant for you. It's kind of tough out in the world, but find a way to say no. . . . It's not always some mysterious person who comes up to you and tempts you to take drugs. Oftentimes, it can be one of your best friends, and that makes it hard, doesn't it? That's when you have to be the hero. That's when you can't look to the movies for your heroes. You have to tell yourself, 'I'm going to say no; I know who I am. I'll find other friends.' It may hurt for a little bit, but if you're going to be a hero, that's what you have to do."

At the end of his talk, the audience jumped up to give Costner a standing ovation, and Williams hurriedly handed him an H. S. Thompson T-shirt. Jean thanked him profusely for coming, and he leaned over and kissed her on the cheek.

"Oooooooh," the kids said.

At the door, Costner paused to compliment the students. "The kids are really nice," he said. "I'm impressed."

In that sentiment, he had plenty of company.

For Jean, one of the most pleasant aspects of her association with *JFK* was the opportunity for her daughter, Jeanne, to play a minor role in it. Toward the end of the filming in the Dallas area, Jeanne arrived from Chicago, and visited the set with her mother to meet members of the cast and crew, watch the action, and be an actual part of it.

Early in the process of developing the script for the film, Stone had been struck by the resemblance in photographs between Jeanne and her mother at Jeanne's age, and he had suggested that Jeanne try out for Jean's role. It was a tantalizing idea, but because the Jean Hill character emerged as one of three major female roles in *JFK*, Stone later decided that it was vital to cast an experienced actress in the part. Jeanne, however, was to play the role of a nurse in the trauma room at Parkland Hospital, where the mortally wounded Kennedy was brought after he was shot.

Packing a bagful of cookies, Jean and Jeanne paid a visit to a set in East Dallas, where the production company was recreating the murder of Off. J. D. Tippit.

Soon after they arrived on the set, Stone spotted them and called out to her: "Jean, what are you doing here?"

"I've brought you some cookies," she said, handing him the bag as he came over to bestow his usual hug.

"Jean Hill's brought me some cookies," Stone announced loudly, facing the crew and holding the bag in the air.

When the cheering and applause died down—Jean was justifiably famous for her cookies by now—Jean introduced her daughter to Stone.

"I could tell this was your daughter," he said, as Jeanne snapped a picture of Jean and Stone together.

Before they left for the wardrobe department to be fitted for costumes for the next day's shooting, Jean handed Stone a card that pointed out various similarities between the assassinations of Abraham Lincoln and John Kennedy. "This is for your son," she said. "I thought he might find it interesting."

Contrary to what many fans believe about the relaxed, late-sleeping lifestyle of movie actors, Jean had learned that filming often begins at an agonizingly early hour and sometimes continues, with only a couple of short breaks for meals, until midnight or after. So it came as no surprise when she and Jeanne were instructed to be in Fort Worth by 7:00 A.M. the next morning to do their separate scenes. Filming was to take place at St. Joseph's Hospital there because it more closely resembled the Parkland Hospital of the 1960s than the vastly changed and enlarged Parkland of the 1990s.

In Jean's scene, she portrayed the stenographer who took

Jean Hill's testimony for the Warren Commission, and although it was not a speaking role, Jean was slightly nervous. Rather than trying to write down on her pad what actress Ellen McElduff was actually saying in the scene, Jean merely scribbled: "Now is the time . . . Oliver Stone . . . Jean Hill . . . He said . . . She said . . . etc."

It was a highly emotional scene, in which Jean Hill is roughly interrogated by the Warren Commission attorney, and when, after a number of retakes, the scene was completed to Stone's satisfaction, Jean and Ellen embraced each other, and both were moved to tears.

"It was very tense . . . very real," Jean recalls. "We couldn't do anything but hold each other and cry."

It was not until this same day that Jean realized what a truly crucial role her character had in the movie. "Before the day was over, some of the extras who had been in bunches of movies came up and said, 'I want to shake your hand,'" Jean says, still slightly awed. "One actor who played a doctor told me, 'I've never wanted an autograph from anyone before, but it would be an honor to have yours.'"

From its inception and her first meeting with Oliver Stone until its completion in mid-summer 1991, the *JFK* movie remained at or near the center of Jean's life for almost a year. When filming was completed in and around Dallas, the production crew moved on to New Orleans to do the major scenes involving Jim Garrison, and although she was again experiencing some health problems, Jean was able to join them there for several days.

As she arrived at the Camelot Productions offices in downtown New Orleans, Jean was armed with her trademark bag of homemade cookies, and she was greeted like a long-lost sister by her many friends in the office. Clayton Townsend jokingly seized the bag and retreated into his office with Jean's cookies, closing the door behind him and clearly implying that he planned to devour them all. However, she was later assured that Townsend did agree to share them with the rest of the staff.

From there, Jean went immediately to the set, an old, two-story residence located in the city's picturesque Garden District and closely resembling the home occupied in the 1960s by Garrison, his wife and five children. There, she enjoyed a spirited reunion with Stone and presented Costner with copies of a highly complimentary newspaper article on his visit to her school. Rory Houston, a fellow teacher, had express-mailed the article to New Orleans after Jean realized she had forgotten to bring it.

"I hope you're going to be here for a while," Costner told her.

Jean assured him that she was.

During the next few days, Jean met and had a long talk with Costner's co-star, Sissy Spacek, who played Mrs. Garrison in the film, and who seemed as fascinated to meet a person of historic significance as Jean was to meet the movie's female lead. She also had a chance to meet several other cast members who hadn't participated in the Dallas portion of the filming.

Crew members took her on a tour of the house, allowing her to watch as set changes were made, and over the next several days, she had numerous chances to see actual scenes being shot and to chat at length between takes with the principals of the film.

Being a part of this epic production and being able to share priceless moments with the most honored names in the movie industry had undeniably been one of the all-time high points of Jean's life.

She was sure that, in years to come, she would relive and cherish those moments hundreds of times. Long after the hoopla was all over, she would treasure a legacy of fond memories of her venture into filmmaking—memories that would stand out in sweet, sharp contrast to those dark recollections of the actual events which the movie portrayed. It was hard to believe, even now, that her most terrible, shattering experiences had given rise to more wonderful and fulfilling times than she had ever thought possible.

For a little while, reality and make-believe had come together in a remarkable union, and out of that marriage Jean

Hill had discovered a richer, more rewarding sense of self-worth than she had ever known before.

For that, she would always be grateful to "Oliver . . . and Co."

CHAPTER FOURTEEN

Where the Nightmare Ends

A small ripple of excitement circulated among the diners at the exclusive Louis XVI Restaurant in the heart of New Orleans' storied Vieux Carre.

"Mr. Garrison's here," the maitre d' barked to the head waiter in an urgent whisper. "Show him to his table."

Heads turned as the tall, courtly figure of one of the most famous residents of one of the world's most cosmopolitan cities made his way slowly across the dining room to the corner table where Jean Hill and two friends waited.

"Mrs. Hill," he said, taking her hand and bowing slightly, "I'm Jim Garrison. It's a great pleasure to meet you."

"Please, let's don't be formal," she said, beaming at him. "I'm just plain Jean, and, believe me, the pleasure is mine."

Thus, on a balmy June evening in 1991, a small bit of history was made. Jean had dreamed of this moment for years, yet doubted that she would ever actually experience it. For close to a quarter-century, the nearest eyewitness to the murder of a president and the prosecutor who risked everything to prove that murder the result of a conspiracy had known each other from afar, but they had never come face to face until right now. Once again, the miracle-making powers of Hollywood had manifested themselves to bring together the former district attorney, whose book, *On the Trail of the Assassins*, formed the main story line for *JFK*, and the woman whose personal trauma provided a starting point for that story. Finally, Jean

243

could say something that had been weighing on her mind ever since 1969.

"I really wanted to come down here and testify for you at the Clay Shaw trial," she said. "I truly did, but I was scared. I'd been through so much by that time that I guess I just lost my nerve."

"I understand," Garrison said. "Your testimony probably wouldn't have changed the outcome of the trial, but if there were more people like Jean Hill, the coverup would never have worked in the first place. You've been very courageous in standing up for the truth, and I wouldn't have wanted you to take any unnecessary risks by appearing at the trial. There've been far too many 'accident' victims as it is. These are bad people we're dealing with. I'm afraid they have the same mentality as the Nazis."

This was the beginning of a heart-to-heart conversation that was to last until almost midnight. It was also the beginning of a genuine friendship.

Garrison left no doubt of his firm belief that tentacles from the same conspiracy that killed JFK continue to entangle elements of the federal government today. He talked openly about his harassment by the Internal Revenue Service:

"They really thought I took money from organized crime— or at least they said they did."

And as he signed copies of his book for his guests, he remarked matter-of-factly:

"I've had terrible problems getting my book distributed. The government has done everything it could to suppress it, and it's still trying, even now. Under the circumstances, Oliver Stone is a very brave man to make this movie. The same people who want to suppress my book are doing their best to kill the movie, but they'll never succeed. I think the movie's going to be the most important thing that's ever happened to get the truth to the American people."

Garrison's talk of continuing official suppression came as a shock to Jean, who by this time was well along in a book project of her own. But instead of being discouraged by his revelations, she drew added resolve from Garrison's experience. If he could succeed against such heavy odds and after the unmerciful battering he had taken before and during the Clay Shaw trial, she told herself, so could she.

"They've done everything in their power to humiliate and discredit us both, Jim," she told him, "but thanks to Oliver, I think we're going to outlast them."

"Yes," Garrison agreed, "Oliver knows this is *the* story of the time, and he knows how important you and I are to it. Even as we talk, Jean, I'm astonished that the people behind this conspiracy still believe they can hide the truth from the American people, that they can shoot a president from the front and then insist that a shot from the back killed him. Soon, thanks to this movie and people like you, there won't be a thinking adult anywhere who doesn't know what really happened."

(One of the most important discoveries by independent assassination investigators involves alterations made in Kennedy's wounds, either in a pointless effort to save his life in Dallas or during autopsy proceedings at Bethesda, Maryland. It is known, for example, that an utterly meaningless tracheostomy was performed on Kennedy in the Parkland Hospital emergency room, in which the apparent bullet entry wound in his throat was needlessly obliterated. One senior medical student who was present at the time was struck by the fact that the necessary tube to restore Kennedy's breathing—if he had been able to breathe—could easily have been inserted in the "perfectly round" hole left by the bullet. "I couldn't understand why the surgeons insisted on cutting the wound open," he said. Whatever their reasons, however, they destroyed vital evidence in the process.)

As the evening drew to a close, Jean tried to find words to tell Garrison how much it meant to her and to express her appreciation.

"This has been one of the high points of my life, Jim," she said. "I hope we'll meet again."

"So do I," Garrison said sincerely. "I want us to stay in touch, and if there's anything I can do to help you with your book—or in any other way—I hope you'll let me know. Your book is going to be a different story about a vanishing breed—a true American—and I wish you the very best with it."

"You make me sound like some kind of heroine, Jim," Jean said, deeply touched, "but I didn't think I was doing anything that any other responsible person wouldn't have done."

"That's the way I felt too," Garrison said, "but I guess not everyone has a one-track mind like you and I. We give no thought to the consequences, but go on and do what we feel we must."

As he rose to make his way to his waiting taxi, Garrison embraced Jean warmly, and his parting words brought tears to her eyes.

"You're what America's all about, Jean," he said, gripping her hand. "You're a genuine patriot."

As great as its impact was on her life and as much as it did to vindicate her beliefs about the Kennedy assassination, Jean's association with the movie, *JFK*, was not to be the conclusion of her story. On the contrary, a whole new era of challenge and opportunity was to grow out of that association, and bold new vistas were destined to open up before her. Not only had Hollywood proved itself capable of recreating one of the most earthshaking moments of history, but for Jean, it had also shown that there is no such thing as an "impossible dream."

As Jean herself puts it: "If someone like Oliver Stone, one of the most important and powerful figures in the entertainment industry, could have faith in me and believe my story—not just accept it as fact, but rely on it as part of the backbone of his finest film—then anything is possible. Of all the benefits I derived from knowing Oliver and working with him, that realization was the greatest one of all."

As the filming neared its conclusion in Dallas, Jean made a decision that friends and associates had been urging on her for years. Since the movie represented only the opening chapter of her story, she decided to present her complete, no-holds-barred personal account of the past 27 years in book form. Knowing that her stature as the most important surviving witness to the assassination—and the last eyewitness to openly dispute the Warren Commission's official findings—was likely to keep her in the public eye indefinitely, Jean wanted every detail of her story thus far to be accurately recorded once and for all.

But not even this book marks the end to that story. Now fortified by the support, insights and resources of the most knowledgeable experts on the Kennedy case—friends like Garrison, Jim Marrs, Larry Howard, Penn Jones, Dr. Cyril Wecht, and others—Jean continues her quest for the ultimate truth.

She makes it clear, however, that despite her access to the broadest existing range of informed opinion on the subject, she has never claimed to be an "expert" in her own right.

"I'm just an ordinary person whom fate happened to place in a certain spot at a certain time," she says. "I'm not a political theorist or even very much of a political person. I don't know anything that most other people don't know about the inner workings of the CIA or the Justice Department or the Mafia or the military-industrial complex. I'm not a rightwinger or a leftwinger; most of the time, I go right down the middle. The only thing I'm 100 percent sure of is what I saw and heard. From that, plus almost 28 years of thinking and reading and studying about it, I think I know what happened in Dealey Plaza at 12:30 P.M. on November 22, 1963. But I'll have to leave the explanations for *who* the killers were and *why* it happened to somebody else."

Jean's basic beliefs about the physical act of murdering Pres. John F. Kennedy can be summed up in five points, each of which stands in total contradiction to official government conclusions:

(1) At least four—and probably six—shots were fired, not three, as the Warren Commission insisted.

(2) At least two—and possibly three—gunmen were involved.

(3) At least one gunman was positioned behind the fence

atop the grassy knoll and fired at least one shot from that location.

(4) The fatal head shot which exploded the president's skull came from the right front (the direction of the knoll), not from the direction of the school book depository.

(5) Some of the shots, including the one that hit Kennedy in the throat, did come from the direction of the depository, but none was fired by Lee Harvey Oswald.

The evidence supporting the first four of these points is clear and undeniable. The fifth point, Jean admits, is only an "educated guess," but it serves to amplify her insistence that all guesswork could be eliminated if the government would act to end the secrecy surrounding the case.

"If the government's files on the assassination remain classified until 2039, as LBJ ordered, there's no way that I or anyone else involved will live to see them released," she says realistically. "But there's no reason why the American people should have to wait until then to find out what's in those files. I don't expect it to happen—not by any stretch of the imagination—but if one executive order can clamp a lid of secrecy on something this important, another executive order should be able to remove it."

Not long ago, Jean traveled to the Texas Hill Country to tour the state park along the scenic Pedernales River which now encompasses portions of the LBJ Ranch, the home of the 36th president of the United States.

"It was a trip I felt I had to make," she says, "something I was almost compelled to do."

As she stood looking down at the grave of Lyndon Johnson, listening to the wind whispering in the live oak trees and the faint rush of the river along its rocky bed, her emotions ranged from bitter sorrow to euphoric nostalgia, and her thoughts drifted far away, then back again.

This, then, was where it all eventually ended for everyone. Whether it was under a spreading bough on a peaceful riverbank, beneath an eternal flame in Arlington National Cemetery, or in some obscure, untended burial plot, our destinations were all essentially the same. Truly, the paths of glory did lead but to the grave.

The Senate and the White House had never really been Lyndon Johnson's destinations; they had merely been stopping places along the way. And whatever ruthless ambitions or calculated malice may have propelled him toward those fleeting, transient goals, they no longer had any importance now. Standing there above the green mound of earth that covered LBJ's mortal remains, Jean realized this great truth as never before.

Life was so terribly fleeting, she thought. That message had been driven home to her with incredible force in the recent past by three deaths that had come in rapid, relentless succession.

The first of these, and by far the hardest for her to accept, had been that of J. B. Marshall, whose life had been snuffed out in a matter of weeks in early 1989 by a fast-spreading form of cancer. Nearly 15 years had passed since the last time she had seen him or heard his voice, but when a friend had called that day to tell her that J. B. was dead, the time seemed to melt away. She could close her eyes and almost feel the warmth of his last embrace, but the sensation brought her no comfort, only a vast emptiness.

In the weeks that followed, Jean had felt herself drawn even closer to Len McGuire, J. B.'s best friend and former partner. While there had never been anything romantic between them, she and Mac had formed a deep bond of friendship over the years. For a long time, Mac had made a habit of stopping by her home once or twice a month to visit and help her with some chore or another. Through him, she had indirectly kept track of J. B., and only a couple of weeks before his death, Mac had told her that J. B. had agreed to do an interview about the assassination with a national historic magazine. It was the first such request he had ever granted.

"God, I can't believe that, Mac," Jean remembered saying at the time. "As far as I know, J. B.'s never once talked to anybody in the media about it. In fact, I remember him threatening to run over one reporter with his motorcycle if the guy didn't quit hassling him for some quotes."

It was so odd, she thought, that he should die so soon after consenting to do something so totally out of character. Now the interview would never take place, and whatever he might have said to the interviewer would forever go unsaid. Was it merely a fateful coincidence, or was it something else?

Even at the height of their relationship, Jean had often suspected that, for whatever reason, J. B. sometimes withheld information from her, especially when it had to do with his own intuition, hunches and "gut" feelings about certain things. Most cops were tightlipped about such matters, she knew. In all the time she had known McGuire, for example, he had never so much as mentioned the assassination in her presence, although, as the lead motorcyclist in the motorcade, he had probably been the most visible officer on the scene that day.

Now, with J. B. gone, she was seized with a compulsive, irresistible urge to try to draw McGuire out on the subject. She couldn't explain why the urge was so strong, or why it was accompanied by a sense of near desperation, but it was.

"Come on, Mac," she urged, "talk to me about it. Tell me what you saw and heard and thought. There's so few of us left who were actually there when it happened, and we're getting fewer all the time. What harm can it do?"

For awhile, McGuire was his usual taciturn self. "Hell, I've never even talked to my wife about it," he told her. "Some things are better left unsaid."

The hint of something covert and mysterious in his words only made her try that much harder. As that spring wore on, she kept prodding him gently about it, and although he revealed absolutely nothing to her, she had the distinct feeling that she was somehow getting closer.

"Hey, I'll bake you the biggest peach cobbler you ever saw if you'll tell me your version of assassination day," she offered.

"Oh, maybe I'll tell you sometime," he said evasively.

The end of the school term arrived and Jean was packing to go out of town for a few weeks when McGuire dropped by to trim some trees for her. Strangely enough, he was the one who brought up the subject that day, even before she had a chance to mention it.

"Tell you what," he said out of the blue. "I've been giving it a good bit of thought, and maybe there are some things I ought to tell you about the Kennedy deal. When you get back from your trip, you can make me that pie, and we'll sit down and go over the whole thing."

She was practically dumbstruck. "You really mean it, Mac?"

"Yeah," he said, winking at her. "I guess it's time I bared my soul to somebody."

When Jean returned home three weeks later, the first thing she did was go into her bedroom and check the answering machine for telephone messages. There were a half-dozen of them on the recorder, and to her pleasant surprise, one had been left two days earlier by McGuire.

"Just checking to see if you were home yet," his laconic, unmistakable voice said. "I'm still ready to talk when you get back. See you soon."

Less than two hours later, Jean received a call from a mutual friend, who told her that Len McGuire had died unexpectedly the previous morning of a heart attack triggered by a blood clot. He had seemed in excellent health but had a previous history of coronary artery disease.

Before the year was out, Patrick Dean, another former Dallas motorcycle officer, who had been a close friend of Mac's and J. B.'s, also died suddenly. Dean had been a few years older than either Mac or J. B., but even he had been only in his early 60s. A fourth motorcade motorcycle officer, Bobby Hargis, the man who had ridden next to J. B. at the rear wheel of the presidential limousine, had suffered permanent brain damage earlier when he was struck by a car.

Three more witnesses, representing three unique and irreplaceable perspectives on the events of November 22, 1963, had been eternally silenced within the span of a single year.

Mere coincidence, she could not help but wonder, or more conspiracy and coverup?

Would the truth be known while there was still a living tongue left to reveal it, or would historians in the distant future have only musty, faded documents on which to base their conclusions?

As she stood at the gravesite beside the Pedernales, Jean prayed for an answer. But there was only the sound of the wind and the river.

Jean Hill, a bespectacled, grandmotherly schoolteacher, stands before a classroom filled with youngsters, most of whose parents were not yet living on November 22, 1963. Many are inner-city minority kids, who inhabit neighborhoods where gunfire, violence and bloodshed are part of the daily routine. Many were not even born in this country, and few have more than the most rudimentary knowledge of American history.

To the casual observer, it might seem unbelievable that this woman could interest this audience in the long-ago story of a handsome young president's visit to their city and the tragedy that befell him there. And yet, as she retells the story once again, as she has so often before in similar settings, the children sit in rapt, wide-eyed attention, clinging to her every word.

". . . and just as the president turned toward me, I heard a sound like a loud pop. I saw the president raise his hands toward his throat and a strange look cross his face, and I realized he had been shot . . ."

As the story goes on, Jean's eyes move around the room from one youthful face to another. She sees a tear roll down the cheek of a little Hispanic girl on the front row. "Poor President Kennedy," the girl whispers.

A gangly, nine-year-old African-American boy reacts with spirited frustration as Jean mentions the shadowy figure of the "shooter" and her dash up the grassy knoll in futile pursuit of him and his suspected accomplice.

"Aw, man, I wish I'd of been there, Mrs. Hill," he says. "If you'd of had me to help you, we could've caught that bad old man for sure!"

From childish reactions such as these, Jean has come to a striking, strangely reassuring conclusion. The courageous investigators like Penn Jones, the tireless researchers like Jim Marrs, the maligned crusaders like Jim Garrison and the dogged eyewitnesses like Jean Hill have done everything they could possibly do. But the final resolution of the Kennedy case was not to be up to them—not to any of them.

If the case was to be resolved at all, it would be up to children like these to see it through to its conclusion. These children would still be relatively young adults in the year 2039. If they cared enough—if the burning questions that were pursued in vain by Jean and her generation remained alive—then no power on earth could keep the truth from coming out.

Jean had believed for a long time that God had spared her for a reason. There was no other explanation for why she had survived when so many others had perished.

Now she knew what her mission was: To keep alive the healthy, questioning curiosity she saw in these children. To teach them to keep asking "why" until they got the answers they deserved. To instill in them the understanding that, no matter how strong and clever, how ruthless and numerous the wrongdoers of the world might be, they still would inevitably have to answer to the forces of right and decency.

The stirring words of the "Battle Hymn of the Republic" ran through her mind: "Mine eyes have seen the glory of the coming of the Lord; He is trampling out the vintage where the grapes of wrath are stor'd. . . . His truth is marching on."

As long as there was truth and someone to seek it, there was hope.

Sometimes in the dark hours after midnight, occasional bad dreams still come—dreams of "shooters" and suspects, vicious callers and interrogators, prowlers and faceless pursuers. In all probability, the dreams will always continue to crop up now and then, but Jean accepts them philosophically as just another inescapable part of the past, and she now knows that she can endure them.

The knowledge that her story has finally been told, as fully and completely as she is capable of telling it, is a source of great comfort and satisfaction to her. For better or worse, it is now a matter of record, and she has no fear of the consequences. She knows now that the real nightmare, the one that dogged her every step for years and drove her to the brink of death, grew out of her inability to break through a veil of secrecy imposed both by herself and others.

That veil is gone now, ripped away for good through the simple process of speaking out with honesty and forthrightness, and the worst of the nightmare is gone too.

Jean feels strongly that her story is different from any of the other published books about the assassination, because it is the story of one ordinary "little" person caught up in a vast, incomprehensible plot; the story of one tiny but unique human thread woven through the tapestry of modern history. And she is glad that, in the final analysis, it will be history—not the federal government or the subsurface power cliques that have so often controlled it during the last half of the twentieth century—which will ultimately determine the merit of her story and the truth of her claims.

"I *am* just an ordinary person," Jean says, "and I'm certainly far from perfect or infallible. I've made my share of selfish, foolish mistakes. Sometimes I've done the wrong thing and suffered as a result, but I hope and believe that most people will be understanding enough to forgive me for it. Besides, whatever may be said or thought about me on a personal level isn't really very important anyhow. If I can help in some small way to reveal facts that have been withheld from the American public for almost 30 years, then I'll be happy and content."

History, Jean believes, will inevitably judge all of us with the kind of merciless objectivity that no human jury could ever possess. It will rule on the historic value of John F. Kennedy and Lyndon B. Johnson, of J. Edgar Hoover and Earl Warren, of Lee Harvey Oswald and Jack Ruby, and of Jim Garrison and Clay Shaw—all with the same relentless, incorruptible fairness.

"And finally, when it gets past all the large rocks and

medium-sized pebbles, and starts sifting through the smallest grains in the sands of time," Jean says, "it will get around to me."

From this point on, Jean Hill is more than willing to let history be her judge as a witness.

"I'm not afraid of the verdict," she says. "I'm not afraid of anything anymore. I rest my case."